STUDYING MUSIC HISTORY

Learning, Reasoning, and Writing about Music History and Literature

DAVID POULTNEY

Illinois State University

PRENTICE-HALL, INC., *ENGLEWOOD CLIFFS, NEW JERSEY 07632*

Library of Congress Cataloging in Publication Data

POULTNEY, DAVID.   (date)
  Studying music history.

  Bibliography: p. 229-242
  1. Music — History and criticism — Outlines,
syllabi, etc.   I. Title.
ML161.P8 1983   780'.9   82-20458
ISBN 0-13-858860-0

Editorial production supervision: Dan Mausner
Cover design: 20/20 Services, Inc.
Cover art: *Symbols Signs & Signets* by Ernst Lehner
        Dover Publications, Inc.
Manufacturing buyer: Raymond Keating

Printed in the United States of America

10 9 8 7 6 5 4 3 2 1

ISBN 0-13-858860-0

PRENTICE-HALL INTERNATIONAL, INC., *London*
PRENTICE-HALL OF AUSTRALIA PTY. LIMITED, *Sydney*
EDITORA PRENTICE-HALL DO BRASIL, LTDA., *Rio de Janeiro*
PRENTICE-HALL CANADA INC., *Toronto*
PRENTICE-HALL OF INDIA PRIVATE LIMITED, *New Delhi*
PRENTICE-HALL OF JAPAN, INC., *Tokyo*
PRENTICE-HALL OF SOUTHEAST ASIA PTE. LTD., *Singapore*
WHITEHALL BOOKS LIMITED, *Wellington, New Zealand*

To Judy,
without whom,
nothing.

Contents

Chapter Two   Renaissance Music   *20*

Chapter Three   Baroque Music   *75*

Chapter Five   Romantic Music   *148*

Chapter Six   Twentieth-Century Music   *175*

Chapter Seven   Writing about Music   *211*

Appendix Four   Scores and Historical Sources Identified   *246*

Preface

By emphasizing learning, reasoning, and writing about music history and literature, the author has sought to create either a valuable supplement to the traditional textbook or, with the aid of class lectures, a viable alternative to it. The difficulty with which students learn from established texts in the field has encouraged the writing of this volume. Here, emphasis is placed upon (1) a systematic approach to the data of music history and literature, (2) identification and interpretation of unidentified music examples and excerpts from historical documents, and (3) properly written expression of musical knowledge and judgment through small-scale writing projects. Adoption of this active approach to gathering, organizing, and assimilating knowledge, applying that knowledge towards revealing musical, historical, or theoretical "mysteries," and writing in support of one's own opinions reduces sharply the student's natural inclination to accept passively the information and perspective, however excellent, of the traditional textbook and lecture.

Learning the information about music history and literature is accomplished best through systematic summaries and tables. Rather than requiring a reader to seek out important facts purposefully embedded in a narrative account and to grope for appropriate questions to ask or categories to consider, this book provides carefully organized frameworks for the assimilation of knowledge. If the student uses this book to help relate his historical knowledge to actual compositions, it will be easier to retain that knowledge. The tables and summaries in the book are intended (1) to serve as models for the student, who can then create new entries for composers, genres, compositions, and terms not included, or simply revise and add new information as needed, and (2) to offer the basic data of music history and literature in a succinct format for study. The density and compact writing of the book require study rather than rapid reading.

Genre Entries   Each entry begins with a definition, if necessary, and a discussion of the genre's development. There may be a table indicating the important composers of the genre, the most characteristic style traits, and the estimated numbers of works by each composer. (These totals, especially those for major composers, are given to establish historical perspective, not as data to be memorized.) A listing of further readings is provided in Appendix Two.

Composer Entries   That a composer's greatest achievement or contribution lies in his music is generally understood without need for comment. It should also be understood that an attempt to list his most significant achievements leads directly to subjective statements that may at times seem biased or, in the light of subsequent research, inaccurate. Nevertheless, these statements reflect critical judgment and the application of historical perspective, both of which require encouragement in the student. If, after study, certain judgments need emendation, the reader should alter them to express his own ideas.

Within the overall systematic format, some freedom of presentation has been retained, particularly in summarizing the works and style of composers for whom either a great deal or too little is known. Some composers are noteworthy only for one genre; others seem to have developed stylistically in well-defined stages. Some have written a great many works that fall into clearly defined categories; others have avoided the standard genres and produced a succession of works difficult to categorize. Where helpful, actual or estimated numbers of compositions have been given, with the intent of offering perspective. Dates are given if they represent important periods in a composer's career or if a work is particularly significant.

The closing section of a composer summary describes his career and outlines his professional life — with whom he studied, how he made his living, where he lived, and, occasionally, the cause of his fame. The chapter bibliographies in Appendix Two invite further research.

The author strongly recommends that concentrated study of glossary terms, entries on major composers, analytical notes for compositions, and genre summaries all precede the study of the parallel chapters in a traditional textbook such as Donald Jay Grout's *History of Western Music.*

Analytical Notes for Selected Compositions   The set of questions that follows is intended as a guide for the student's use in adding other works to the selected repertory of compositions. In applying these questions it should be kept in mind that technical grasp of a composition or style enhances appreciation, since what happens in the realm of style and structure can usually be described and communicated fairly adequately in words. At least as important is the listener's emotional and aesthetic response, which ought to be recorded. Scores for the works discussed are not contained in this text. They should be consulted by the student.

Transparencies or slides of the scores could be shown in class while the compositions are played from recordings or sung.

Historical Perspective

1. When was the composition written? What is its place in the history of the genre?
2. What kind of composition is it? What is the plot or text, if any?
3. For whom, or for what function, or reason was it composed?

Description of Style

1. Who plays (sings)? Relative importance of tone color and dynamics? Noteworthy sound events?
2. Scale or mode, range, nature of motion? Continuous (spun-out) or clearly articulated phrases? Tempo constant or changing? Meter regular or irregular?
3. Modal, tonal, atonal? Texture homophonic or contrapuntal or mixed? Nature of chord vocabulary, of harmonic rhythm, of dissonance treatment, of cadences?

Analysis of Structure

1. Number of movements or sections and nature of interrelationships?
2. Growth process by spinning-out of motives, thematic development, contrast and recurrence, variation, thematic transformation?
3. Type of formal principle employed: sonata form, rondo, fugue, variation, or other?

Rather than attempting to deal with all these questions at once, the listener might well approach new compositions in the following stages:

1. Achievement of familiarity through repeated hearings, with reference to the appropriate genre summary in this book. Find the necessary information to answer the first group of questions.
2. Use of scores while listening, to make more concrete the mental image of musical events. Answer the second group of questions, consulting published sources if needed. Some freedom is desirable in the application and ordering of the questions. (Some questions will not be pertinent for all works, and some works will require formulation of additional questions.)
3. Response to the last group of questions, with reference to published sources for assistance.
4. Comparison of a given performance of a composition with other performances by different artists.

Reasoning about music is encouraged in this book through the use of unidentified excerpts from compositions and from historical documents. Testing a student's knowledge of style and repertory by using unidentified music excerpts has long been a valuable classroom tool. Questions are provided that deal with historical period, genre, elements of style, and likely composer. Employing unidentified historical prose excerpts in a similar way requires that the student draw from his or her own knowledge whatever must be added to the internal evidence to help identify the excerpt and to reason out an "interpretation" (that is, to project what has been discovered onto the canvas of music history past and present). Opportunity is thus given to apply one's knowledge and historical perspective.

Several kinds of historical documents are represented, most of which call not only for interpretation but also for identification of the author or subject. Just as in dealing with unidentified music, precise identification of the prose excerpt is less important than are the processes of deduction and interpretation. (To provide a broader choice of historical period in the solving of the "mysteries," musical and historical excerpts for neighboring periods have been combined in Chapters Two, Four, and Six.) For those stymied, hints are offered. Brief explanations — leaving room for further discussion — and complete identification of all excerpts are contained in Appendix Four. Instructors using this text should help students practice on the excerpts given and find new ones for examination purposes.

Writing adequately about music depends upon having a message, reasoning out a logical structure, and learning the value of the art of bibliography. Familiarity with the basic reference and research tools cited in Appendix Two will help reduce the effort of writing, as will use of the study ideas and research paper suggestions given in Appendix Three. Every student should learn as soon as possible through experience of the inestimable value of mastering bibliographic skills.

D.P.

Chapter One

Medieval Music

The Middle Ages lie between the glories of the Greek and Roman ancient world and the rebirth of Greek-inspired humanism in the fifteenth century. They were a dark time of poverty and illiteracy, feudalism and peasant revolts, and unremitting violence (barbarian raids, the Crusades, the Hundred Years' War), of flagrant social injustice and disease (the Black Death), and yet also a time of refinement (chivalry), of religious piety focused on life after death (monasteries and convents), and even of reason, logic, and learning, as reflected in scholasticism and in the Latin culture that remained alive and even rose to relative heights in the twelfth century. After the fall of the Western Roman Empire in A.D. 476, a new cultural synthesis was forged by the alliance in the later seventh century of the emerging Carolingian dynasty with the Christian Church. The Church dominated life in the period, its strength growing constantly until reaching its peak in the thirteenth century. However, corruption caused the Church's overambitious attempt to guide secular as well as spiritual activity to founder in the fourteenth century, resulting in the papal captivity and the Great Schism. The later Middle Ages also saw the collapse of the nominal secular power, the Holy Roman Empire, and the consequent rise of the modern European nations and languages. New forces were at work in the growth of cities, in the beginnings of capitalism, and in the foundation of the great Medieval universities, reflecting the growing secularity of life and resulting in the general recognition of the separation of church and state.

In the Medieval period, music's importance was primarily three-fold: in philosophy, where it was treated as a science; in worship, as the bearer of the Church liturgy; and in society, for its value in entertainment, self-expression, and artistic creativity. The cultural and educational values of the period were derived mainly from such Greek philosophers as Pythagoras, Plato, and Aristotle through the work of Latin scholars like Boethius (c. 480-524), whose treatise *De institutione musica* laid the foundation for Medieval education in music. Since no actual Greek music was known, it was Greek philosophy about music that influenced later ages. Boethius wrote of music as exemplifying the acoustic and mathematical relationships that govern the harmonious microcosmic arrangement of man and the earth as well as the macrocosm of the universe. Largely speculative in nature and much concerned with music's influence on character and morals, his treatise placed little emphasis on the concerns of performers and composers.

The role of the Medieval Church as the primary music institution, serving as patron, educator, and concert hall, was of indelible importance for the development of music. As the bearer of the sacred liturgy in the form of CHANT,* music served a functional purpose in the Church. Innovations in musical style came slowly and were dedicated to the greater glory of God, with early composers remaining anonymous. Music notation, greatly enhanced by the development of the music staff by Guido of Arezzo (c. 1025), was developed to codify the use of liturgical chant, as were the **church modes**. Notation marked a momentous departure from the oral tradition of the ancient world. **Polyphony**, the most distinguishing feature of Western music after about A.D. 1000 and one dependent upon notation, was apparently developed to enhance special chants and feast days in the liturgy. Like the **trope**, the **sequence**, and the **liturgical drama**, indeed like theology itself, polyphony served the much-loved Medieval practice of commentary on a sacred text. **Cantus-firmus** technique, the foundation of the most Medieval polyphony, entailed the use of the melodies of the sacred liturgy as the basis for the chief polyphonic genres of the period — **organum**, MOTET, and MASS.

Organum, the earliest polyphonic music, was cultivated most extensively at the monasteries of St. Martial in Limoges and Santiago of Compostela in northern Spain, and in the churches of Paris, rising to its greatest heights in the twelfth- and thirteenth-century compositions of LÉONIN and PÉROTIN. The adoption of metrical rhythm, so important for Western music, took place in organum in the form of the six **rhythmic modes** that apparently govern the performance of the later repertory. In addition, through the substitute **clausula** inserted into organa was born the motet. In the motet developed **mensural notation**, codified by Franco of Cologne in the thirteenth century and still the basis of Western rhythmic notation. The Medieval motet reflects an additive method of composition, in which each voice was written out completely before the next voice was composed. Since a third voice would need only be consonant with one or the other of the original voices but not necessarily both, this horizontal or linear method resulted in considerable incidental dissonance, a significant Medieval characteristic. The increasing technical complexity of the motet culminated in the technique of **isorhythm**, a late Medieval style trait that became prominent in the

---

*Capital letters for a genre or a composer's name indicate that a detailed entry on the subject appears later in the chapter.

Boldface type indicates that the term so marked is defined in the glossary at the end of the chapter.

works of Philippe de Vitry (1291-1361). Isorhythm also played an important role in the most famous Medieval Mass, the *Mass of Notre Dame* by GUILLAUME DE MACHAUT. Settings of single or paired Mass movements, as opposed to complete Mass Ordinaries, were customary throughout the period, as in the works of Johannes Ciconia (c. 1335-1411). Whereas the sacred polyphony of Guillaume de Machaut (c. 1300-1377) represents the height of French contrapuntal intricacy wedded to intensity and depth of expression, that of Ciconia presages the Renaissance in its Italianate lyricism, occasionally homogeneous texture, use of **responsorial polyphony**, and musically-related Gloria-Credo pairs.

Secular **monophony** undoubtedly played a much greater role in Medieval life than did sacred polyphony. Unfortunately, little of this music is preserved. Instrumental music from the period, since it was largely improvised, is very rare indeed. It consists mainly of dance types like the **estampie** and the **saltarello**, all of which generally unfold in short repeated sections within a fairly limited pitch range. Polyphonic dances are also found, but are few in number. In the realm of vocal monophony, the Latin song (**goliard song**) apparently flourished throughout the early Middle Ages, but few are extant. The important courtly art of vernacular poetry and song began with the CHANSONS of the twelfth-century **troubadours**, poet-musicians from southern France. A flowering of vernacular song ensued, including chansons by **trouvères** in northern France, lieder by **Minnesinger** and **Meistersinger** in Germany, **cantigas** in Spain, and **laude** in Italy. The poems of these secular songs are many and of great variety; the melodies are far fewer, basically syllabic in character, loosely organized in the church modes, and varying in style from chantlike to frankly popular and even folklike. Some became popular when they were played by wandering **jongleurs**. The imprecise rhythmic notation of all Medieval monophony makes modern transcription and performance problematical and subjective.

The development of Medieval secular polyphony took place largely in France. The polytextual motet of the thirteenth century had a chant basis but secular French texts in its upper parts. Some apparently quoted texts to refrains of monophonic songs. A great change, known as the **ars nova**, came to secular polyphony in the fourteenth century. The new secular polyphony was increasingly concerned with the vertical or harmonic element in music. In the thirteenth century the **conductus** broke away from sacred polyphonic practice not only by its non-chant tenor but also by its equally active voices and homogeneous texture. Now a treble-dominated or so-called **ballade style** developed in which one or two lower voices accompany a principal melody in the top part. The vertical emphasis is strengthened by greater use of thirds and sixths, which largely replace the "perfect" consonances (octave, fifth, fourth, and unison) except at cadences. Of great importance are new notational features based upon both the traditional triple division of the basic beat and a new full acceptance of duple division of the basic beats (see **mensural notation**), the new notation making possible a greater freedom of rhythmic expression. The major secular or chanson types in the ars nova were the **ballade**, the **rondeau**, and the **virelai**, collectively referred to as the fixed or **refrain forms** (*formes fixes*). Their great master was Machaut, not only one of the first to cultivate the polyphonic chanson but mainly responsible for the new ballade style. Perhaps of greater significance was his new process of composition, in which he composed the treble melody first and then added the other voices. By the end of the period the French love of rhythmic complexity was to culminate in the highly mannered chanson art of composers such as Baude Cordier.

The sudden flowering of Italian secular polyphony in the fourteenth century seems to have stemmed from the art of singing with improvised instrumental accompaniment and from the outpouring of lyric poetry by Petrarch and other poets. The principal composers, including Jacopo da Bologna and FRANCESCO LANDINO, were governed by the unique principles of Italian notation as codified by Marchettus of Padua. They achieved in the MADRIGAL, the **ballata**, and the **caccia** a new and distinctive rhythmic style as well as a noteworthy and thoroughly Italianate lyricism. Nevertheless, in the process of synthesis between French and Italian styles that began in the latter part of the century and was to be so important for the music of the Renaissance, Italian secular polyphony declined as rapidly as it had risen and played little part in the fifteenth century.

By the end of the *ars nova* period, which marked the close of the Middle Ages, leadership in music had shifted from the Church to the secular court and from sacred polyphony written in praise of God by anonymous composers to the ballata and, especially, the chanson, written with an attitude of art for art's sake and man's sake. Man had again become free to formulate and pursue earthly pleasures and goals.

PRINCIPAL MEDIEVAL GENRES

Chant

Chant, or plainsong, is monophonic music sung in the celebration of Christian liturgy. In the early Christian churches of both East and West, chant was composed anonymously for the purpose of conveying the sacred Word. Like the non-musical elements of the liturgy, it seems to have been modelled on the musical styles and forms of the Jewish synagogue. The most significant of Eastern bodies of chant is that of the Byzantine Church, while the Western plainsong heritage includes principally Gregorian (Rome), Ambrosian (Milan), Gallican (France), Mozarabic (Spain), and Sarum (England) chant.

Gregorian chant is the official liturgical monophony of the Roman Catholic Church and is generally regarded as one of the greatest Medieval cultural accomplishments. It was named after Pope Gregory I (reigned 590–604), who reorganized the liturgy and instituted a movement toward musical uniformity throughout the Western church. However, the earliest preserved Gregorian chant appears in manuscripts written three or more centuries later, by which time it apparently had been so altered by usage in France that some music historians refer to it as Franco-Roman chant. Despite periods of low prestige and influence from changing musical styles, Gregorian chant remained functionally important until the twentieth century; a rapid decline in use followed the Second Vatican Council (1962–65), when Latin was replaced in the Catholic liturgy by vernacular languages. About 3000 Gregorian chant melodies are extant. They remain of great importance as the basis of most Medieval and much Renaissance sacred music.

Overview c. 675–c. 1420

	FRANCE		ITALY		ENGLAND	
	Sacred	*Secular*	*Sacred*	*Secular*	*Sacred*	*Secular*
Early Medieval	chant	folk music	chant	folk music	chant	folk music
Late 12th Century	organum (Léonin)	Latin or goliard song; troubadour chanson (Guiraut de Bornelh)	organum	Latin song	organum	Latin and French song
Early 13th Century	discant conductus (Pérotin)	trouvère chanson (Thibaut de Champagne)	organum	vernacular song	discant	Latin and French song
Late 13th Century	motet (Franco of Cologne)	motet hocket estampie	lauda	vernacular song and instrumental dance	gymel	vernacular song
Early 14th Century	motet (Philippe de Vitry) (Machaut)	motet (Machaut); polyphonic chanson (Machaut)	polyphonic liturgical settings	madrigal ballata caccia (Jacopo da Bologna)	motet	rondellus
Late 14th Century	Mass Mass sections (Machaut)	polyphonic chanson (Baude Cordier)	motet Mass sections (Ciconia)	madrigal ballata (Landino)	motet Mass sections	instrumental dance

Chant Style and Structure   The rhythmic interpretation of chant remains uncertain. The approved modern practice calls for performance in equal note-values, but there is historical evidence for use of unequal note-values, perhaps even in metrical patterns, according to the accentuation of the words. Melodically, phrases or sections of chant commonly begin by ascending to a high point and then descending gradually to rest again at the end. As in Jewish practice, Gregorian chant is drawn from a common fund of short melodic patterns appropriate for a specific mode, but it does not necessarily remain strictly within the theoretical framework of the eight **church modes**.

Chant may be written basically one note per syllable (syllabic style), as in the **recitation tones** for performing psalms, or several notes per syllable (neumatic style), as in most chants for the Sanctus, or many notes per syllable (melismatic style), as in many settings of the Kyrie. It may be sung entirely by a soloist or group (direct), or by soloist and chorus in alternation (responsorial), or by two alternating choirs (antiphonal). The forms of chant include (1) partite structures with recurring sections, (2) freely composed chants, (3) strophic types (basically hymns), and (4) the characteristic balancing pairs of phrases found in psalm settings. The use of recitation tones, responsorial and antiphonal psalmody, refrains such as the Alleluia, and hymns are all features of the traditional Jewish service.

An Outline of the Gregorian Liturgy   Services in the Roman Catholic Church are of two kinds, the **Office** (the service of the eight canonical hours) and the Mass (the service commemorating the Last Supper). The texts for certain sections of the Mass (the Ordinary) are repeated unchanged at every service, while those for other sections (the Proper) change according to the occasion or season. The texts are either prose (usually Biblical) or poetry (such as hymns and sequences). The most important musical parts of the Gregorian liturgy are listed in the table below. Music for the Mass is contained in the *Gradual*, music for the Office (except Matins) in the *Antiphonal*. A selection of music from both Gradual and Antiphonal (plus Matins) and of spoken texts, all arranged in their appropriate order for the entire service, is contained in the *Liber usualis*.

Mass

The Mass is a commemoration and re-creation of the last Supper (the Eucharist); it is the most solemn service of the Roman Catholic Church and the one normally attended by the public. It consists of texts that vary according to the day (the Mass Proper) and texts that remain the same (the Mass Ordinary). The Mass may be celebrated with singing (High Mass) or without (Low Mass). Musical settings of the liturgy range from plainchant to complex works for soloists, chorus, and orchestra, and a service may well offer a mixture of various styles. For a list of the most important musical sections of the Mass, see page 7.

In common musical parlance, the term Mass refers to the principal sung sections of the Ordinary: Kyrie, Gloria, Credo, Sanctus (including the Benedictus), and Agnus Dei. Polyphonic settings of the Ordinary began in the fourteenth century, some being compilations of independent pieces, some comprising only two sections of the Ordinary, and a very few constituting a musical whole — most notably the *Mass of Notre Dame* by Machaut. Not until the fifteenth century and the appearance of the cyclic Mass does the genre become a major artistic form.

MASS ORDINARY	MASS PROPER
	1–Introit
2–Kyrie	
3–Gloria	
	4–Gradual
	5–Alleluia
6–Credo	
	7–Offertory
8–Sanctus (Benedictus)	
9–Agnus Dei	
	10–Communion

OFFICE

Matins (Te Deum)
Lauds (Benedictus Dominus)
Prime
Terce
Sext
None
Vespers (Magnificat)
Compline (Nunc dimittis)
         (Marian antiphons)

Motet

The motet is a genre whose nature has changed greatly with each historical period. It orginated when words (*mots* in French) were added to the upper part (*motetus*) of a clausula passage in organum. The motet began in thirteenth-century France as a liturgical composition with the Gregorian cantus firmus; by the end of the century, however, motets were being performed in both secular and sacred contexts, sometimes with as many as three different secular texts simultaneously and even a refrain. Their linear character was reflected in greater rhythmic differentiation among voices, as in the motets of Franco of Cologne and Petrus de Cruce, and later in the isorhythmic polytextual motets of the fourteenth century. But the later ars nova also brought to the motet an increasing use of a single text and a treble-dominated style with one principal melody and two supporting parts. The major motet composers of the period were both Frenchmen, Philippe de Vitry (15 motets extant) and Guillaume de Machaut (23 motets).

Chanson

Chanson is the French word for song, whether popular or art song, monophonic or polyphonic. Twelfth- and thirteenth-century monophonic secular chansons were cultivated by poet-musicians known as troubadours (active in Southern France), among them Guiraut de Bornelh and Bernart de Ventadorn. In the late twelfth century came the trouvères (active in northern France), including such musicians as Thibaut de Champagne and Gace Brulé. Of the approximately 2000 chanson texts for which melodies exist, most are love songs of many poetic types, the most frequent musical form being A A B. Unfortunately, their rhythmic interpretation remains uncertain.

The fourteenth-century secular chanson was usually composed in one of the three formes fixes—the **rondeau**, the **ballade**, and the **virelai**—in a treble-dominated, three-voice texture. Style in the fourteenth century was ordinarily contrapuntal and rhythmically complex, as in the works of Machaut, the most famous of those who wrote in the trouvère tradition.

Madrigal

The Medieval madrigal originated in the fourteenth-century as a secular song for two (or three) voices, in an ornamented conductus style; its text usually consisted of two strophes of three lines each, followed by a final strophe of two lines called the ritornello. The musical form of the Medieval madrigal is thus usually A A B. Major composers include Jacopo da Bologna and Giovanni da Cascia. A more important composer was Francesco Landino, whose madrigals are few. The Italian style of the ars nova is found at its best in his many ballatas, a secular genre written in the form of the French virelai. The ballata rose to popularity about 1350, but by the end of the century both madrigal and ballata had fallen prey to increasing influence from the French chanson.

MAJOR COMPOSERS AND SELECTED COMPOSITIONS

Léonin (Leoninus)   French   flourished c. 1163–1190

Achievement

1. Léonin is the first significant composer of polyphony who is known to music history. It was apparently he who extended the use of **organum** to the entire liturgical repertory.

2. He was described by the thirteenth-century theorist Anonymous IV as the creator of the famous *Magnus liber organi* (the "great book of organum") and as *optimus organista* ("greatest composer [or perhaps only singer?] of organum"). In fact, his name does not appear in surviving musical sources, and his exact role regarding the *Magnus liber* is unknown. Perhaps his role was more that of notater of an essentially improvisatory singing tradition than composer.

3. He was perhaps among the first composers to employ modal rhythm systematically. However, although the contents of the *Magnus liber* have been tentatively established, the music exists solely in later versions from the thirteenth and fourteenth centuries. Whether the passages in modal rhythm, especially those in **discant style**, stem from the original manuscript has not been definitely established.

Works and Style Summary   Léonin may have composed many organa, these works being contained principally in the *Magnus liber*. The book comprises Graduals, Alleluias, and responsories for the entire church year (in all, 33 pieces for the Mass and 13 for the Office) and was designed to augment and enrich the divine service.

As preserved in later sources, the collection features two-voice organum, either in melismatic style or in discant style. Melismatic style consists of an improvisatory upper part in the first rhythmic mode over a sustained tenor part in large, unmeasured note-values. In discant style both parts are measured, with the upper moving mainly in the first mode and the tenor in equal note-values. Noteworthy in Léonin's organa are the artistic phrasing and the recurring motives in the upper part. Octave, unison, and fifth are the harmonic intervals usually heard at cadential points, whereas the fourth and even the third and sixth may be used at phrase beginnings. The composer alternates polyphony (for the portions of chant intended for two soloists) with plainsong (for the choral sections).

Career   It seems likely that Léonin learned music while serving as a choirboy. His activity as a musician was probably mainly in Paris.

Pérotin (Perotinus)   French   c. 1160/70–c. 1205/25

Achievement

1. Pérotin was certainly the outstanding composer of his time. His organa in three or four voices written about the year 1200 constitute an extraordinary landmark in Western music history.
2. He was renowned as a composer of clausulae (passages of organum in discant style), in which he further developed the principle of modal rhythm and contributed to the establishment of mensural notation. The thirteenth-century theorist Anonymous IV described him as *optimus discantor*, the greatest composer (singer?) of discant.
3. The composer revised the *Magnus liber* of Léonin, adding a third and sometimes even a fourth voice-part.

Works and Style Summary

Organa: "Viderunt omnes" (a four-voice gradual for the Feast of the Circumcision) and the "Sederunt principes" (a four-voice gradual for St. Stephen's Day) are the most famous

Clausulae: principally, his revisions for Léonin's *Magnus liber*

Conducti: both polyphonic and monophonic, most notably the three-voice "Salvatoris hodie" and the two-voice "Dum sigillum summi patris"

Pérotin composed in three (occasionally four) voice-parts, either with two faster voices moving over a sustained tenor or with all three parts in the rhythmic modes. His compositional technique is essentially an additive one in which each upper voice is set against the tenor independently, without concern for the dissonant clashes between the upper voices except on strong beats. Short, reiterated patterns are frequent, foreshadowing at times the technique of isorhythm and bringing greater rhythmic precision. Contrasting textures and rhythmic modes are employed to create tension; major sections are articulated by a rhythmic **drive to the cadence** (a closing gesture characterized by greater rhythmic and harmonic activity). Pérotin maintained the customary alternation of unison plainchant and polyphony, but with more use of discant style in place of melismatic organum.

Career   The composer probably received his musical training in the church. The common assumption that he worked at Notre Dame Cathedral, or its predecessor, the Cathedral of the Beatae Mariae Virginis in Paris, has not been substantiated.

Guillaume de Machaut   French   c. 1300–1377

Achievement

1. Machaut was the dominant French composer of the ars nova as well as a famous poet. Fame came chiefly through his polyphonic ballades, rondeaux, and virelais, which served as models for other composers.
2. The process of composing the treble melody first and then the lower voices, resulting in a treble-dominated texture often called ballade style, was established by Machaut. It represented an important change from the cantus-firmus method.
3. The composer was apparently the first to set the complete Mass Ordinary in polyphony.
4. At the end of his life Machaut caused six large manuscripts of his music (plus two more of his poetry) to be compiled, thus becoming the first composer to preserve his complete works.

Works and Style Summary   There are about 150 compositions altogether, including:

> *Polyphonic chansons* in the formes fixes: ballades (42), rondeaux (21), and virelais (8)
> *Motets:* 23, mostly French rather than Latin, and all but 3 isorhythmic
> *Mass of Notre Dame* (in four voices)
> *Double hocket:* the "Hoquetus David"
> *Monophonic pieces:* lais (17) and virelais (25) in the trouvère tradition

In his polyphonic works Machaut generally wrote either in three voices with the melody in the top part (ballade style), or in equal-voice counterpoint in three or four voices with more complex rhythms (including isorhythm and hocket) and much incidental dissonance. Fifth and octave remain the principal consonances, although the third and sixth are common in rhythmically un-stressed positions. In the secular works the lower parts, freed from the rhythmic patterns typical of motet tenors, adopt the rhythmic nature of the more lyrical treble. The composer's music reflects the new ars nova possibilities of time and prolation, especially the use of duple meter. Rhythmic variety, particularly the use of **syncopation**, characterizes his style, with much intricate motivic work over a somewhat extended vocal range. The chansons are generally lighter in tone as well as texture, and they rely on use of musical rhyme.

Career   Machaut apparently received his musical training in the church. He took holy orders at an early age, then became an ordained priest. He was granted several canonries, the last at Rheims in 1333. He also received the university degree of *Magister*. For many years (1323–1346) he was a civil servant under King John of Bohemia. Later, he served the future Charles V of France as well as various other high French nobles. In a letter of 3 November 1363 to his beloved Péronnelle, the aged Machaut wrote of sending her two of his finest four-voice ballades: "My sweetest heart, I am sending you the two *ballades* which you once saw — and which were made for you — in writing. And so I humbly beg that you learn them: for I have heard them several times and like them very much."[1] Only a teenager, Péronnelle was favored with perhaps the first explicit reference indicating that music must please the ear of the composer.

QUI ES PROMESSES/HA! FORTUNE/ET NON EST

The score of the motet is found in two anthologies, CSM I, p. 62 and AMM, p. 134. (See key to anthology abbreviations, pp. 229.)

Historical Perspective Machaut composed 23 motets. "Qui es promesses/Ha! Fortune/Et non est," so titled because it has three different texts, belongs among the group of fifteen that have different French texts in the *triplum* (top voice) and *duplum* (middle voice) over a Latin cantus firmus apparently drawn from chant. In its polytextuality, secular character, impressive length, and use of isorhythm, it is typical of its time. The text of the triplum says that he who has faith in Fortune's promises is a fool, since Fortune is unreliable. The duplum text depicts the poet at sea in a small boat at the mercy of Fortune. The tenor consists of only a few words, which are clearly related to the themes of the upper voices: "And there is none to help."

Description of Style The linear nature of the three-voice texture, particularly the voice-crossing of the equally active triplum and duplum, requires contrasting timbres for clarity in performance. The much larger note-values and lack of text in the lowest voice invite instrumental realization. The voice ranges are basically alto, high tenor, and bass, the upper two being within the capabilities of modern countertenors. Each of the upper voices appears to have been conceived separately against the lowest voice; the relationship between the two upper voices and the harmonic result of all three voices are less important. From this Medieval intervallic approach stems an incidental rather than expressive treatment of dissonance that results in occasional parallel movement in perfect **consonances**, weak-beat **suspensions** (including some to the octave), unusual changing-tone clashes[2], accented **neighbor-tones**, accented **passing-tones**, and strikingly dissonant **escape-tones** — the last two sometimes occurring simultaneously. Rhythm plays a greater role in the composition of each line than pitch materials, beginning with the basic distinction between the active and varied nature of the upper voices in duple mèter and the regular, modal-sounding (second rhythmic mode) slow triple meter of the cantus firmus. Characteristically, the music surges forward in small note-values in the upper voices, only to pull back suddenly to larger note-values followed by renewed activity.

---

[1]Piero Weiss, *Letters of Composers through Six Centuries* (Philadelphia: Chilton Book Co., 1967), p. 3.

[2]See Chapter 2 Glossary, Cambiata.

Analysis of Structure   The form of an isorhythmic motet is determined by the organization of a repeated tenor melody (the *color*) and a repeated rhythmic pattern (the *talea*). In this motet Machaut composed the tenor melody (the color), comprising four statements of one short rhythmic pattern, in three identical phrases of twelve measures in triple time. The upper voices, however, use only nine measures of the tenor (three statements of the short rhythm's pattern) as their talea, transforming the apparent simplicity of the tenor into an asymmetrical design in which, over the course of the motet, three colors (3 × 12) equal four taleas (4 × 9). The upper voices are only isometric rather than isorhythmic because melodic repetition occurs unsystematically and in short motives, whereas rhythmic patterns recur frequently and with isorhythmic regularity before each of the cadences. Several minor rhythmic changes appear in the duplum simply to accommodate new lines of text. The clear periodicity of the structure is emphasized by syncopated passages (carried out at two levels of motion) before each major cadence, by the same descending melodic motive appearing in the triplum before the last three statements of the talea, and most importantly, by the strong cadence at the conclusion of each talea; final tenor pitches at these structural cadences are F, C, F-sharp, and F, which tend to establish F as the modal center. (See **modal/modality**.) Since, however, the motet begins in D dorian, which has no flats, and then introduces several into the duplum, it poses a dilemma for the singer who performs the triplum: whether, and to what extent, to employ the art of **musica ficta** by adding unwritten accidentals in the course of performance. In "Qui es promesses" Machaut contradicts the final F several times with important F-sharps, most prominently in the cantus firmus itself.

Francesco Landino   Italian   c.1335–1397

Achievement

1. Landino was the most famous and apparently the most prolific Italian composer of the *Trecento* (fourteenth century), his works comprising about one-fourth of those known from the period.

2. In his later works the composer succeeded in synthesizing his extraordinary Italian gift for lyrical melody with a French-influenced concern for rhythmic variety, thus creating the style of his greatest works.

3. Landino was an admired poet and perhaps the author of many of his own texts.

Works and Style Summary   There are 154 extant compositions by Landino, all of them secular. Most of these are contained in the famous Squarcialupi Codex. Little is known regarding their chronological order.

Ballatas: 90 in two voices, 42 in three voices, 8 which exist in both two- and three-voice settings

Other secular works: twelve madrigals (written for two and three voices), one caccia, one French virelai, and several works of doubtful authenticity

The composer wrote two- and three-voice polyphony with a lyrical and ornamented upper part over one or two less active parts. There is much euphonious use of thirds and sixths, although perfect intervals are still preferred at important cadences, which generally employ an upward leap of a third in the melodic line (the **Landino cadence**). Penultimate syllables of phrases and sometimes initial ones receive long melismas. In those works closest to the French style, there is much less ornamentation, making the voices somewhat more equal in motion and style; in addition, melodies are built from shorter motives, and there is more use of syncopation. The late works reveal a regular use of imitation at the beginnings of phrases as well as an increasingly vertical approach to texture in which the distribution of consonance and dissonance within the measure produce notably smoother effects than in contemporary French music.

Career   Landino may have been a pupil of Jacopo da Bologna. Although blind from childhood, he mastered music theory and played many musical instruments, including the lute, guitar, and recorder. He was a celebrated organist and also built and tuned organs. In addition to music, he studied philosophy and astrology. For many years he served as organist at the Church of San Lorenzo in Florence, where he was born. His fame was achieved largely through entertaining aristocratic Florentines with secular music.

GRAM PIANT'AGLI OCHI
The score is in MSO I, p. 27.

Historical Perspective   "Gram piant'agli ochi" is a ballata, the Italian equivalent of the French virelai. It is one of 42 extant three-voice ballatas by Landino. The text deals with a parting of lovers. With "eyes full of tears and a wounded heart" the singer calls in vain for death and promises fidelity while life remains. Although none of the composer's works are dated, the three-voice texture of this ballata may indicate that it was composed sometime after 1365.

Description of Style   The beautiful melody of "Gram piant'agli ochi" lies in the top voice. It moves largely by step with gradually increasing rhythmic motion within each phrase, culminating in long melismas ending in cadences. Rhythmically, it is more active than the supporting voices and, for all its smoothness, does engage occasionally in syncopation. The melody of the refrain rises twice to the dominant, each time falling back to the supertonic, before completing its arch from tonic up to dominant and back to tonic. In the middle section, initial motion is again upwards, reaching both higher and lower than previously, before undulating between dominant and tonic and closing with the same cadence as the refrain. The melody in the top voice is accompanied by two less active voices of lower range, resulting in precisely the texture of the French ballade. Unlike contemporary French composers, however, Landino cultivates neither rhythmic complexity nor dissonance. His accompanying parts offer harmonic support for the melody, including many full triads as well as thirds and sixths. Initial strong beats of phrases and closing chords of cadences still consist of perfect intervals. The piece has a **partial signature**: The mode is essentially major, so the tenor — being based on F — carries one flat; the upper parts, with their higher ranges, do not have problems with the tritone B–F and so do not require the flat in the signature. Of the three voices, only the contratenor does not carry the text; this omission, and the angularity of the line, suggest that the contratenor should be performed instrumentally. The tenor may either be sung or played.

Analysis of Structure   "Gram piant'agli ochi" begins and ends with a musical and textual refrain. The music of the contrasting middle section is repeated to accommodate two different passages of text. Prior to the return of the refrain text, its music is heard with a different text. The form may be represented by means of capital and lower case letters. If we allow a given letter (for example, "a") to stand for the music of a section, and the same letter capitalized ("A") to stand for that music in conjunction with a repeated text, then the musical-textual form can be easily represented. The form of this ballata, like all ballatas and virelais, can thus be represented as AbbaA. Both A and b sections close with identical vii^6–I cadences.

GLOSSARY

anticipation   an unaccented nonharmonic tone (taken either by step or leap) that immediately precedes the harmony of which it is a part, and that is repeated at the arrival of the harmony. (See Ch. 2, Ex. 1, m. 4, beats 2–3 in the treble.)

antiphon   refers properly to short syllabic pieces that precede and follow a psalm or canticle, but loosely used to include longer works of processional nature as well as settings of four texts dealing with the Virgin Mary (the Marian Antiphons; see Ch. 2 — Dufay, "Ave regina coelorum").

antiphonal   singing or playing in alternating choruses.

ars nova (Lat., "new art")   Although the term derives from a treatise from c. 1325 by Philippe de Vitry dealing with notation, it has come to be used for music of the fourteenth century.

augmentation   proportional enlargement of rhythmic values. (See Ch. 2, Ex. 16, mm. 3–4 and 8–9 in the tenor.)

ballade (Fr.)   a prominent Medieval type of chanson, one of the three *formes fixes* (or refrain forms); its musical scheme is either AAB or AABB.

ballade style   refers to three-voiced music of the fourteenth and fifteenth centuries in which the top part sings the melody over the accompaniment of two lower voices in larger note-values (thus treble-dominated); the lower parts are often played by instruments.

ballata (It.)   a major Medieval Italian genre whose form (like the French virelai) is usually AbbaA. (See Ch. 1 — Landino, "Gram piant'agli ochi.")

bar form   an AAB form found frequently in the songs of the Minnesinger and Meistersinger. (See Ch. 2, Ex. 12.)

caccia (It.)   a canon in two parts with a free supporting tenor, often dealing with the hunt; it flourished during the fourteenth century.

cadence   a closing pattern or formula that terminates a phrase, a section, or a composition. Traditionally, cadences are termed authentic if dominant to tonic (**V–I**) and plagal if subdominant to tonic (**IV–I**). Typical Medieval cadences include the 2-1/7-8 close (found in two- or three-part polyphony) in which the lower voice descends by step to the tonic while the upper voice is ascending one step to the tonic, the **Landino cadence**, the double leading-tone cadence (Ch. 2, Ex. 10, mm. 62-63), and the phrygian cadence (Ex. 10, mm. 74-75.)

canon, canonic   an imitative device consisting of the exact repetition of a melody in one or more additional voices which enter soon after the initial statement begins.

cantiga (Sp.)   a monophonic song from Medieval Spain, usually in honor of the Virgin Mary.

cantilena style   See **ballade style**.

cantus ecclesiasticus (Lat.)   Gregorian chant.

cantus firmus (Lat.)   a given melody, often drawn from chant, which is used as the basis of a new polyphonic composition. (See Ch. 2, Exs. 3, 7, 15.)

chace or chasse (Fr.)   a three-voice French Medieval canon, generally dealing with the hunt.

church modes   See **modal/modality**.

clausula (Lat.)   a short section of polyphony in an otherwise monophonic chant.

concentus (Lat.)   in polyphony, a concord (consonant harmony).

conductus (Lat.)   either (1) a Medieval monophonic strophic song with Latin text, or (2) a polyphonic genre of the same period, noteworthy for being freely composed in all voices (that is, not employing plainsong for a cantus firmus) and for its chordal style (often called conductus style).

consonance/dissonance   Notes creating tension and requiring resolution are called nonharmonic tones or dissonances, and notes that create repose or resolve tension are consonances. Different historical periods have differing understandings of consonance and dissonance. Generally speaking, the perfect consonances are the unison, fourth (in Medieval music), fifth, and octave, the imperfect consonances being the third and sixth. For a list of dissonances, see under **nonharmonic tones**.

counterpoint/contrapuntal   describe music in two or more parts that have a certain degree of individuality or linear integrity, as opposed to parts in a **homophonic**, or essentially chordal relationship; sometimes used interchangeably with **polyphony/polyphonic**.

diatonic   refers to the seven notes that belong to a scale or mode, as opposed to the chromatic notes that do not belong.

diminution   proportional reduction of rhythmic values.

discant/discant style   note-against-note counterpoint in the rhythmic modes (often improvised in two voices, the lower being a chant cantus firmus); usually in contrary motion and mostly in imperfect consonances.

dissonance   See **consonance** above.

ecclesiastical tones   See **church modes**.

escape tone   a dissonance, normally weak metrically, that is approached by step and left by leap, usually in the opposite direction. (See Ch. 2, Ex. 1, mm. 4-5 in treble.)

estampie (Fr.)   a stamping dance of the Medieval period consisting of a succession of repeated sections (aabbcc. . .).

formes fixes (Fr.)   See **refrain forms**.

Geisslerlied (Ger.)   a folklike song sung by Medieval German flagellants.

goliard song   a type of monophonic song composed to Latin texts by Medieval students.

gymel   two-voice counterpoint composed in English discant style.

heterogeneous   unlike, or contrasting, tone colors or textures within a work.

heterophony   incidental polyphony produced by simultaneous performance of a melody and one or more variants of the same melody.

hexachord   in Medieval practice, one of three six-note scales with identical interval structure, beginning on C, G, and F. See **solmization**.

hocket   a Medieval technique whereby two or three voice-parts take turns singing the notes of a melody, one note at a time. It also designates a composition that makes much use of such a technique. (See Ch. 2, Ex. 10, mm. 68-69.)

homogeneous   similar tone colors or textures within a work.

homophony/homophonic   music in which the parts move more or less together (chordal, homorhythmic, or familiar style), or in which one prominent melody is given basically chordal accompaniment.

isometric   a term used for chordal motion in the same rhythmic values (as in homorhythmic), or to indicate unsystematic repetition of short melodic motives as opposed to true isorhythm.

isorhythm   a Medieval principle by which a repeated rhythmic pattern (the talea) unifies the structure of a composition. It often appears in the tenor, but may include all parts, and it is often interlocked with a melodic pattern (the color) of a different length, the two coinciding only intermittently and at the end of the piece. (See Ch. 1, Machaut, "Qui es promesses.")

jongleur (Fr.)   a Medieval French minstrel and entertainer.

Landino cadence   a cadence in which the upper voice sings the leading tone, the sixth degree, and then the tonic (thus 7–6–1); common both before and after the time of Landino. (See Ch. 2, Ex. 1, mm. 32-33.)

lauda (It.)   an Italian hymn of praise and devotion.

liturgical drama   a Medieval play on a Biblical subject using (occasionally) monophonic music.

Meistersinger (Ger.)   middle-class German composers of secular monophony who flourished in the Renaissance.

melisma   a passage in which many notes are sung to one syllable of text.

mensural notation   a system of writing down music in such a manner that the shapes of the notes themselves indicate their relative durations. Established by Franco of Cologne in the thirteenth century on the basis of triple meter, mensural notation expanded to include duple meter in the ars nova by the division into two or three of its note-values: the long (the level of modus), the breve (the level of tempus), and the semibreve (the level of prolation). With the introduction of shorter note-values, the minim and the semiminim, there developed four standard meters, as follows:

SYMBOL	EXPLANATION	LATER EQUIVALENTS
⊙	perfect tempus, greater prolation	9/8
⊙	imperfect tempus, greater prolation	6/8
○	perfect tempus, lesser prolation	3/4
C	imperfect tempus, lesser prolation	2/4

Minnesinger (Ger.)   noble German poet-musicians who, in emulation of the **trouvères**, cultivated secular monophony in the late Middle Ages.

modal/modality   refer to music based on the church modes, which governed Western polyphony before the advent of tonality. There were two closely related scale arrangements of four basic modes: dorian, phrygian, lydian, and mixolydian.

(To hear them, play the diatonic scale of C major on, respectively, the pitches D, E, F, and G. For a composition in dorian mode, see Ch. 2, Ex. 12.) In the Renaissance came recognition of major (ionian) and minor (aeolian) modes, the basis of tonal music from the Baroque period to the present.

modulation   movement from one mode to another. In tonal music, movement from one key to another.

monophony   music composed for a single, unaccompanied voice or unison choir (See Ch. 2, Ex. 3).

musica ficta (Lat.) altered pitches or nondiatonic pitches introduced into the church modes (beginning with B-flat, as in Ch. 2, Ex. 3) and ultimately transforming them. The apparent need to add accidentals to early music, or to improvise them, brought about the modern editorial practice of placing them above the notes in question. (See Ch. 2, Ex. 1.)

neighbor tone   an adjacent nonharmonic tone heard between two statements of the same note.

neumatic   a style of performing chant with which two to four notes are often used on one syllable.

nonharmonic tones   notes foreign to the prevailing harmony, among them **anticipation, escape tone, neighbor tone, passing tone**, and **suspension**.

Office   The Office, or the Canonical hours, is that portion of the Roman Catholic liturgy usually observed by those in monasteries and convents. Its musical significance, which was greatest in the early Middle Ages, stemmed from being given far more frequently than was the Mass. The Office consists largely of prayers, readings, and psalm singing—the entire body of 150 psalms is covered every week. Two types of music are found in the Office—elaborate settings of psalms and other Scriptural passages, and a simpler style in which texts are sung on **recitation tones**. (See CHANT.) Although psalms represent the chief musical interest, there are also other Biblical texts called canticles (songs of praise) and such songs of devotion as the Marian antiphons (in honor of the Virgin Mary).

organum (Lat.) the earliest form of polyphony; based upon chant as **cantus firmus**. Organum may be parallel, free (admitting oblique and contrary motion), melismatic (the upper part containing many notes against one tenor note), or measured (with motion in both voices according to the **rhythmic modes**). The great master of organum was LÉONIN.

partial signature   when the voice-parts of a polyphonic composition have differing key signatures, as in Ch. 2, Ex. 4.

passing tone   a nonharmonic tone heard usually on a weak beat between two harmonic tones a third apart.

plainsong   See CHANT.

polyphony   music with more than one voice-part.

prolation   See **mensural notation**.

recitation tone   a melodic pattern centered on the fifth note of the appropriate church mode; it was used to intone long liturgical texts such as the Epistle. Music notation may possibly have begun with the symbols used above the text to show where the basic pitch was raised or lowered.

refrain forms   Medieval vocal forms which include a recurring section of music and text, like the French **ballade, rondeau**, and **virelai** and the Italian **ballata** and **madrigal**.

responsorial polyphony   alternation of sections for a small group of two or more with choral sections in three or four voice-parts (apparently first employed by Ciconia at the end of the ars nova).

rhythmic modes a rhythmic system based upon the meters of poetry and employed — not without some flexibility — in the thirteenth century before the advent of **mensural notation**:

1st (trochaic) - ♩ ♪♩ ♪	4th (anapestic) - ♪♩ ♩.
2nd (iambic) - ♪♩ ♪♩	5th (spondaic) - ♩. ♩.
3rd (dactylic) - ♩. ♪♩	6th (tribrachic) - ♪♪♪♪♪♪

rondeau (Fr.) a significant Medieval type of chanson of the form ABaAabAB; one of the **formes fixes** or **refrain forms**. (See Ch. 2, Ex. 1.)

rondellus (Lat.) a composition with two or three simultaneously sung lines performed by each voice in turn, as in a round; also called voice-exchange.

saltarello (It.) as a Medieval genre, a fast monophonic dance not unlike the **estampie**. In the Renaissance, a fast leaping dance in triple meter; often preceded by the slower, processional passamezzo.

sequence (a) repetition of a melody (or of all parts) at a different pitch level in the same voice(s); (b) a poetic and musical **trope** added in Medieval times to the Gregorian Alleluia.

solmization designation of the tones of the **hexachord** by the names ut, re, mi, fa, sol, la; devised by Guido of Arezzo as an aid to singers.

strophic form refers to a composition in which several verses of the text are sung to the same music.

suspension a nonharmonic tone that is normally "prepared" by being stated as a consonance, is then "suspended" by being held over beyond the duration of the harmony to which it belongs, and is finally "resolved" by stepwise descent to another consonance. Common types are the 7-6 (Ch. 2, Ex. 8, m. 1) and 4-3 (Ch. 2, Ex. 6, m. 4 between soprano and bass).

syncopation the disruption of the normal accent in a measure by shifting it to an unexpected beat.

tempus (Lat.) See **mensural notation**.

texture the relationship of the voice-parts in a composition or a section thereof. Some common Medieval textures are **contrapuntal, homophonic, ballade-style, discant-style,** and **isorhythmic**.

timbre/tone color the specific quality of a tone imparted by the voice or instrument that sings or plays it.

trope a textual and/or musical interpolation into the liturgy and its established musical repertory. A notable example is the **sequence**.

troubadour (Fr.) a Medieval poet-musician from the south of France, often of noble status; significant for creating a large body of secular monophonic chansons.

trouvère (Fr.) the successor to the troubadour; active in the north of France in the late twelfth and early thirteenth centuries.

virelai (Fr.) an important Medieval variety of chanson, one of the three formes fixes or **refrain forms**; its musical-textual scheme can be represented as AbbaA.

Instruments

bagpipes an instrument with a number of reed pipes, one or two with sound holes and the rest as drones, plus a windbag for air pressure.

dulcimer a stringed instrument whose ten or more parallel strings are struck by hammers rather than plucked.

fiddle any Medieval stringed instrument played with a bow whose body and neck were clearly divided, particularly the Medieval fiddle (*Fiedel* in Ger.; *vielle* in Fr.). It had a flat back, and from two to six strings, was unfretted, and was played at the shoulder. (See **rebec**.)

harp a plucked instrument, its many strings perpendicular to the soundboard; typically has an arched neck.

hurdy-gurdy a popular mechanical instrument whose four to six strings were activated by a wheel turned by a crank.

organistrum **hurdy-gurdy.**

portative (organ) a portable organ small enough so that one player could operate the bellows with his left hand and the keyboard with his right.

psaltery a many-stringed plucked instrument with a flat soundboard, like a zither.

rebec a several-stringed, bowed instrument with an arched back and no clear separation between body and neck.

sackbut the Medieval trombone, whose narrower bell gave it a mellower sound than its successor.

shawm a double-reed ancestor to the oboe, generally employed in the Medieval period with "loud" outdoor instruments.

tabor a Medieval drum.

vielle (Fr.) a Medieval term used for both the viol and the fiddle, the latter being the most popular bowed string instrument of the thirteenth and fourteenth centuries.

Chapter Two
Renaissance Music

The aristocracy of secular wealth and power produced by rising capitalism in the Renaissance resulted in a newly emergent feeling of personal freedom from religious authoritarianism and a consequent emphasis upon the pleasures of the senses. The period was proclaimed by leading humanists of the time as one of rebirth of the classic virtues of antiquity, primarily with reference to the visual arts and literature. Despite the gradual recovery of Greek theory and philosophy concerning music, however, the flowering of a new musical style stemmed mainly from its recognition as an autonomous art of sound unshackled by Medieval restraints imposed by liturgical or secular function and by the structure of the text. The influence of socio-political developments spurred the classical revival by bringing Byzantine scholars to Europe in the wake of the Turkish threat to Constantinople and its eventual fall in 1453. Of much greater significance for music, however, was the Anglo-Burgundian alliance of the fifteenth century, which forged musical as well as political links and helped establish an age of dominance by Northern European composers—the Burgundians, Dutch, Flemish, and Northern Frenchmen who comprised the several generations of composers known as the Netherlanders. The dominant event of the sixteenth century, the Protestant Reformation (1517), was as much political as religious, at least in its consequences. With the onset of the Catholic Counter Reformation, battlelines were drawn for a power struggle of two centuries whose effects are still being felt. Musically, the Protestant chorale melodies and their polyphonic settings were answered in musical kind by the magnificent late flowering of Catholic Mass and motet.

"The culture of the Renaissance was filled with music, permeated by it, probably to a much higher degree than the culture of any other period . . . ."[1] Music was cultivated at every level of society, with perhaps more great composers, more kinds of instruments, and more participation by both professional and amateur musicians than in any other age. The ceremonial aspects of both secular and religious life required music. Although church patronage, enhanced by the need for new liturgies, remained at a high level, the great early Renaissance musical establishments were the "chapels" of such noble patrons as Duke Philip the Good of Burgundy, Henry VI of England, Francis I of France, and Emperor Maximilian I. In addition to civil and religious ceremonies, the twenty or so vocal and instrumental musicians of noble chapels supplied music for evening entertainment, for dancing, for dining, and for private church services. To know music at least well enough to sing part-music at sight seems to have become a social necessity in the higher circles of society. Noble performers of note included Duke Philip of Burgundy, Henry VIII of England, and many others; noble composers included Henry V of England, Charles the Bold of Burgundy, and even Pope Leo X. Aristocratic patrons also supported music by commissioning works for churches and religious groups, and through participation in **academies** (exclusive societies of intellectuals and connoisseurs), many of which enjoyed chamber concerts. Amateur music-making flourished at all levels of society, in the form of domestic chamber music for the middle classes, municipal music, and popular and folk music for the lower classes. Untrained minstrels made a great deal of music, which was seldom written down. Those minstrels in the service of the courts and towns were gradually replaced during the Renaissance by trained musicians.

Renaissance composers took a new attitude towards sonority, basing their music firmly on the interval of the third rather than the perfect consonances, and firmly regulating the treatment of dissonance. Counterpoint was leavened with generous use of homophony, and polyphony was now simultaneously conceived rather than composed part by part. Along with these changes there emerged the practice of true choral polyphony, using a full vocal range from soprano to bass, and also a trend towards a homogeneous use of voices and of instruments. Those Medieval techniques that endured, such as cantus firmus, were adapted to a new aesthetic purpose; the structural control of music through the poetic text, as in the refrain forms of the ars nova, gradually disappeared, as did isorhythm. A desire to reflect both the prosody of the text and its meaning, the latter largely through **tone-painting**, reflects the strong impact of Renaissance humanism.

In its consonant tertian sonority, which revealed the influence of **faux-bourdon** in its carefully restricted use of dissonance and its greater homogeneity and fluidity of rhythm, the Burgundian CHANSON of GUILLAUME DUFAY represents the first great musical achievement of the Renaissance. Influenced by the English sound as represented by JOHN DUNSTABLE, Dufay and Gilles Binchois created an elegant chanson art perfectly suited for the fifteenth-century

---

[1]Friedrich Blume, *Renaissance and Baroque Music*. Translated by M. D. Herter Norton (New York: W. W. Norton, 1967), p. 69.

court. By way of contrast, the Netherlands chanson of JOSQUIN DES PREZ and ORLANDUS LASSUS generally reflected the influence of the motet, while the lighter tone and more democratic realm of chordal homophony and declamatory rhythms in the sixteenth-century Parisian chanson seems to have been aimed more at pleasing the music-makers than an aristocratic audience. The chanson, known at the end of the Renaissance as the **air de cour**, offered one of the few direct musical links to humanism via the late Renaissance style known as *musique mesurée à l'antique*. Following the prosody of the words of such neo–classic poets as Jean-Antoine de Baïf and Pierre de Ronsard, composers such as Claude Le Jeune employed irregular groupings of two or three beats rather than fitting the words to regular musical meters.

The creation of a unified MASS Ordinary was perhaps the greatest structural triumph of Renaissance composers. Transformation of the Medieval cantus-firmus technique from liturgically proper use in one movement in an inner voice-part into the foundation of a five-movement cycle clearly placed aesthetic above liturgical concerns and indicated the emergence of music as an art. Placing the cantus firmus in the top voice; altering it freely by using the **paraphrase** technique; introducing liturgically improper cantus firmi, including secular melodies; and composing original melodies — all represent the Early Renaissance trend towards greater artistic freedom. In the High Renaissance the **parody** technique reflected still greater freedom, but at the same time a residual craftsman-like pride in building from a pre-existent basis. New is a greater love for sonority, as manifested in the growing pleasure in textural contrast and varied chord-voicings and spacings, and in the newfound delight in tonal (as opposed to modal) chord successions. Through the achievements of Dufay and, especially, JOHANNES OCKEGHEM, the Mass Ordinary became the touchstone of competence for a composer, a position it maintained in the High Renaissance works of Josquin des Prez and Lassus (for whom it took second place to the motet in interest) and especially in the extraordinary masterpieces of PALESTRINA and Victoria.

The leading genre for new style developments in the early sixteenth century was the MOTET. Its greater concern for the expression of the words reflected the spirit of humanism, as did its thorough equalization of voice-parts. Equality of voices in their thematic roles, with any voice permitted to carry the principal theme, symbolized the change from the hierarchical structure of Medieval society to a freer spirit that recognized and valued individual genius in the arts as being equivalent in its way to rank conferred by birth. Systematic use of carefully graded and interlinked **points of imitation** characterize the principal technique explored in the Renaissance motet, an art of thematic manipulation very distant from Medieval structural devices. The Netherlanders, most prominently Josquin and Lassus, developed the style of imitative counterpoint and carried it all over Europe. Subtle refinements of text expression, referred to by the enigmatic term *musica reservata*, characterize the development of the Netherlands motet, to the point that the works of Lassus can be analyzed by using musico-poetic figures formulated by analogy with the humanistic art of rhetoric. In Italy another Netherlander, ADRIAN WILLAERT, cultivated a more dramatic style in his motets, creating the Venetian polychoral art that was to culminate in the Late Renaissance **concertato**[2] style of GIOVANNI GABRIELI.

During the High Renaissance the rise of vernacular genres across Europe fragmented what was ostensibly a universal musical language — the Netherlands style — and created numerous new secular genres: the Parisian chanson and *air de cour* in France; the **villancico** in Spain; the polyphonic **Lied** in Germany; the **canzonet, ballett,** English MADRIGAL, and song in England; and the **frottola, canzonetta, villanella, balletto,** and others in Italy. Although not without influence from the French chanson and the motet, the meteoric rise of the Italian madrigal reveals two concerns of paramount interest for the Late Renaissance, the desire both to create an emotional response in the listener and to offer a more sensuous sonorous experience. In the madrigal, as represented in its maturity by LUCA MARENZIO, tone-painting was enhanced by expressive use of chromaticism, freer treatment of dissonance, sensitivity to verbal declamation, and, in performance (according to some theorists), by altering tempo and dynamics when appropriate. By the end of the century the style was exaggerated by Gesualdo and Monteverdi to the point of abandoning the classic virtues of clarity, balance, and moderation. In these works the modes, and even the growing force of tonality, were suspended at times. Nevertheless, the flow of influence was now from the madrigal back to the motet and the chanson. Further, the use of ensemble (as opposed to choral) polyphony in the madrigal led to the accompanied (or *continuo*) madrigal for a soloist with accompaniment, and a consequent polarity between melody and bass, both of which constitute basically Baroque traits. The solo-with-accompaniment texture is indicative of the amateur's need for solo music, which led to arrangements of chansons and madrigals, just as it had earlier produced the solo frottola.

In the shadow of the magnificent body of Renaissance vocal polyphony, there arose for the first time an independent instrumental music. Beginning with the idiomatic organ works by the Germans Conrad Paumann and Paul Hofhaimer in the fifteenth century, instrumental genres gradually established themselves and thus strengthened the autonomous nature of the art of music. Solo genres included preludes and embellished cantus-firmus works for organ (Girolamo Cavazzoni), various keyboard arrangements of vocal works (Jean de Macque), keyboard variations (Antonio de Cabezón and WILLIAM BYRD), and such improvisatory types as the **fantasia** (Luis Milán) and the toccata (Claudio Merulo). Dance music flourished in the Renaissance, in works for lute or keyboard, in improvisatory dance-types like the **basse danse**, and in suites for ensembles of instruments. The most popular pairs of dances were the **pavane–galliard** and **passamezzo–saltarello**. The foremost ensemble genres were modelled on vocal types, the **ricercare** and the imitative **fantasia** on the motet and the **canzona** on the chanson (Andrea and Giovanni Gabrieli). The usual Renaissance consort of instruments consisted of a homogeneous family of

[2]See Chapter 3 Glossary.

recorders or of viols, or of various ensembles including **crumhorns, cornetti,** shawms, **sackbuts,** and **lutes** — all made in various sizes and shapes.

Whereas the change from the Renaissance to the Baroque offers a clear contrast in vocal music, the leading instrumental genres basically continued their gradual evolution. Significantly, Italy, which had attracted most of the principal Netherlanders but produced few important native composers, was in the forefront of developments in instrumental music. So prevalent was instrumental performance of vocal works in Italy that Ottaviano de Petrucci, one of the first music printers of the early sixteenth century and clearly the most influential, published many sets of part-books of vocal music without the texts. Music printing helped disseminate the art of music to a wider circle of music-lovers, both professional and amateur. The rise of a growing professional class of musicians who were not bound to the church brought greater freedom and respect for music, and also enhanced the social status of composers, though not generally to the level of the great Renaissance artists and writers. The rise of amateur music-making can be traced by the appearance of a succession of how-to-learn-music books such as *Musica getutscht* (1511) by Sebastian Virdung. The leading English treatise, Thomas Morley's *Plaine and Easie Introduction to Practicall Musicke* (1597), reflects the spirit of his age — the Elizabethan era — as well as the amateur's thirst for musical instruction. Significantly, the leading theorists of the Early Renaissance — Johannes Tinctoris and Franchino Gafuri — were also composers. Such later theorists of importance as Pietro Aron, Gioseffo Zarlino, and, to a lesser extent, Nicola Vicentino not only were highly practical in much of their approach but also wrote in the vernacular language rather than in Latin.

The dominant Renaissance attitude towards music was articulated in the later Renaissance as follows: "The proper aim of the musician, like that of the poet, is to please and delight." With these words Zarlino (*Istituzione armoniche,* 1558) not only recognized music as an autonomous art, but placed the craft of composition — which, as the science of counterpoint, required much training and many rules — in a subsidiary position to the creation of *belezza* (beauty). From contemporary sources, even as early as this, it is clear that the composer may break the rules so long as he pleases the ear. The next step, that from delighting the hearer to inducing a stronger emotional response, leads directly into the Baroque period.

PRINCIPAL RENAISSANCE GENRES

Mass

The structure of the Mass is given in the Medieval entry. Although a few complete Mass Ordinaries were composed in the fourteenth century, it was not until the fifteenth century that the cyclic Mass enabled the genre to emerge as a major aesthetic vehicle for musical expression. Two kinds of Mass other than the sung Ordinary were often composed during the Renaissance. The Requiem Mass is a musical setting of the Mass for the Dead, which differs somewhat in its Ordinary and includes various musical sections in its Proper, among them the famous sequence "Dies irae." An organ Mass is a polyphonic setting of the Mass, usually restricted to the Ordinary, for organ in alternation with chant.

Overview c. 1420–c. 1600

	ITALY	FRANCE AND BURGUNDY	ENGLAND	GERMANY
	(many cities)	*(Paris & other cities)*	*(London)*	*(Munich & Vienna)*
Early 15th Century	Dufay (Mass) (motet)	Dufay (chanson) (Mass) (motet) Binchois (chanson)	Dunstable (motet) (song)	
Mid 15th Century		Ockeghem (Mass) (chanson)		Hofhaimer (Lied) Isaac (motet) (Mass) (Lied)
Late 15th to Early 16th Century	Josquin (motet) (Mass) Willaert (Mass) (motet) (madrigal)	Sermisy (chanson) Certon (chanson) Janequin (chanson)	Taverner (Mass) (motet) Tallis (Mass) (motet)	Gombert (motet) (Mass) Senfl (motet) (Mass) (Lied)
Mid to Late 16th Century	Palestrina (Mass) (motet) Victoria (Mass) (motet) Marenzio (madrigal) Gesualdo (madrigal) G. Gabrieli (motet)	Mauduit (chanson) Le Jeune (chanson)	Byrd (motet) (Mass) (song) Gibbons (anthem-motet) Wilbye (English madrigal)	Lassus (motet) (Mass) (chanson) (madrigal) (Lied)

Renaissance Mass Composers

	COMPOSER-NATIONALITY*	NO. OF MASSES	PRINCIPAL TECHNIQUES
Early	John Dunstable (Eng.)	20 Mass movements (some in pairs); 2 complete Masses?	isorhythm; tenor cantus-firmus
	Guillaume Dufay (Fr.-Fl.)	8, plus 37 sections (some in related pairs and some forming Masses)	tenor cantus-firmus; motto
	Gilles Binchois (Fr.-Fl.)	28 Mass movements (8 in related pairs)	treble cantus-firmus and paraphrase
	Johannes Ockeghem (Fr.-Fl.)	10 complete and 3 incomplete	tenor cantus-firmus; canon
	Antoine Busnois (Fr.)	2 complete Masses	tenor cantus-firmus
Middle	Josquin des Prez (Fr.-Fl.)	18	tenor cantus-firmus; paraphrase; parody; canon
	Heinrich Isaac (Fr.-Fl.)	c. 40	tenor cantus-firmus
	Jean Mouton (Fr.)	16	14 cantus-firmus; 2 parody
	Pierre de La Rue (Fr.-Fl.)	c. 30, plus single movements	tenor cantus-firmus; motto; parody; canon
	John Taverner (Eng.)	8, and movements	cantus-firmus
	Adrian Willaert (Fr.-Fl.)	9	parody
	Claudin de Sermisy (Fr.)	12	parody; paraphrase
	Cristóbal de Morales (Sp.)	23	cantus-firmus; paraphrase; parody
	Nicholas Gombert (Fr.-Fl.)	10	8 parody; 2 paraphrase
	Clemens non Papa (Fr.-Fl.)	15	parody
	Pierre Certon (Fr.)	8	6 parody; 2 paraphrase
Late	Philippe de Monte (Fr.-Fl.)	38	parody
	Giovanni da Palestrina (It.)	104	51 parody; 35 paraphrase; 7 tenor cantus-firmus; 6 free; 5 canon
	Orlandus Lassus (Fr.-Fl.)	c. 60	parody
	William Byrd (Eng.)	3	motto
	Tomás Luis de Victoria (Sp.)	20	15 parody; 4 chant paraphrase; 1 mostly free

*Abbreviations used here and following: Franco-Flemish (Fr.-Fl.), French (Fr.), Italian (It.), English (Eng.), German (Ger.), Spanish (Sp.).

The Renaissance was the golden age of Mass composition, the contrapuntal style of the genre suiting the gravity of the text, and the importance of the Church as patron ensuring extensive cultivation. Important types included the plainsong Mass (with various appropriate chants as cantus firmi), the cantus-firmus Mass (with one basic melody, often borrowed from secular music, for all movements), the motto Mass (with the same motive at the beginning of each movement), the paraphrase Mass (with a paraphrased or embellished cantus firmus from chant, chanson, or motet), and the parody or imitation Mass (which borrowed polyphonic material—more than just the melody—from a motet, chanson, or even a madrigal). More than one of these techniques could be employed in a single composition. With the advent of monody and the concertato style in the early seventeenth century, the Mass, whose unvarying texts offered little inspiration, gradually declined in importance, thereby reflecting the decline of the Church as patron.

Motet

The term *motet* is commonly used in its late Renaissance meaning—a choral piece in imitative style on a Latin extra-liturgical text. In the fifteenth century there was a gradual demise of the Medieval technique of isorhythm and, near the turn of the century, a decline in importance of cantus-firmus technique in favor of a freely-composed piece on one text, which could be virtually any Latin religious text not from the Mass Ordinary. Treble-dominated style remained prominent with the Burgundians, whose top part could well be an elaborated Gregorian melody; they also adopted a new dissonance treatment based on triadic harmony. By 1500 the motet had typically increased in size (to two or three sections), number of voices (now four or five), and importance, superseding the Mass as the focus of style change. The influence of humanism came to be reflected in greater care for declamation (including occasional use of a syllabic chordal style), more tone-painting (depiction of words in music), and, in Reformation Germany, in use of vernacular religious texts. The chorale motet was an elaboration upon the basic material provided by a chorale melody. Of great significance for the motet was the adoption of point imitation as a structural principle in the works of Josquin des Prez. It marked the full equalization of all voices and pointed towards a new and more homogeneous approach to timbre, which is reflected particularly in sections of homophonic declamation. After about 1550, Adrian Willaert and his Venetian followers developed the polychoral motet. The major composers of motets in every European country were Netherlanders, the greatest among them being generally regarded as Josquin des Prez and Lassus. Emphasis upon expressive musical depiction of the text characterizes the motet masterpieces of Lassus, whereas those of his famous contemporary Palestrina represent a more conservative tradition.

Following the late Renaissance style of Giovanni Gabrieli, the adoption of concertato and monodic elements, including independent instrumental parts, resulted in the concertato motets of the seventeenth century.[3] In general, however, the term *motet* came to be reserved for a more conservative composition for

[3]Sacred concertos for virtuoso singer or singers with basso continuo and possibly obbligato instruments.

Renaissance Motet Composers

	ITALY	GERMANY	FRANCE	ENGLAND
Early	* Jacob Obrecht, 13	Heinrich Finck, c. 40	* Guillaume Dufay, c. 90	John Dunstable, c. 40
	* Alexander Agricola, c. 20	Conrad Paumann, several	* Johannes Ockeghem, 9	Leonel Power, c. 20
	Loyset Compère, c. 45	* Heinrich Isaac, c. 350	Antoine Busnois, 8	Robert Fayrfax, 10
Middle	* Josquin des Prez, c. 100	* Nicolas Gombert, 160+	Jean Mouton, 100+	William Cornysh, 6
	* Adrian Willaert, 173	* Thomas Créquillon, 100+	* Pierre de La Rue, 30+	Christopher Tye, 10
	Cristóbal de Morales, 100+	Ludwig Senfl, c. 100	* Clemens non Papa, c. 230	John Traverner, c. 25
Late	Giovanni da Palestrina, c. 375	* Jacobus de Kerle, c. 75	Claudin de Sermisy, 70+	Thomas Tallis, c. 30
	Tomás Luis de Victoria, 50+	* Orlandus Lassus, 500+	Pierre Certon, 40+	Alfonso Ferrabosco, c. 75
	Giovanni Gabrieli, c. 90	* Philippe de Monte, 250+	Claude Le Jeune, 11	William Byrd, 175+

* Netherlanders

chorus without obbligato instrumental parts, a genre which soon ceased to play an important role in the evolution of musical style.

Chanson

The Renaissance brought graceful accompanied melody to the chanson in the works of the great early Burgundian composers, Guillaume Dufay (over 70 chansons) and Gilles Binchois (c. 60). Despite their traditional use of the formes fixes, especially of the rondeau, the style of the Burgundian chanson does reflect the new courtly preference for simpler rhythmic motion and more lyrical and

Development of the Renaissance Chanson

PERIODS	MAJOR COMPOSERS	STYLE
1440 to *1480*	Guillaume Dufay (Fr.-Fl.) Gilles Binchois (Fr.-Fl.) Antoine Busnois (Fr.)	Generally a courtly and elegant lyrical type in a treble-dominated texture, but with increasing rhythmic freedom and independence of the voices, occasional imitation and sequence, and much use of parallel imperfect consonances (thirds and sixths).
1480 to *1520*	Josquin des Prez (Fr.-Fl.) Loyset Compère (Fr.) Pierre de La Rue (Fr.-Fl.)	Composed in dignified four-voice Flemish imitative counterpoint similar to the style of the motet, but more clearly sectional and occasionally using short homophonic phrases for contrast and more vivid expression.
1520 to *1560*	Clément Janequin (Fr.) Claudin de Sermisy (Fr.) Pierre Certon (Fr.)	A lighter, simpler, and more elegant — at times even frivolous — type known as the Parisian chanson. Distinctively French, with dancelike and declamatory rhythms in a basically chordal texture. There is some use of realistic tone-painting, especially in the programmatic chansons of Janequin.
1560 to *1600*	Jacob Arcadelt (Fr.-Fl.) Orlandus Lassus (Fr.-Fl.) Claude Le Jeune (Fr.)	Varied styles, from the light, homophonic, and strophic to a more imitative and serious Franco-Flemish style, sometimes expanded to five or six voices. There is even a *chanson spirituelle* cultivated by French Protestants. Stimulated by the poets Baif and Ronsard, some composers follow poetic rhythms closely, while others make more use of madrigalian tone-painting.

memorable melodic lines. In the second half of the fifteenth century the leading Burgundian composer was Antoine Busnois (c. 60), who wrote longer and more complex melodies and achieved greater textural homogeneity. Some of his chansons were composed in four voices, and some use not only imitation but canonic writing. In France, Ockeghem (c. 20) composed his chansons in a more or less equal-voiced style without the clearly articulated phrases of the Dufay generation.

The late-fifteenth- and early sixteenth-century secular chanson was usually composed basically in imitative style by Netherlanders and in a homophonic fashion by native Frenchmen. Because the refrain forms were no longer employed, these chansons are called free. They served the same social function in France as the madrigal did in Italy and England. They were printed in great numbers by Pierre Attaingnant and Jacques Moderne, and were also arranged by the hundreds for German and Italian lute and keyboard books. The example chosen for analysis to exemplify the genre was composed in the later Renaissance by the extraordinarily versatile Netherlander Orlandus Lassus.

Madrigal

The classic Italian madrigal is a sixteenth-century secular form in four to six voices, in contrasting chordal and imitative textures, using poetry developed from fourteenth-century models but avoiding a fixed form or rhyme scheme. It has no fixed musical structure and no musical relationship with the Medieval madrigal. Sung in upper- and upper-middle-class social gatherings, at meetings of academies, and on special occasions, the madrigal was the most progressive genre of the Late Renaissance and also the most numerous, with several thousand collections having been printed. It served as a model for similar kinds of music throughout Europe and especially in England.

Special types of Italian madrigal include the *madrigale spirituale*, a devotional song sometimes in monodic rather than polyphonic style; many were simply contrafacta of secular madrigals. In addition, there was the *continuo madrigal*, which featured an early Baroque "polarized" texture (emphasizing the melody and the bass) and was written for one or two solo voices and basso continuo; Monteverdi was the major composer of this genre. Finally, a humorous genre consisting of a series of madrigals linked by a plot has become known as the *madrigal comedy*; its leading composers were Orazio Vecchi and Adriano Banchieri.

MAJOR COMPOSERS AND SELECTED COMPOSITIONS

John Dunstable   English   c. 1390–1453

Achievement

1. Generally regarded as the best composer of his generation, Dunstable was especially noteworthy for combining characteristic English features—a love for thirds and sixths, and for full triads—with the French polyphonic tradition. Historically, he has received much of the credit for innovations common to the entire English school of his period.

Development of the Renaissance Madrigal

PERIODS	MAJOR COMPOSERS	STYLE
1520 **to** **1550**	Adrian Willaert (Fr.-Fl.) Philippe Verdelot (Fr.-Fl.) Jacob Arcadelt (Fr.-Fl.)	Written in 3 or 4 voices, with much imitation but prevailing chordal sound and restrained expression. Much concern for balancing musical and textual values.
1550 **to** **1580**	Cipriano de Rore (Fr.-Fl.) Philippe de Monte (Fr.-Fl.) Giaches de Wert (Fr.-Fl.)	Composed in 4 or 5 voices. More thoroughly imitative and longer, with more intense expression of words and meanings through harmonic means and through greater freedom in setting the text.
1580 **to** **1610**	Luca Marenzio (It.) Carlo Gesualdo (It.) Claudio Monteverdi (It.)	Often in 5 or 6 voices. Virtuoso imitative and chordal writing, with a new freedom of technique and expression employing greater chromaticism, improvised embellishment, tone-painting, and dramatic effects of dissonance, color, and declamation.
1600 **to** **1630**	Thomas Morley (Eng.) John Wilbye (Eng.) Thomas Weelkes (Eng.)	In 4 or 5 voices, both imitative and chordal textures, somewhat less radical than the late Italians; English character evident in touches of gaity and melancholy, as well as by use of cross-relations.

2. He and his English contemporaries exerted great influence upon the history of music by establishing the structural and harmonic traits later adopted by the Burgundians.

Works and Style Summary

Motets: c. 40, the largest number of them not using plainchant, 12 having isorhythm (mostly polytextual) with the plainchant in any of the three voices

Mass sections: c. 20, some apparently in related pairs, some single movements, and 2 possible cycles (or collections of single movements)

Secular songs: a few, and some carols of questionable provenance

Dunstable's style is characterized by its beautifully shaped, long-breathed melodies and the strongly consonant sound of its full triads. Apart from the isorhythmic works, which generally involve all four voices in the isorhythm, the textures alternate between equal-voice two-part counterpoint and treble-dominated three-voice polyphony. Rhythmic imitation is frequent, although brief. Within his strong major-mode harmonic emphasis upon thirds and sixths, dissonance is very carefully controlled. Metrically, pieces nearly always begin (and often end) in triple meter, and usually contain a duple section in the middle. There was apparently little development in his style, but its evolution remains unclear.

Career   Dunstable probably learned music as a choirboy. Apparently he received scientific training as well, since he later won renown as a mathematician and astronomer. He may have been in the service of the Duke of Bedford, who governed various English holdings in France from 1422 to 1435. In addition to this opportunity to know the Burgundians at first hand, Dunstable may have spent some years in Italy, but this has not been confirmed.

Guillaume Dufay   Franco-Flemish   c. 1400–1474

Achievement

1. Dufay was celebrated well before his death and long after as the greatest composer of his time, dominant by reason of his technical skill and the catholicity of his outlook and accomplishment (covering secular as well as sacred music, to Latin, French, and even Italian texts), by the importance of his positions and commissions, and by the extensive performance and preservation of his compositions (about seventy surviving manuscripts).

2. He was the most important figure in the creation of the expressive and vertically oriented Burgundian style, a synthesis that leavened the subtle French contrapuntal art of the ars nova with the simpler, more mellifluous melodic art of the Italians and the homogeneous triadic textures of the English. He played an important role in the development of **fauxbourdon**.

3. The composer was prominent in the development of the new cyclic concept of the Mass Ordinary as a large-scale, musically unified whole based on a borrowed cantus firmus. So impressive were his tenor Masses (so called from the location of the cantus firmus) that this remained the leading type of Mass well into the sixteenth century. Dufay was perhaps the first to use a secular melody as a cantus firmus for a Mass.

Works and Style Summary   There are about two hundred works altogether, in the following principal categories:

> *Masses and Mass sections*: at least 8 complete Masses (including perhaps the first written on the tune "L'homme armé"), 6 or so pairs of movements from the Mass Ordinary, and many single Mass sections
>
> *Chansons*: over 70, three-fourths of them rondeaux (for instance, "Adieu m'amour"), written in all periods of his life
>
> *Motets*: about 90 (including his famous four-voice "Ave Regina coelorum")
>
> *Miscellaneous works*: some Italian canzone ("Vergine bella"), and other works.

In his youth Dufay wrote old-fashioned isorhythmic motets with plainchant tenors and chanson-like motets, as well as three-voice hymns in fauxbourdon style. Harmonizations of elaborated liturgical melodies in a basically homorhythmic style make up more than half of the composer's works; most of the works of this type were apparently intended for use in Vespers or in the Mass. The early chansons are in three voices and are composed in treble-dominated style with **Burgundian cadences**. After about 1450, the most notable works are the Masses, which are in a more or less equalized four-voice SATB texture with either strict or paraphrased use of the cantus firmus. The texture is triadic, with carefully controlled use of dissonance and greater rhythmic independence of the voices than earlier in his career; Dufay's skill in handling four voices demonstrates his leading rank. The three-voice chansons are still treble-dominated, but in them his remarkable melodic genius depends more on stepwise motion and freer, more complex, and yet smoother treatment of rhythm. In this period there is more frequent use of imitation, more care in setting the text, more textural contrast between counterpoint and homophony, and some **V–I** cadences. More significant are the evidences of structural use of **tonality**.[4]

Career The composer served as a choirboy at Cambrai Cathedral (1409–12), where he may have studied with Richard Loqueville. He apparently became an ordained priest in 1420. Dufay's career was launched through the patronage of the bishop of Cambrai. Between 1419 and 1437 he was mostly in Italy, one of his posts being in the papal chapel (1428–33). He was welcomed at many European courts between 1433 and 1457, including Ferrara, Savoy, and Burgundy. In about 1445 he received a degree in jurisprudence at the University of Turin. For years he served as canon at both Mons and Cambrai; he often returned to the latter throughout his life, and chose to remain there after 1440, except for some years in Savoy (1451–58).

AVE REGINA COELORUM

The score is available in an edition by Manfred Bukofzer (New York: Mercury Music, 1949).

Historical Perspective "Ave Regina coelorum" was composed about 1464, near the end of the remarkable Burgundian flowering so closely linked with Dufay's name. The text is that of a Marian antiphon (a chant in honor of the Virgin Mary sung at Compline). Some words are deleted, but added is a textual trope containing the composer's name (pronounced Du-fá-ee). In his will Dufay stipulated that this motet should be sung at his deathbed; that proved impossible however; it was sung at his funeral.

Description of Style Dufay freely paraphrased the liturgical chant of the Marian antiphon for this text, treating it most strictly in the tenor. Remarkable for his time is the extent to which the chant melody permeates the other vocal parts. With the exception of some chromatic inflections and possible **musica ficta**, the melodic line is essentially modal. Its phrases flow irregularly, with much use of syncopation, but they are correlated closely with the text and articulated clearly by rests and cadences. All four voice-parts (SATB) have a vocal

[4]See Chapter 3 Glossary.

character and, although they are not quite equalized and balanced as in sixteenth-century practice, they do achieve a homogeneity unusual for the time.

The texture is generally free counterpoint, but with some imitation and some very affective block chords (at the word "miserere," with its striking assumption of minor mode). Much use is made of paired voices (two-voice writing in a work for several voices) and of three-voice writing. The triad is the main harmonic combination of intervals, and dissonance is largely regulated: chords on strong beats are either consonances or include suspensions that resolve, while other dissonances occur on weak beats or subdivisions of the beat and are of a passing nature. Chord progressions between cadences follow a melodic or linear principle rather than functional logic, and cadences themselves have a more melodic than harmonic function.

Analysis of Structure   The motet is written in two large parts, the former with two sections (in triple meter) and the latter with three sections (mostly in duple meter). The first three sections employ two lines of text each and the last two just one. All sections end with strong cadences on C, the third cadence being plagal and the others authentic. A striking increase in rhythmic activity marks the penultimate section. Unity stems from the proportional balance among sections (for example, the second and third sections both unfold in phrases of nine, ten, and twelve measures), from similar contrapuntal treatment, and, above all, from the liturgical cantus firmus, whose phrases generate points of imitation that generally end freely in cadences.

	LINES OF TEXT	MUSICAL SECTIONS	MEASURES	METERS	CADENCES
Part I	1 & 2	A	1–44	3 6 2, 4	C (V–I)
	3 & 4	B	45–76	3 6 2, 4	C (V–I)
Part II	5 & 6	C	77–108	4 4	C (IV–I)
	7	D¹ & D²	109–149	4 4	C (V–I)
	8	E	150–170	3 6 4 2, 4, 4	C (V–I)

Johannes Ockeghem   **Franco-Flemish**   **c. 1420–1497**

Achievement

1. Ockeghem was the leader of the second generation of Netherlands composers. In his works he demonstrated unsurpassed creativity and won universal respect, including the title "Prince of Music" from composers and theorists, many of whom he taught either directly or through his compositions. He was honored

during his lifetime not only as a composer and teacher, but also as a choirmaster and singer.

2. The composer raised the Mass to the principal form of composition of his time, imbuing it with a mystic otherworldliness and concealing in it with extraordinary skill such technical devices as double mensuration canons (*Missa Prolationum*) and music that can be sung in any mode merely by changing the clefs (*Missa Cuiusvis Toni*).

3. He achieved a free contrapuntal style in four thoroughly equalized voices within an expanded vocal range, the bass voice exploring new depths.

4. Ockeghem was significant in establishing an instrumental type of piece based on one or more parts from a pre-existing chanson (e.g., on his own "Fors seulement").

Works and Style Summary   Ockeghem did not compose a great deal of music.

> *Masses*: 13 cyclic Mass Ordinaries (3 of them incomplete), which constitute his chief claim to fame; one Requiem Mass (the earliest extant Requiem in a polyphonic setting)
>
> *Chansons*: about 20, most of them in three voices and written in the traditional *formes fixes*, especially the rondeau ("Ma maistresse")
>
> *Motets*: 9, most of them on texts in honor of the Virgin Mary ("Alma redemptoris mater")

In his church music Ockeghem created an original and generally continuous contrapuntal style in four independent voices (SATB) with infrequent cadences, avoidance of sequences (except for special effect), clear phrase formation, strict use of the modes, and rare or merely incidental use of imitation. Several traits that prefigure later practice are (1) the presence of a rhythmic drive to the final cadence (usually involving subdivision of the beat), (2) the use of contrasting textures (especially by varying the number of voices) to achieve a cumulative effect, (3) occasional homophonic or even declamatory passages, (4) sequential technique employed to produce a climax, (5) tone-painting, and (6) parody technique. Three of the Masses are apparently free of borrowed material, an unusual feature since a cantus firmus (either sacred or secular) was customary. The secular pieces stay closer to the common practice of the time than do the sacred ones. In them he employs a treble-dominated style in three voices, and he uses imitation frequently. In both his secular and sacred music, Ockeghem's style implies a simultaneous rather than successive method of composition.

Career   It is possible that Ockeghem received his early training as a choirboy in Bruges and that he was a pupil of Gilles Binchois, perhaps even of Dufay as well. Tinctoris praises him as a composer and as a fine singer with one of the best bass voices he had ever heard. His career was spent largely in the chapel of three successive kings of France (from 1452 to 1476, perhaps even to 1495); from about 1454 on, he was the highly esteemed master of the chapel. Earlier, he had served at Antwerp Cathedral and in the chapel of the Duke of Bourbon. Among his honors received from the King of France were appointments as treasurer of

St. Martin-de-Tours and canon at Notre Dame Cathedral. Expressions of grief at his death lament the loss of an exceptionally fine person.

MISSA CAPUT

The score has been published in an edition by Gabor Darvas (Zurich: Eulenburg, 1972).

Historical Perspective   As a composer of Masses, Ockeghem ranks among the best from any historical period. His *Missa Caput* is a cantus-firmus Mass on the same theme as the Masses by the same name of Dufay and Obrecht. The melody comes from a melisma on the last word of an antiphon entitled "Venit ad Petrum." (The antiphon, which is sung during the washing of the feet on Maundy Thursday, is found in this version only in the Processional and Gradual of the Sarum rite in England.) None of Ockeghem's works carry dates. If this Mass was indeed modelled after Dufay's *Missa Caput*, then it may well have been composed in the 1460s.

Description of Style   Ockeghem seems to have liked dark vocal colors. Not only is the lowest part extended downward to become a real bass part, but all four voices — arranged SATB — lie low in their ranges. Since the composer wrote for a combination of singers and instrumentalists, the lower parts may be played instead of sung, or any vocal part may be doubled by an instrument. Each voice maintains rhythmic independence within a fairly smooth but unpredictable flow that seldom finds the parts cadencing together. When they do, at final cadences, the approach involves an increased pace often referred to as the Netherlands "drive to the cadence." The range of the melodies is not large, and skips are normally followed by the notes that were skipped. The cantus firmus is thoroughly assimilated in Ockeghem's non-imitative, equal-voiced counterpoint. The usual modality of his harmony is emphasized in this Mass by the placement of the cantus firmus in the bass part. Dissonance is treated strictly, with preparation and resolution (sometimes ornamental) of suspensions and other such conventional devices as the **cambiata** and the passing-tone.

Analysis of Structure   In composing his *Missa Caput*, Ockeghem drew upon the *Missa Caput* of Dufay, altering his model by making selections from its cantus firmus and by varying the number of intervening rests in its presentation. He retained the major divisions, the phrase structure, the disposition of the text, even the exact melodic and rhythmic shape of Dufay's cantus firmus.[5] As in Dufay's Mass, Ockeghem's Kyrie — lacking the opening duet and motto — stands alone, his Gloria and Credo forming one pair, and his Sanctus and Agnus Dei another. Ockeghem broke away from his model in three important ways: (1) he placed the cantus firmus in the bass voice; (2) although he retained a Mixolydian cantus firmus, the Mass is in the Dorian mode; and (3) he employed the cantus firmus only once in the Kyrie, combining the two versions of Dufay into one with some omissions. Unusual for Ockeghem is the fact that the cantus firmus is presented in the

[5]Manfred Bukofzer, "Caput: A Liturgico-Musical Study," in *Studies in Medieval and Renaissance Music* (New York: W. W. Norton, 1950), pp. 217-310.

same form in each movement. In Ockeghem's Mass, as in Dufay's, the cantus firmus is heard twice in each of the last four movements, the first time in triple meter and the second in duple. Furthermore, as in the model, the same movements all begin with a fairly extended two-voice passage that in each case contains a short motto beginning. An effect of cyclic unity is achieved not only by the cantus firmus and the motto but also by a third element, the $vii^{6o}-I$ cadence with which he ends each movement of his Mass.

Josquin des Prez   Franco-Flemish   c. 1440–1521

Achievement

1. Josquin was universally admired and celebrated as the greatest composer of his time while still alive, and was of great influence upon succeeding composers (including such important figures as Gombert and Willaert); his fame has never been eclipsed. Renaissance publications of his music reveal in their number the high degree of contemporaneous and posthumous esteem for his works.

2. The composer gave greater attention to prosody than had his predecessors; his music also expresses the meaning of the words to a degree never before attempted, thus reflecting the impact of humanism.

3. Josquin was perhaps the first to use systematic point imitation as the basis for composition, a style that became standard for the remainder of the Renaissance.

4. A master of the motet, he made it the leading musical genre, as well as the most progressive, by responding ever more creatively to the challenge of its constantly new texts.

5. He was the greatest chanson composer of his time, often foregoing the formes fixes and employing the imitative style of the motet.

Works and Style Summary

Motets: c. 100; generally imitative, some are based on a cantus firmus ("Ave verum"), some use paraphrase technique ("Salve Regina"), some are free ("Absalon, fili mi")

Masses: 18, mostly based upon secular cantus firmi (whether tenor or paraphrase Masses); often full of technical ingenuity, such as canon, ostinato technique, and the derivation of themes from the letters of significant words; use of parody technique

Chansons: c. 70 ("Mille regretz"); miscellaneous secular works such as frottole, plus works that seem instrumental in nature

Despite his fame, Josquin's career was so long and his art so prolific that — in the absence of external evidence on the manuscripts themselves — it remains difficult to posit either a chronology of his works or a total picture of his musical development. His music displays remarkable inventive power and an equally noteworthy ability to control large-scale structure. He gradually moved away from the free melismatic counterpoint of his early works towards a systematic use of imitation, with contrasting passages in familiar (chordal) style, always displaying considerable concern for expressive depiction of the text. Josquin usually wrote in four or five fully equalized voices combined in interlocking phrases, often using double counterpoint, canons, ostinatos, and what initially seem to be very unpromising cantus firmi. He clearly demonstrated that he could shape a large-scale composition with or without the conventional aid of a cantus firmus. The later works bring greater motivic density and a more tightly controlled sense of pace (for instance, note-values may be progressively reduced to build a climax, and even the cantus firmus itself may gradually begin to move faster). The expressiveness of his music derived from his skill in matching both melodic and harmonic materials to the text, which came to occupy more and more of his attention.

Career   The composer was apparently a choirboy at St. Quentin. Although it seems unlikely, he may have studied with Ockeghem. During his career he travelled frequently and widely, assuming numerous important posts in Italy (with the papal chapel), the Sforza family, and the Este family in Ferrara, where he reached artistic maturity, in France (the royal court), and in Burgundy, and may also have been employed by the Netherlands court. Evidence suggests that the mature Josquin composed only when and as he wished, and that his displeasure could fall like lightning upon his choristers.

MISERERE MEI, DEUS

The score is No. 37 in vol. VIII of the composer's *Complete Works*, ed. Albert Smijers.

Historical Perspective   The text of "Miserere mei, Deus" comprises the entire twenty verses of Psalm 50 in the Vulgate, with a few minor alterations. A deeply moving song of David for the remission of sins, the psalm is sung on several occasions in the Roman Catholic Church, including the burial service. The motet was composed for Duke Hercules I of Ferrara, probably sometime after Josquin's return to Ferrara in 1503. Well before this time, the genre of the motet had become, through its textual variety and expressive scope, the composer's principal vehicle for realizing his humanistic ideals in music.

Description of Style   The liturgical psalm tone for intoning this text may have been the source for Josquin's terse cantus firmus, a two-pitch pattern (sometimes a major second, sometimes minor) stated twenty-one times and serving as a refrain after each new phrase of text. One voice, the second tenor, is added to the basic SATB texture specifically to sing the cantus firmus. The long and stark text is rarely extended by melismas, the setting remaining almost strictly syllabic. The rhythmic activity is sometimes intricate, as in the canonic passages, and at other times simple and declamatory. Continuity is maintained by avoiding perfect cadences within each major section, while the final cadences are each preceded by a notable increase of rhythmic activity. The text is suitably matched by the solemnity of the predominant Phrygian mode and by the harsh suspensions of minor second and major seventh that occur naturally in it. The composer's craft is revealed particularly in his masterful handling of texture. The cantus firmus is equally suited to homophonic or imitative treatment; the constantly full texture of the refrain forms pillars of structural support between the verse settings. Musical expansion is generated by imitation, which is used in a seemingly endless variety of ways. Many phrases begin with paired voices, which may enter either simultaneously with different materials or separately with imitation of a common line. Important points of imitation are maintained strictly for a longer time, at larger time intervals, and at perfect pitch intervals. Especially noteworthy is the composer's mastery of the art of transition between phrases of contrasting themes and textures. Among the wonderful moments when music and text unite with affecting purpose is a canon which—in illustration of the text—causes the phrase "ecce enim veritatem dilexisti" to "lack truth in its inward parts."

Analysis of Structure The motet has three large parts, comprising eight, seven, and five verses of the psalm. In Part I the cantus firmus is sung first beginning on e', then again on each descending step of the Phrygian scale to the octave below. The procedure is reversed in Part II, as the cantus firmus in diminution by half ascends through the same scale. (Verse 14 is divided in two to permit the necessary eight statements.) Part III finds it descending by step from e' to a final cadence on a. Imitation and antiphonal repetition of whole phrases emphasize purely musical factors in Part III, producing a feeling of breadth and climax as well as conveying the text's course from intense supplication to humble faith in God's mercy. In addition, similar motives of stepwise ascent (man's supplication) mark the verses of Part I, and motives featuring stepwise descent (God's mercy) characterize Part III.

Adrian Willaert   Franco-Flemish   c. 1490–1562

Achievement

1. Willaert was a greatly admired and highly influential composer who brought Venice to the musical forefront and taught many notable composers, among them Cipriano de Rore, Andrea Gabrieli, and Jacques Buus, as well as the great theorist Gioseffo Zarlino.
2. Along with Philippe Verdelot and Jacob Arcadelt, Willaert was among the earliest group of important Renaissance madrigalists and among the first to employ extensive harmonic chromaticism. Of special significance was his new sensitivity to the text, a feature of Willaert's music for which he was highly praised by his contemporaries.
3. Although his antiphonal psalm settings were not the first of their kind, they established firmly the practice of **cori spezzati** (divided choirs), which was to remain characteristic of Venetian church music.
4. Willaert was among the first to publish collections of instrumental ricercari.

Works and Style Summary

Motets: c. 175 (the last of them published in his famous *Musica nova* of 1559), some thoroughly imitative in texture and some based upon the older cantus firmus technique

Madrigals: 25 in *Musica nova*, revealing a synthesis of Italian and Franco-Flemish traits

Masses: c. 10 (half of them in four voices), mainly of the parody type

Chansons: (c. 75) composed in the richest Franco-Flemish manner

Instrumental works: both ricercari and fantasie, composed in a highly imitative style

Willaert fused his native Franco-Flemish tradition of imitative counterpoint with the Venetian love for richness of harmony and tone color. On the one hand, he achieves expressive and scrupulously correct declamation of the text, even to the point of lessening the imitative density; on the other, he exhibits a truly characteristic Franco-Flemish penchant for canon and contrapuntal complexity.

Career   Willaert studied law at the University of Paris, where he became a music student of Jean Mouton, a disciple of Josquin des Prez. His most important positions were all in Italy, in musical service to the Duke of Ferrara (1520–25) and Cardinal d'Este in Milan (1525–27) and, most significantly, as *maestro di cappella* at St. Mark's in Venice (1527–62).

Giovanni Pierluigi da Palestrina   Italian   c. 1525–1594

Achievement

1. Palestrina created an exemplary style of church music expressing the spirit of the Counter-Reformation, a style upheld as a model during his lifetime as well as by succeeding generations, consciously imitated by later composers, and officially sanctioned by the Church. Ultimately, it became the basis of the so-called *stile antico* (the "old style").
2. He was the first Renaissance composer whose works were published in a complete edition (by Breitkopf & Härtel in Leipzig, 1862–1903).
3. Along with Annibale Zoilo, Palestrina was entrusted in 1577 with a revision of the Gregorian chant in the Gradual and the Antiphonal; although some revisions were made, the task was not completed.

Works and Style Summary

Masses: 104, comprising 7 on a tenor cantus firmus, 35 paraphrase Masses, 51 parody Masses, 5 canonic Masses, 6 freely composed Masses (*Missa Papae Marcelli*)
Motets: More than 375, many of them freely composed, including 35 Magnificats, 68 Offertories, 4 or 5 Lamentations, and 65 hymns
Madrigals: c. 140, 83 of them secular and the remainder *spirituale*

Palestrina composed in a wondrously smooth and exquisitely balanced style that marked in its own way a refined culmination of the traditional Netherlands imitative technique. Treatment of both rhythm and harmony is completely controlled; nothing is allowed to disturb the smooth, continuous flow, and all dissonances except suspensions are carefully placed on unstressed beats. Whether long or short, the melodies unfold in balancing curves, with infrequent large leaps that are immediately countered by a change of direction in the melodic line. The text settings always faithfully reflect natural accentuation, but never in an immoderate way. Textures range from chordal to many-voiced imitation; even in imitative passages the composer achieves clarity of texture by means of interlocking entries, antiphonal writing, reduction in the number of parts, invertible counterpoint, repetition of material, and careful spacing and voicing of the parts. Despite his careful restrictions on personal and subjective expression, few composers have approached the refined eloquence of Palestrina.

Career   Palestrina, who learned music as a choirboy at Santa Maria Maggiore in Rome, may have studied with Mallapert and Firmin Le Bel, both Frenchmen. A tenor and an organist, he became an excellent church musician. After 1551, his career was spent entirely in Rome, where he served at the Capella Giulia in St. Peter's, in the papal Capella Sistina, at St. John Lateran, and at Santa Maria Maggiore. In later life he became a successful fur merchant as well.

MISSA PAPAE MARCELLI

Score available in Lewis Lockwood, *Palestrina: Pope Marcellus Mass* (Norton Critical Score, 1975), and MSO I, p. 61.

Historical Perspective   This is apparently a "free" Mass, based on a new and original theme rather than a pre-existing one, an unusual practice for Palestrina. The increased use of chordal writing reflects the composer's concern for the intelligibility of the text, a major issue for church musicians during the Council of Trent. The title (after Pope Marcellus, who reigned for only three weeks in 1555) apparently stemmed from that pope's views concerning the necessity for textual clarity in church music. Published in 1567, in Book II of Palestrina's Masses, the *Pope Marcellus Mass* was composed perhaps five years before that.

Description of Style   There are basically six voice-parts (SATTBB), with a seventh (S) added for the second Agnus Dei. By way of contrast, the Crucifixus (SATB) and Benedictus (SATT) employ only four voices. As always with Palestrina, the spacing and voicing of the chords as well as the varying linear relationships among the voices create an amazingly varied and expressive sound spectrum. Stepwise motion within a limited range is normal in the upper parts, with leaps being followed by conjunct (stepwise) motion in the opposite direction.[6] The lower parts, on the other hand, leap about freely (though avoiding sixths and sevenths), providing harmonic support. Phrases may be balanced—the Kyrie, for example, begins with phrases of four bars plus four bars, then three plus three—but are of no regular size. Phrases usually begin with imitation, become freer as they unfold, and overlap with their successors in an inexhaustible variety of ways. The **tactus** remains steady and the meter duple, but voices usually differ in rhythmic accent. Ionian mode is always strongly confirmed following mixolydian openings (except in the Sanctus). The Gloria and the Credo are more chordal and less linear than usual for Palestrina, and therefore more succinct. Contrapuntal complexity is limited throughout, although imitation is normal and paired imitative entries frequent. Dissonance is totally controlled, and consists largely of passing-tones and suspensions. Cadences occur on various scale degrees but the variety of cadential chords is relatively circumscribed. Somewhat surprisingly, root progression is generally by fifths and fourths with a recurrent emphasis on plagal (**IV–I**) motion, thus reflecting, on a larger scale, the characteristic interval of the opening theme.

---

[6]See, for example, the ascending fourth of the opening theme.

Analysis of Structure   Palestrina followed most of the standard structural procedures of the period: three-fold Kyrie, Sanctus with fewer-voiced Benedictus and repeated Hosanna, two-fold Agnus Dei (the second with more voices and greater complexity). But because of chordal declamation, both Gloria (in two sections) and Credo (in three, including a four-voice Crucifixus) are simpler and shorter than usual. The unifying opening theme is heard in the Kyrie, Credo, and both Agnus Dei sections, and is clearly suggested in the Gloria and the Benedictus. Growth is characteristically achieved by imitative counterpoint. A striking feature (which is mentioned by Lockwood) is the structural use of contrasting sonorities; for instance, in both the Gloria and the Credo alternating voice-groups are employed until the climactic moment, when a full choral texture is finally permitted.

Orlandus Lassus   Franco-Flemish   1532–1594

Achievement

1. Lassus was the culminating figure in the great line of Franco-Flemish composers, and the most versatile and cosmopolitan of them all. He composed idiomatically in all genres and styles from the most elevated to the most popular. A peerless master of the motet and the chanson, he was referred to by his contemporaries as the "Prince of Music."
2. Lassus succeeded in musically expressing the meaning of his texts so effectively that his work served as a model and inspiration in this regard for many of his younger contemporaries.

Works and Style Summary   Lassus certainly composed at least 1250 works (and possibly as many as 2000) of all types, both sacred and secular, large and small, and he set texts in four languages.

> *Motets*: more than 500 (the largest published collection being the *Magnum opus musicum*, 1604)
> *Masses*: about 60, as well as about 100 Magnificats, many of both genres employing parody technique
> *Miscellaneous sacred works*: psalms, hymns, Passions, spiritual madrigals, and others
> *Secular works*: c. 150 chansons, c. 150 madrigals, c. 100 Lieder (many of these sacred)

A chronology of the composer's works and a detailed history of his stylistic evolution are not yet possible. His amazing ability to grasp the essence of each style he undertook is evident from his youth, when he assimilated the style of popular Italian composers such as Cipriano de Rore. During his career he mastered the Italian madrigal, both Netherlands and Parisian types of French chanson, and even the somewhat more rugged style of the German polyphonic Lied. His expressive scope ranged with ease from utmost gravity to high humor. His ability to move the listener's emotions was likened in his time to the affective art of rhetoric, the devices of which he translated into musical devices, but without sacrificing the consummate beauty and technical perfection of his music. His native style of Netherlands imitative counterpoint was brilliantly employed from his youth, with emphasis upon very free imitative techniques and the use of parody, and he was also skilled at the older technique of cantus-firmus writing. Thematic originality and mastery of vocal scoring characterize his style, in which texture, rhythmic motion, phrase length, melodic contour, and harmonic progressions all serve the dramatic depiction of his texts. Motives are often short and clearly derived from particular words, and there is much use of wide leaps, dotted rhythms, and various kinds of homophony, including much chordal declamation. Many works are labelled "apt for voices and instruments." Rather than adopting forward-looking Baroque features at the end of his career, he chose to refine his art, using less declamation and turning instead to greater density and complexity of contrapuntal texture.

Career   Lassus may have learned music as a choirboy at the Church of St. Nicholas in Mons. His talent was so remarkable that he is said to have been kidnapped several times to serve as a boy soprano, spending much of his youth in various Italian cities. From 1544 he served in a musical capacity to the Viceroy of Sicily. In 1550 he was employed by the Marchese della Terza. At the extraordinarily early age of 21, he became *maestro di cappella* at the Church of St. John Lateran in Rome. In 1555 he took up residence in Antwerp, where he published several important works. Finally, in 1556, he went to Munich to serve the Duke of Bavaria, at first as a singer (a tenor) and then, in 1563, as Kapellmeister. He spent the rest of his life in this post (though he still travelled widely), being honored with knighthood and by magnificent publications of many of his works.

O FAIBLE ESPRIT

The score is published as No. 7 in vol. XIII of *Das Chorwerk*, ed. Heinrich Besseler (Berlin: Möseler Verlag, 1931).

Historical Perspective   Highly characteristic of the composer, Lassus' chansons reveal clearly his protean aspect and his unsurpassed range of styles, including those of the madrigal, Lied, and motet. Humorous, amorous, declamatory, religious, pastoral, love-lorn — there is no better introduction to the musical aesthetic and achievement of the High Renaissance. One of approximately 150 chansons by the composer, "O faible esprit" (published in 1571) is a madrigalian setting of a sonnet by Joachim du Bellay. "A feeble spirit, burdened by the sorrows of love," apparently seeks to arouse pity in the breast of the beloved. The poet wonders that he does not rest in the grave, that his heart does not turn to ashes, that his eyes do not become fountains. "O God, who permits me to dare attempt so much, why do you make my undertakings fruitless?" In the second part of the song, after criticizing Cupid for his unerring aim and for setting the poet's soul aflame, he addresses his beloved: "O face of an angel, O heart of stone, at least behold the anguish I endure."

Description of Style   Each phrase of text receives its own setting without obvious recurrences of thematic material. Melodies are shaped and rhythms paced so as to emphasize textual passages of particular concern. Except for the opening motives of a few phrases, melodic motion in the top voice is predominantly conjunct, striking leaps being reserved for tone-painting (for example, an octave descent at the words "under the earth," measure 13) or intensifying the text. Other parts engage freely in harmonically designed disjunct motion. The mode, nominally dorian, is usually altered by accidentals and swings freely between major and minor. Rhythmically, the note-values are largest at the beginning, then basically half as large, and finally, in Part II, diminished once again by half. The chanson closes with a characteristic drive to the cadence. The texture ranges from predominantly non-imitative counterpoint to an ingenious simulated polyphony that proves an excellent vehicle for conveying the text. The harmonic language is a rich amalgam from two sources — a modal one, seen in the step progressions and linear voice-leading, and a tonal one, signified by two strong descending circles of fifths that lead, in each part, toward a final cadence (I, mm. 42–46; II, mm. 73–78). Suspensions are employed both for tone-painting (*faible*, *peines*, *dure*) and as typical devices in **V–I** cadences.

The original clefs identify the voices as sopranos I and II, altos I and II, and baritone. Whereas the outer voices are seldom crossed by the inner ones, the three inner parts overlap a great deal, creating a rich triadic texture. Both Parts I and II of the chanson begin in four voices, expand to five with the entrance of the baritone, offer varied groupings among the voices, and ultimately return to a full five-voice texture.

Analysis of Structure   The emotional course of the poem, from melancholy resignation through active concern to anguished anxiety, is reflected in the twice-diminished unit of rhythmic motion, as mentioned above. Parts I and II both begin syllabically and later introduce some melismas and repetitions of phrases; both also end with full five-voice texture. About midway in each part occur very similar phrygian half-cadences on E (as **V** of **V**). By way of contrast, Part I, the larger of the two, moves from tonic to dominant, whereas Part II begins and ends in the tonic. The melodic climax (and the only identical repeat of a sizable phrase) occurs at the end of Part II.

William Byrd   English   1543–1623

Achievement

1. Byrd was the finest of Elizabethan composers and widely recognized as such by his contemporaries. Not only was he responsible for continuing the great tradition of English vocal polyphony, but he excelled in all branches of composition. "After Shakespeare, Byrd is without doubt the most imposing figure of the English Renaissance."[7]

2. His influence on English composers was exerted by his own music, by his monopoly on music printing in England, and by his teaching. His pupils included Thomas Morley and Thomas Tomkins, and perhaps Peter Philips, Thomas Weelkes, and John Bull. His principles of music were clearly set forth in Morley's *Plaine and Easie Introduction to Practicall Musicke* (1597).

[7]Paul Henry Lang, *Music in Western Civilization* (N.Y.: W. W. Norton, 1940), p. 286.

3. "The perfection of English virginal music from primitive beginnings" was perhaps "his greatest single accomplishment."[8]
4. Byrd may have invented the **verse anthem** for the new Anglican service.

Works and Style Summary

Latin church music: 3 Masses and many motets (two famous collections of motets are entitled *Cantiones* and *Gradualia*, the latter comprising 100 motets or motet sections, which together provide complete Mass Propers for the principal feasts of the entire church year)

English church music: including both Great and Short **Services** as well as anthems

Miscellaneous vocal music: both sacred and secular, a major type being his songs for one and two voices accompanied by a consort of viols, a genre of which he was the principal composer

Keyboard music: virginal (harpsichord) works (such as variations and pavans and galliards, in the collections *The Fitzwilliam Virginal Book* and *My Ladye Nevells Booke*), and organ music (principally preludes, hymns, and antiphons)

Byrd achieved consummate mastery of the four- and five-voice contrapuntal art of the Netherlanders, the first English composer to do so; nevertheless, his art was thoroughly, even obstinately, original and as full of character as his stormy life as a staunch Catholic during an age of open persecution of that church in England. Byrd's vocal music is distinguished by his vivid text interpretation, by his English bent for harmonic effects and expressive chromaticism, by his highly expressive thematic material, and, especially, by his special gift for molding the shape of a phrase, a section, or a composition. Having systematically mastered many styles and genres early in his career (using the works of Thomas Tallis, Christopher Tye, and Alfonso Ferrabosco as models) he ranged freely among them and made major contributions to each. As the hitherto least developed type, virginal music stands foremost among his achievements, occupying his attention mainly at the beginning and end of his career. In keeping with the more devotional and less penitential nature of his later texts, Byrd turned away from intense expressiveness in his vocal music composed after 1590 towards a simpler and more concise style with more homophony and unassuming binary forms. Tone-painting is present, but the composer avoids **madrigalism**. Characteristically, the last Masses are highly original, the composer disdaining to use the conventional parody technique as his structural basis.

Career   The composer was a pupil and later a business partner of Thomas Tallis. He was also a close friend of Alfonso Ferrabosco, who taught him Netherlands imitative counterpoint. After serving as organist and choirmaster at Lincoln Cathedral from 1563 to 1572, he became a member and eventually organist of the Chapel Royal in London. In 1575 he and Tallis acquired the monopoly of printing and selling music in England, a privilege which he retained until 1596. In his later years he spent less time with the Chapel Royal, devoting himself more to music for the Catholic Church.

[8]Joseph Kerman, "Byrd," *New Grove Dictionary* III, 538.

Luca Marenzio　　**Italian**　　**1553–1599**

Achievement

1. Marenzio was "perhaps the greatest Italian composer of the century" (Edward Dent). He was certainly among the best, and was also the most popular and influential of all the madrigalists. His first book of madrigals (Venice, 1580) achieved at least ten editions between 1580 and 1610. In his works may be seen complete technical mastery wedded to sensitive and scrupulous setting of the text. The later books of madrigals reveal greater depth and more advanced harmonic treatment.

2. Through his madrigals that were published in Yonge's *Musica Transalpina* (1588), Marenzio served as an important model for the development of the English madrigal. One English view was expressed in Henry Peacham's *Compleat Gentleman* (1622): "For delicious Aire and sweet Invention in Madrigals, Luca Marenzio excelleth all others whatsoever."

Works and Style Summary　A notably prolific composer, Marenzio published twelve of his sixteen books of madrigals within the years from 1580 to 1585.

Madrigals: 16 books, 9 for five voices and 6 for six voices

Popular types: 5 books of **villanellas** for three voices, as well as various other genres

Madrigali spirituali: 1 book for five voices

Motets: 3 books, 2 of them for four voices (about 75 motets altogether)

Masses: 3

Marenzio made masterful use of all the various trends in madrigal writing of his time — from light to serious, from simple to complex, even the brilliant and declamatory Venetian manner — all as required for the setting of the individual text. His early style featured contrapuntal ingenuity and a light and lyrical pastoral character, whereas the later works use more melancholy tones to go with more serious texts. The change in his style is noted in the preface to his 1588 collection of madrigals. From this collection on, the treatment of tonality, of dissonance, and of tone-painting was subordinated to a more integrated structure and a smoother rhythmic flow. In addition, he gained a darker sonority by employing two tenors rather than two sopranos in his five-voice settings. His progressive nature was reflected in the large cycles of madrigals written late in his career and in his use of the Venetian polychoral style in some of the motets.

Career　Marenzio served as a choirboy at the Cathedral of Brescia. He was apparently a pupil of Giovanni Contini. As a young musician, he was known primarily for his singing, and he seems to have remained in demand as a performer. His career, apart from service at the Polish court, was spent largely in Rome, where his patrons included three cardinals (most notably Cardinal Luigi d'Este). He also established ties in the highly musical cities of Ferrara, Mantua, and Florence.

CRUDELE ACERBA
The score is in CM, p. 33 and in Denis Arnold's *Marenzio: Ten Madrigals* (London: Oxford University Press, 1966).

Historical Perspective   Although Marenzio's later books of madrigals, in particular that of 1599, were well-received in his time, his reputation has rested for many years on his earlier works and has only recently been enhanced by a full regard for the complexities of his later madrigal collections. "Crudele acerba" was published in the ninth book of five-voice madrigals printed by Angelo Gardano (Venice, 1599). Dedicated to the Duke of Mantua, this volume was the last of the composer's publications. The poem is by Petrarch. It deals with "cruel death," which permits no happiness and leaves the poet to spend "his darkened days and anguished nights in weeping;" sorrows and sighs will not result in verse, and painful torment stifles any manner of expression.

Description of Style   Whereas Marenzio essentially composes each line of this text with different musical materials, he carefully maintains rhythmic continuity within the three sections of the piece and also, with conspicuous disjunct exceptions, he achieves melodic integration by almost constant stepwise motion in either the top voice or the lowest voice, or both. The composer here excels in the subtle use of harmony to underline the text, in the ease with which textures change, and in the large-scale control of the twin harmonic poles of F major and A. End-of-the-century mannerism found expression in Marenzio largely as harsh chromaticism spiced occasionally with cross-relations (for example, mm. 16–18 and 44–45), accented passing-tones, and chains of suspensions — some of them unprepared. As opposed to the earlier practice of a low-range fifth voice, Marenzio here wrote for two sopranos, alto, tenor, and bass. Often one voice rests, or two voices are paired against the other three; several times, especially near the end, the upper two voices are paired in thirds in the Baroque manner.

Analysis of Structure   "Crudele acerba" is a concise madrigal in three distinct sections articulated by contrasting themes and, in particular, by strong cadences. Each section sets two lines of text. The first (mm. 1–25) begins with a freely-treated point of imitation marked by a disjunct motive, large note-values (whole-notes), and a cumulative texture. The section continues with an expansive, quasi-sequential setting of the second line of text, which leads to a melodic climax followed by a V–I⁶ deceptive cadence strengthened by a 7–6 suspension.
   In the second section (mm. 26–57), the basic note-value is the half-note, and there is much syncopation. The word "pianto" (weeping) is illustrated by syncopation, suspension, and the traditional motive of stepwise descent, highlighted at its repetition by the use of fauxbourdon (mm. 27–40). The setting of "giorni oscuri" (darkened days), which is melodically like the theme that began the section, brings forth chromatic tone-painting that is further heightened by a suspension with dissonant preparation. The expanded setting of line four of the poem leads through an extraordinary harmonic progression fraught with chordal resolutions of suspensions to a V–I cadence in F major.

The third section (mm. 58–89) begins and ends with the upper voices moving in parallel thirds over the other parts. After a dramatic pause by the upper voices underscores "sospir" (sighs), the composer increases rhythmic activity by introducing eighth-note motion for a point of imitation that is made even more striking by its disjunct motive and cumulative entries. The last line of the poem reintroduces syncopation, now over a conjunct bass line, and, after some musical expansion, the section and the piece close with a somewhat surprising (to modern ears) Phrygian cadence on A.

Giovanni Gabrieli   Italian   c. 1556–1612

Achievement

1. Gabrieli is significant for having established a truly instrumental style in his **canzonas** and sonatas. He was perhaps the first to write vocal works with independent instrumental accompaniment, and one of the first to designate specific instruments for pieces (as in the *Sonata pian' e forte*) as well as specific dynamics.
2. The Venetian vocal and instrumental traditions of the High Renaissance were brought to their culmination by Gabrieli, who expanded the motet into a work for two, three, four, even five choirs (some of them vocal, some instrumental), employed in **concertato** fashion.
3. He was a famous and influential teacher; Heinrich Schütz, Michael Praetorius, and numerous other Northerners are numbered among his pupils.

Works and Style Summary   The composer published two collections of music jointly with his uncle Andrea Gabrieli, and six more of his own, three of which appeared posthumously.

> *Motets in concertato style*: Sacrae symphoniae, Books I and II, including works for between twelve and twenty performers
> *Instrumental ensemble works*: canzonas, many sonatas (a term which, in this period, generally denoted a genre similar to the old-fashioned **ricercare**) and other works
> *Organ music*: ricercari, canzonas, **fantasias**, **toccatas**[9]
> *Madrigals*: c. 30, some written for two groups of four voices each

Gabrieli composed in a colorful, polychoral idiom, using both instrumental and vocal choirs, as well as soloists, in concertato textures. His works display progressive features such as strong reliance on speech rhythms, freer dissonance treatment, and much use of short contrasting motives. Syncopation and cross-rhythms are present from the beginning of the composer's career, as is his preference for full homophonic textures and a diatonic idiom. Use of *cori spezzati* diminishes in his later works, which reveal idiomatic use of instruments as well as voices, and emphasize contrast by section rather than by phrase. An effect of unity is often achieved by use of the rondo principle. Unlike most of the major composers of the Late Renaissance, Gabrieli restricted himself to a relatively small number of genres, concentrating in each of them upon the element of sonority.

[9]See Chapter 3, Organ Music.

Career   Giovanni was almost certainly a pupil of his Uncle Andrea (who had in turn been a student of Willaert) and may also have studied with Lassus during his service from 1576 to 1580 at the ducal court in Munich. From 1585 until his death, he served as second organist at St. Mark's in Venice, and also as organist and director of music for the religious order of San Rocco.

GLOSSARY

a cappella (It.)   without instrumental accompaniment (with reference to choral performance); literally, "in the chapel."

academy   a learned society, founded in imitation of Plato's Academy for the purpose of furthering the arts, literature, or science. In the Renaissance the idea of the academy took root in France and Italy. The Baroque period brought the establishment of academies all over Italy, many of which cultivated music and even gave private and public concerts.

air de cour (Fr.)   an accompanied French strophic song for one or two voices from the Late Renaissance and Baroque periods.

anthem (Eng.)   The anthem evolved from the Latin motet after the Reformation. Despite Latin titles, it was sung in English, assuming the role of the motet in English Anglican and Protestant services. Anthems are usually simpler, more homophonic in style than the motet, more solicitous of conveying the text clearly. The verse-anthem, a late Renaissance genre introduced by Byrd, alternates solo sections with sections for full choir.

balletto (It.)   a dance-like vocal piece in homophonic style. Many balletti were composed in the late Renaissance by Giovanni Gastoldi. In English and German the form is called a ballett.

basse danse (Fr.)   one of a family of Renaissance dances which apparently used a gliding or walking step; the music seems to have been mostly improvised, and very little is extant.

Burgundian cadence   a disguised **V-I** cadence often used by the Burgundians in three-part music. The highest voice moves from the seventh to the octave (perhaps, in Landino fashion, by way of the sixth), the middle voice leaps up an octave from the dominant, and the lowest voice descends one step to the tonic. (See Ch. 2, Ex. 1, mm. 24-5.)

cambiata (It.)   changing-tone dissonance in which one or two rhythmically weak nonharmonic pitches lie between consonant ones, usually with a prominent reversal of direction in the vocal line. (See Ch. 2, Ex. 6, m. 18, bass.)

canzona (It.)   a type of instrumental composition derived from the chanson and retaining that genre's sectional structure, varied textures, and lively rhythms.

canzonetta/canzonet (It.)   a short composition of the canzona type for voices; noteworthy for its light character.

chorale   a Protestant hymn, a form cultivated especially during the Renaissance and Baroque periods; their tunes were frequently employed by composers as cantus firmi.

chromatic, chromaticism   refer to the use of tones outside of a given diatonic framework; narrowly speaking, they denote the use of different forms of the same pitch name, such as C and C-sharp.

consort (Eng.)   a term used in the seventeenth century for a small instrumental ensemble. A consort is said to be "whole" (for example, a chest of viols or a nest of recorders) or "broken" (an ensemble with contrasting instruments).

consort song   a late sixteenth- and early seventeenth-century composition that features one or two voices with the accompaniment of a consort, often of viols. A prominent composer of consort songs was William Byrd.

contrafactum (Lat.)   the substitution of a new text for the original one, often of a sacred for a secular one, as in the borrowing of secular tunes for use with Protestant chorale texts.

cori spezzati (It.)   divided choirs, a practice which originated in sixteenth-century Venice. Music for cori spezzati is referred to as polychoral.

cross-relation   the appearance of a note in two versions, one chromatically altered, within the space of a measure or so in two different voices; also used to describe the effect produced by the presence of the tritone.

cyclic principle   the use of the same or closely-related thematic material in some or all of the movements of a large-scale composition, as in the Renaissance Mass.

diminutions   improvised embellishment of a melodic line by introducing faster motion, running passages, etc.

enharmonic   refers to notes that sound the same but are written differently (for instance, C-sharp and D-flat).

familiar style   refers to passages in vocal music sung in chordal or homophonic fashion; used in contrast to a learned, or contrapuntal, style.

fantasia (It.)   a term that encompasses a great variety of works in improvisatory style from the Renaissance to the Romantic period; generally denotes solo pieces for lute or keyboard instrument of the late sixteenth and seventeenth centuries.

fauxbourdon (Fr.)   a controversial term referring to a technique that results in three voices singing basically in first inversion (or sixth) chords; employed frequently by Dufay.

figured music   used before 1600 to denote polyphony (versus plainchant) and especially the style of the Netherlanders.

frottola (It.)   an Italian secular song of the middle Renaissance; usually set in a treble-dominated style of lighter tone and texture than the Renaissance madrigal, which it precedes historically.

galliard (Fr.)   a leaping dance in fairly fast triple meter; often preceded by a **pavane** in a paired set.

gorgia (It.)   see **diminution**; used in vocal music.

imitation   a form of repetition in which a melody is re-stated in different voice-parts.

improvisation   spontaneously created music, as in a fantasia or a cadenza, or just spontaneous re-creation of a given melody.

inversion   melodically, a mirrorlike exchange of ascending and descending intervals of a theme.

Lied (Ger.)   Late in getting started, German polyphonic song flowered in the Renaissance, assisted greatly by such Netherlanders as Isaac and Lassus. It soon acquired a national character and distinction in the works of Heinrick Finck and Paul Hofhaimer.

madrigalism/madrigalian   the highly developed use of tone-painting in the madrigal, a characteristic that then appeared in both chanson and motet.

motto theme   In the Renaissance the term refers to a motive that appears at the beginning of the movements of a Mass.

paraphrase   a varied version of a given melody in the Renaissance; the technique was often used by Dunstable, Dufay, and Josquin.

parody   the practice of reworking a polyphonic composition (such as a motet or chanson) so that it forms the basis for a Mass.

passamezzo (It.)   a moderately fast dance in quadruple meter; often followed by a **saltarello**.

pavane (Fr.)   a dignified courtly dance in slow duple meter; frequently paired with the **galliard**.

pedal point   a sustained note, usually in the bass, over which harmonies change; often employed just before or during a cadence.

points of imitation   See **imitation**. Sections beginning contrapuntally with the same motive in each voice.

polychoral   employing two or perhaps more distinct choirs of voices and/or instruments, as in the works of Giovanni Gabrieli.

psalter   a book of musical settings for Protestant congregational singing.

ricercare (It.)   a term for several types of instrumental pieces; the most significant type is a work for keyboard or ensemble of the sixteenth century which resembles the motet in its use of successive points of imitation. Since ricercare were often composed on a single theme, they anticipate the later fugue.

service   the musical portions of the Anglican liturgy, including the portions from the Mass Ordinary. In the Renaissance the Service was cultivated by Tye, Tallis and Byrd in two forms — Short (if set concisely and syllabically) and Great (if set in expansive counterpoint).

sortisatio (It.)   improvisation of counterpoint on a given part; also known as *discantus supra librum* and *contrappunto alla mente*.

tablature   one of several systems of notation using various symbols rather than notes on a staff; often used for lute music.

tactus (Lat.)   a continuing but unaccented pulse, a Renaissance concept differing from the later concept of beat by being relatively fixed in duration rather than extremely flexible (as in later music).

throughcomposed   a term used for musical forms in which repetition of sections is eschewed in favor of new music.

tone-painting   depicting natural sounds or word-meanings in musical tones.

variations   a type of composition based upon varied repetition of a theme or a harmonic pattern, the overall structure of phrases and sections generally being maintained throughout. Variation emerged in Spain and England during the Renaissance, their most noteworthy exponents being, respectively, Cabezon and Byrd. Influenced by the English was the Dutchman Sweelinck, whose variations represent the culmination of Renaissance types. Two kinds of variations were favored in the period, one unfolding in discrete sections on a melodic theme and the other proceeding more continuously on a repeated bass or on a harmonic pattern.

verse anthem   See **anthem**.

villancico (Sp.)   Spanish song of the Renaissance in a form similar to the Italian ballata; written for three and four voices, and for accompanied solo voice.

villanella (It.)   a popular type of chordal song composed in the Renaissance.

Instruments

cornetto (It.; in German, Zink)   a tubular wooden instrument with fingerholes and a cup-shaped mouthpiece; in use from the Middle Ages until the Baroque period.

crumhorn   a curved double-reed Renaissance instrument with a nearly cylindri-
cal pipe and a wind cap to cover the reeds; also spelled as *Krumhorn* (Ger.) and
cromorne (Fr.).

douchaine (Fr.)   probably a straight-capped shawm with a mellower, softer sound.

lute   an important plucked stringed instrument; its fingerboard was fretted and it
usually had eleven strings tuned to six different pitches which were plucked. It was
characterized by a pear-shaped body and a bent-back pegbox.

recorder   a wooden flute with a beaked mouthpiece played in a vertical position
(often called simply *flauto* in early scores).

regal   a small reed organ.

vihuela (Sp.)   a Spanish guitar of the sixteenth century.

viol   a bowed stringed instrument with frets; an ensemble instrument (as opposed
to the more brilliant violin) that found considerable favor in the sixteenth and
seventeenth centuries.

UNIDENTIFIED MUSICAL EXAMPLES

The use of scores sharpens the ear by making musical events and styles visible as
well as audible, and therefore more memorable. Finding and reading the scores
of the compositions discussed in Chapters 1 and 2 should precede study of the
analytical notes and comments given there. In addition, identifying the score excerpts that follow requires thorough study of the Comparative Style Table on
pages 54 and 55. For those still needing assistance, hints are provided. Studying
one of the anthologies listed in the bibliography for the first two chapters, particularly one for which recordings are available, will also provide valuable practice in
score-reading. Finally, the key to all of the unidentified materials in the chapter is
given after the Historical Sources. For the best results in doing these exercises in
the unknown, the questions below should be answered in writing and in detail:

1 What is the style period of the example, and what musical (and historical) factors —
specifically, which elements of tone color, of melody and rhythm, and of harmony
and texture — support your answer?

2 What kind of composition is it: chant, organum, motet, Mass, monophonic or
polyphonic chanson, madrigal, instrumental dance? What musical, historical, and
textual factors support your choice?

3 Who among the major composers of the period in question is the most likely composer, and why?

Hints for Score Examples

Ex. 1.   Observe particularly the texture, the simple rhythm, the lack of incidental dissonance, and the cadence in measures 24–25. Note the structure of the piece
and the language of its text.

Ex. 2.   There are two movements shown, each with regular, balancing, four-measure
phrases. What does their relationship by meter, theme, and key suggest?

Ex. 3.   Begin with the rhythm and texture; identify the text's language. (Keep the text
of this example in mind for later reference.)

Ex. 4.   Compare the texture, the nature of the rhythm, and especially the harmony
(mm. 23–24) with Ex. 1. Can you recognize the language?

Ex. 5. Read the excerpt in a fast tempo and lively manner. What kind of composition is homophonic with lively syncopation, dotted rhythms, and French text?

Ex. 6. How many voice parts? Are they related to each other? What is the nature of the rhythm (smooth or irregular) and dissonance treatment (incidental or regulated)? Do you recognize the text?

Ex. 7. Of primary importance are the fairly rigid rhythm (measured notation, or a rhythmic mode?), the harmonies at the beginnings and ends of phrases, and the lowest part (the text is "*omnes*"), whose last note is sustained for the remainder of the page (and eight lines thereafter).

Ex. 8. A single factor reveals period, genre, and even likely composer; examine the pitch materials (diatonic versus chromatic) and their use (conventional harmonic progressions or unconventional).

Ex. 9. Is the texture imitative or nonimitative? How frequent are the cadences? Does there seem to be a cantus firmus? The four-voice texture is standard for the period.

Ex. 10. Do you suppose that the parts were conceived simultaneously or one at a time? What term might be used to describe the activity of the upper voices in measures 68–69 and 76–77?

Ex. 11. Read it *presto*; note the simple meter (rhythmic mode?), and the intervals on first beats.

Ex. 12. Note the location of the melismas, the preferred intervals during the verses, and, of course, the layout of the verses themselves.

Ex. 13. Work from the number of voice parts, their relationship to each other (the texture), and the language of the text. Assume a famous composer noted especially for this genre.

Ex. 14. Note the texture, the rhythm, the mode, and the language of the text.

Ex. 15. The middle section flows evenly (in a meter or a rhythmic mode?), but what is the texture of the beginning and end? The syllable given is part of the word "*omnes*."

Ex. 16. Is the texture freely imitative or not? What instrumental genre arose from the model of the motet?

Comparative Style Table

PERIOD	TONE COLOR	TEXTURE	HARMONY
Mid-Medieval Period: 900–1300	Unspecified: heterogeneous ensembles assumed. Solo polyphony vs. choral chant. Light, nasal vocal quality and high range conjectured.	Monophonic/heterophonic. Polyphonic: parallel perfect intervals; melismatic solo over sustained tenor; discant style; conductus style; unequally-active voices over slower cantus firmus (some voice-exchange). Two, later three, voices usual.	Modal polyphony. Intervallic concept of voice relationships. Incidental dissonance (including 2nds & 7ths). Dominance of perfect consonances (including 4th) at important beats, resulting in typical "open" (3rd-less) sound. Cadences usually 2-1/7-8 (in polyphony) on various scale degrees. Some musica ficta.
Late Medieval Period: 1300–1420 (ars nova)	Instrumental doubling of voice(s), especially in secular music. Loud outdoor instruments: shawm, sackbut, rebec, organistrum, tabor. Soft indoor instruments: harp, psaltery, vielle.	Unequal-voice free counterpoint with overlapping ranges over slower cantus firmus; isorhythmic/isometric texture; ballade style. Use of hocket and canon. From two to four voices, with three usual.	Modal, intervallic polyphony. Milder incidental dissonance: escape tones, accented passing-tones, weak-beat suspensions. 3rds, 6ths, full triads now common. Cadences: Landino type; double-leading-tone; occasional V–I. Use of partial signature and musica ficta.
Early Renaissance: 1420–1480 (Burgundian)	Unspecified: usually heterogeneous. Inception of choral polyphony (SATB) in sacred music. Instrumental doubling of voices, soft colors including viol, recorder, douchaine, lute.	Homorhythmic textures include more harmonic ballade style and fauxbourdon; more or less equal-voice counterpoint over cantus firmus with occasional imitation; isorhythmic/isometric texture. Three or four voices, but reduced to two or three in some sections.	Modal, but much Ionian & Aeolian. Intervallic concept but some chordal sound. Expressive, regulated use of less dissonance: escape tones, anticipations, accented passing-tones, proper suspensions. Full triads except at important cadences. Cadences: Landino type; disguised V–I; double-leading-tone; occasional IV–I. Musica ficta (seldom in Ockeghem).
High Renaissance: 1480–1600	Unspecified: homogeneous use of families of instruments and voices. A capella ideal. Choral sacred music, solo secular. Vast variety of colors, including cornetto, crumhorn, guitar, harpsichord.	Imitative counterpoint and some canon (fully equalized voices) contrasted with homophonic textures (familiar style); accompanied solo texture; polychoral and concertato styles. Four voices (secular); five, then six or more (sacred), with some sections of smaller number.	Modal (and some tonal) polyphony. Chordal sound with some harmonic sequence. Highly regulated, expressive dissonance, stressing passing- and neighbor-tones, suspensions, and pedal points. Harmonic tone-painting reflected in chromaticism and cross-relations. Cadences usually V–I, with IV–I at important places. Some double counterpoint. Clear rules for applying musica ficta.

RHYTHM	MELODY	FORM
Original chant rhythm unknown: generally sung today in equal note values without accents, but some performances use accents, unequal values, even meter. Secular monophony apparently sung in a rhythmic mode or metrically. Rhythmic modes likely for organum. Later, mensural rhythm (triple meter). Irregular phrases with repeated short rhythmic patterns.	Motion basically conjunct (some 3rds, few larger leaps), based on hexachords with some mutation. Contour often archlike, revolving around dominant. Use of church modes (and major mode). Mainly syllabic with melismas for expression. Character ranges from folklike to highly sophisticated.	Text-dominated forms (through-composed, sectional, strophic) with secular ones including refrain types and bar form (AAB). Cantus-firmus forms. Dance music in chain of repeated sections.
French rhythm varied and complex, due to independence of voices and isorhythm. Motion irregular. Phrasing irregular, articulated by rests & cadences. Introduction of duple meter. Much syncopation and some diminution.	Mostly conjunct motion in relatively small range, but more leaps in supporting voices (lines are unrelated). Melismatic treble (especially in Italy). Phrases follow length of poetic line, with some short phrases and recurring rhythmic motives.	Text-dominated secular forms, especially refrain types with musical rhyme. Cantus-firmus forms. Isorhythmic structures. Dance music in repeated sections.
Less complex and varied; smoother flowing but with restless continuity and irregular quality (sacred more complex than secular). Phrases articulated by rests and cadences (unless these are avoided, as in Ockeghem). Much use of duple meter. Considerable syncopation. Some accent in pieces with metrical text. Netherlands drive to the cadence common.	Flowing diatonic motion based on the 3rd, with leaps then filled in and penultimate melismas. Chant often paraphrased in the treble. Ockeghem's melodic lines seldom sequence or cadence. Tenor and contratenor frequently unvocal. Basic range of part still an octave.	Text-dominated secular forms but decline of the *formes fixes*. Cantus firmus often ornamented in treble, sometimes in tenor (often in larger note-values). Isorhythm now rare. Sectional motet forms (repetition & contrast.)
Smooth regular flow (Palestrina) or restless continuity. French-type chanson and dance strongly metrical. Meter generally unstressed. Phrases complex and interlocking. Use of constant tactus. Ostinato, syncopation, and dotted rhythms. Concern for text declamation. Carefully graded levels of rhythmic activity by section: with Netherlands drive to the cadence.	Contrapuntal lines either mainly conjunct and relatively unarticulated, or shaped in well-defined themes with memorable intervals and rhythms. Much tone-painting by way of ascending and descending lines, chromaticism, and unusual intervals of larger size. Melody with accompaniment often given balanced phrasing.	Systematic point imitation. Cantus-firmus structures (often on secular tunes). Sectional forms clearly defined, and some use of tonal unity. Text-dominated forms used, but not *formes fixes*. Instrumental forms based on repeated sections, imitation, variation.

Ex. 1

Ex. 2

Ex. 3

Ex. 4

Ex. 5

Ex. 6

Ex. 7

Ex. 8

Ex. 9

Ex. 10

Ex. 11

Ex. 12

1. Al - ler - êrst leb'___ ich mir   wer - de, ___ 2. sît mîn
hê - re lant unt ___ ouch die ___   er - de, 4. der man

sün - dic ou - ge___   siht ___ 3. daz
sô vil___ ê - ren   5. mirst ge -

-sche - hen des___ ich ie___ bat: 6. ich bin___ ko - men___
giht.___

an die___ stat, 7. dâ Got men - nisch - lî - chen___ trat.___

Ex. 13

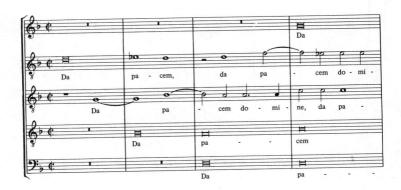

Ex. 14

Reis glo-ri - os, ve — rais lums — e clar - tatz, —
Deus po-de - ros, sen - her, si — a vos — platz, — Al — meu com -
-panh si - as fi zels a - iu - da, Qu'eu non lo vi — pos la
noitz — fon ven - gu - da, Et a - des se - ra — l'al - ba.

Ex. 15

om -

40

Ex. 16

Unidentified Historical Sources

After studying the essays and entries for Chapters 1 and 2, read the unidentified historical sources that follow, mark the clues that reveal their identity and meaning, and then answer the questions below. Consult the list of hints given after the sources, if necessary. Answer each question in writing; indicate specific clues in the text by using the line numbers.

1. What kind of source is it, primary (letter, diary, legal document, practical or speculative music theory, dating from the period described) or secondary (music history, theory, or criticism by a later author)? What evidence supports your answer?
2. What is the style period of the source (Mid-Medieval, Late Medieval, Early Renaissance, High Renaissance), and what is your proof?
3. Summarize the message of the source as briefly as you can.
4. How might you interpret or apply what you have learned from the excerpt?
5. Who might be the author of the source? (In No. 5, which famous composer is described, and how do you know?)

Consult the chapter glossaries for definitions of unfamiliar terms.

HISTORICAL SOURCE NO. 1

We turn to the doctrine of counterpoint. Through this a simple song, most beautiful by nature, is artificially varied in many ways and thereby becomes much more beautiful and smooth and of infinite sweetness to the listeners who partake of it. We call counterpoint a procedure containing in itself diverse variations of sing-
5 able sounds with certain reason in proportions and measure of time. It is called counterpoint from point against point, that is, note against note, because the notes are placed one against the other, and a harmonic concordance of the extreme sounds which correspond together arises.

The consonances of counterpoint are unison, major third, minor third, fifth,
10 major sixth, and minor sixth . . . . Consonance (as Boethius says in his *Music* in the third chapter in the end) is defined as a concord of voices different from each other and reduced together . . . .

Many composers used to have the idea that the cantus should be fashioned first, then the tenor, and after the tenor the contrabass. This happened because
15 they lacked the order and understanding of what was required in making the contralto, and thus they made many difficulties in their compositions, because this inconvenience forced them to use unisons, rests, and ascending and descending leaps difficult for the singer, so that their songs remained with little smoothness or harmony. For when the cantus or soprano was written first and then the tenor, some-
20 times there would be no space left for the contrabass after the tenor was written, and after the contrabass was written some notes in the alto would lack a place. Thus, when one considers only part by part, that is, when you attend only to the concord of the tenor when composing that part, and the same for the contrabass, each part may necessarily suffer the loss of its concordant positions.
25 The moderns have considered better in this matter . . . because they consider all the parts at once rather than by the method described above.

HISTORICAL SOURCE NO. 2

Certain disciples of the new school, much occupying themselves with the measured dividing of the *tempora*, display their prolation in notes which are new to us, preferring to devise methods of their own rather than to continue singing in the old way; the music therefore of the Divine Office is now performed with semibreves
5　and minims, and with these notes of small value every composition is pestered. Moreover, they truncate the melodies with hockets, they deprave them with discants, sometimes even they stuff them with upper parts made out of secular songs. So that often they must be losing sight of the fundamental sources of our melodies in the Antiphoner and Gradual, and may thus forget what that is upon which their
10　superstructure is raised. They may become entirely ignorant concerning the ecclesiastical Tones, which they already no longer distinguish, and the limits of which they even confound, since, in the multitude of their notes, the modest risings and temperate descents of the plainsong, by which the scales themselves are to be known from one another, must be entirely obscured. Their voices are incessantly
15　running to and fro, intoxicating the ear, not soothing it, while the men themselves endeavor to convey by their gestures the sentiment of the music they utter. As a consequence of all this, devotion, the true end of worship, is little thought of, and wantonness, which ought to be eschewed, increases.

This state of things, hitherto the common one, we and our brethren have
20　regarded as standing in need of correction; and we now hasten therefore to banish those methods, nay rather to cast them entirely away, and to put them to flight more effectually than heretofore, far from the house of God. Wherefore, having taken counsel with our brethren, we straitly command that no one henceforward shall think himself at liberty to attempt those methods, or methods like them, in the
25　aforesaid Offices, and especialy in the canonical hours, or in the solemn celebrations of the Mass.

And if any be disobedient, let him, on the authority of this Canon, be punished by a suspension from office of eight days . . . .

Yet, for all this, it is not our intention to forbid, occasionally — and especially
30　upon feast days or in the solemn celebration of the Mass and in the aforesaid Divine Offices — the use of some consonances, for example the eighth, fifth, and fourth, which heighten the beauty of the melody; such intervals therefore may be sung above the plain *cantus ecclesiasticus*, yet so that the integrity of the *cantus* itself remain intact, and that nothing in the authoritative music be changed. Used in
35　such sort the consonances would more than by any other method both soothe the hearer and arouse his devotion, and also would not destroy religious feeling in the minds of the singers.

HISTORICAL SOURCE NO. 3

In every good composition, there are required many things, and one may say that it would be imperfect if one of them were lacking.

The first of these is the subject, without which one can do nothing . . . . . Just as the poet . . . takes as the subject of his poem some history or fable, discovered
5　by himself or borrowed from others, which he adorns and polishes with various manners, . . .so the musician . . . takes the subject and founds upon it his com-

position, which he adorns with various modulations and various harmonies in such
a way that he offers welcome pleasure to his hearers.

10   The second condition is that the composition should be principally composed of consonances; in addition, it should incidentally include many dissonances, suitably arranged in accordance with the rules . . . .

The third is that the procedure of the parts should be good, that is, that the
modulations (that is, the movements from one sound to another by means of various intervals) should proceed by true and legitimate intervals arising from the
15   sonorous numbers, so that through them may be acquired the usage of good harmonies.

The fourth condition to be sought is that the modulations and the concentus
be varied, for harmony has no other source than the diversity of the modulations
and the diversity of the consonances variously combined.

20   The fifth is that the composition should be subject to a prescribed and determined harmony, mode, or tone, . . . and that it should not be disordered.

The sixth and last . . . is that the harmony it contains should be so adapted
to the speech, that is, to the words, that in joyous matters the harmony will not be
mournful, and vice versa, that in mournful ones the harmony will not be joy-
25   ful . . . .

In every musical composition, what we call the subject is that part from
which the composer derives the invention to make the other parts of the work, however many they may be. Such a subject may take many forms, as the composer
may prefer and in accordance with the loftiness of his imagination: it may be his
30   own invention; . . . again, it may be that he has borrowed it from the works of
others, adapting it to his work and adorning it with various parts and various
modulations. And such a subject may be of several kinds: it may be a tenor or some
other part of any composition you please, whether of plainsong or of figured music;
again, it may be two or more parts of which one follows another in consequence or
35   in some other way, for the various forms of such subjects are innumerable . . . . And when the composer . . . derives one part from another and goes
on to write the work all at once, . . . that small part which he derives without the
others and upon which he then composes the parts of his composition will always be
called the subject. This manner of composing practical musicians call "composing
40   from fantasy," although it may also be called "counterpointing," or as they say,
"making counterpoint."

HISTORICAL SOURCE NO. 4

Compositions differ according to the subject on which they are made, and
very often certain singers are not aware of this, singing any composition whatever
without any consideration and always in their own way, according to their nature
and practice. Works that are written on various subjects and various fantasias
5   carry within them different manners of composition, and so the singer must consider what the musical poet has in mind, and whether the poet writes in Latin or
the vulgar tongue, and with his voice express the composition and use diverse ways
of singing, like the diverse manners of composition. If he will use such ways, he will
be judged by auditors who are men of judgment to have many styles of singing and
10   demonstrate that he has an abundant and rich store of manners of singing by the
disposition of *gorgia*, or diminutions . . . .

Such [poor singers] as these will point out that the diminutions, which are of
the kind used in more than four voices, will appear good [only] if they are done in

appropriate places and in tempo; because the diminution always loses many conso-
15   nances and strikes many dissonances . . . . It will be more satisfactory if, during
the diminution, the instruments that are playing the piece play it as it is notated,
without embellishments, so that the harmony cannot be lost with the diminution,
for the instruments will keep the consonances in their proper form. And as to those
who wish to embellish a composition singing and playing together, if both do not
20   make the same diminutions at the same time they will sound well together. Then in
the compositions which are sung without instruments, the diminutions will be good
in compositions for more than four voices, because wherever a consonance is lacking, the other part will have it in the octave or unison and there will not be a poverty of harmony . . . .
25   And every singer will take care, when he sings lamentations or other compositions of a sad nature, not to make any diminutions, because then the sorrowful
composition would appear joyful; and the opposite is true also, for he should not
sing in a sad manner the joyful things, either in the vulgar tongue or in Latin . . . .
And sometimes one uses a certain way of proceeding in the composition that can-
30   not be written down—such as to sing *piano* and *forte*, and to sing *presto* and *tardo*,
moving the measure according to the words to demonstrate the effects of the passions of the words and of the harmony. And it should not appear strange to anyone,
this manner of changing tempo suddenly in singing, since it is so understood in
performance that where it is necessary to change tempo it is not an error. And the
35   composition sung with changes of tempo is more pleasing in its variety than that
which is sung without being varied all the way to the end. And a trial of this manner of singing will prove it to everyone, for in secular pieces it will be found that
such procedure will please the hearers more than when the measure continues
always unvaried.

HISTORICAL SOURCE NO. 5

Book I opens with a definition of "counterpoint," to which a further explanation is added in Book II, Chapter XX. The second passage makes it plain that
"counterpoint" is not only a generic term, embracing both improvisation (*super
librum cantare*) and written music (*res facta*), but also a specific term, used as a syno-
5   nym for "improvisation." . . . . The unison, fourth, fifth, octave, and their compounds are perfect consonances; the major and minor thirds and sixths and their
compounds, imperfect. But _____ has little liking for the fourth and its compounds—in music *a 2* [in two parts], indeed, he removes them from improvised
counterpoint . . . .
10   Book II deals with the dissonances, . . . the second, tritone, seventh, and
their compounds. Then . . . the diminished and augmented fifth and octave and
their compounds . . . . One important difference is pointed out between dissonance treatment in *res facta* and in improvisation; in the former, the voices, whatever their number, must observe their mutual obligations to one another according
15   to the rules; in the latter, it suffices if the improvised lines are made to fit the tenor.
Nevertheless, if the singers have some understanding among themselves in advance, that is worthy of praise rather than blame . . . .
Book III presents eight general rules:
(1) A perfect consonance should be used at the beginning and end, but an imperfect
20   consonance may be employed at the opening if the music starts on an upbeat, and
at the end (except that the consonance must not be a sixth) if several singers are im-
provising.

(2) A part may accompany the tenor with several imperfect consonances of the same size but not with successions of like perfect consonances, unless these are required by strict imitation or a particularly beautiful effect results.

(3) If a tenor reiterates a note, concords of the same kind, perfect or imperfect, may be repeated against it. "However, where other concords can be interpolated, the singing of this kind of counterpoint over the *cantus planus* (in improvisation) is diligently to be avoided." But in *res facta* one may have repetition, especially of thirds and sixths, if it makes for smooth setting of the words.

(4) The added part should have a small range and move conjunctly, even if the tenor leaps. But there may be exceptions in the interest of beauty.

(5) A cadence should not be introduced on any note—high, medium, or low—if it breaks up the development of the melody.

(6) The same melodic note-group should not be repeated in improvisation, especially if the *cantus firmus* has such a repetition. However, in written music repetitions are permissible in imitation of bells, trumpets, etc.

(7) One should avoid two or more consecutive cadences on the same degree, even when the *cantus firmus* seems to lend itself to this. *Cantus firmi* calling for such resemblances to repetition should be selected only when necessary.

(8) One should seek variety by using different note-values and cadences, by writing sometimes conjunctly, sometimes not, both with and without syncopations, canon, rests, etc. This rule is applicable most to a Mass, less to a motet, least to a *cantilena* (the simplest type).

Hints for Historical Sources

Ex. 1. If we recognize that changes in musical style generally precede theoretical writing about them, then the period of the source can be deduced from lines 9–10, 13–14 and, above all 25–26.

Ex. 2. The development of music in the Church confronted composers with unique problems, not all of them artistic. Who can issue such commands as those found in lines 24–26 and 27–28, and what will such an attitude mean for the future of church music? The clues for the period are found in lines 2, 6–7, and 31–34.

Ex. 3. This apparently innocuous page describes a giant step towards emancipation of music from forms imposed by the text (lines 36–41). What would be the texture of music written in the manner described? How long after such a texture became common would theorists write of it as recommended practice? Who is perhaps the most significant music theorist between Aristoxenus and Rameau?

Ex. 4. What historical period is indicated by the references to "more than four voices"?

Ex. 5. This excerpt is taken from a very famous treatise. Key clues are the importance of improvisation (lines 2–5, 12–17, 19–22, 35–37), the reliance upon a cantus firmus (35–40), and the author's attitude toward consonance and dissonance (especially 5–8, 12–15, 19–22, 23–24).

Chapter Three

Baroque Music

The Baroque period was an age of discovery by scientists such as Galileo and Newton, of religious conflict between Catholics and Protestants, and of political absolutism. Each of these factors was reflected in musical life. The experiment of monody led to the creation of dramatic music, the religious hostility found music serving the purpose of proselytism, and the concentration of power and wealth in the hands of educated nobles stimulated music patronage. Emulating the magnificance of the courts of the Medici in Florence, Louis XIV of France, and other noble patrons of the arts, secular and ecclesiastical aristocrats everywhere enlisted artists (such as Caravaggio), architects (Borromini), poets (Metastasio), and musicians in their quests for prestige and personal satisfaction. Educated in an age of humanism and inclined towards the expressive, many of these wealthy nobles were very willing to patronize music. Some, like Count Giovanni de' Bardi of the Florentine **Camerata**, even collaborated with composers by providing texts for their music.

A fundamental belief in the power of music to move the listener distinguished the Baroque. By seeking to discover a musical equivalent for each state of feeling, for poetic images, and for the rhythms of the words, theorists and composers gradually compiled a standardized musical rhetoric—the so-called **doctrine of the affections**. Enthusiasm for this rational art of emotional expression in music, combined with music's inherent capacity for touching the soul, enabled music to become perhaps the most popular of the fine arts among both the nobility and the growing middle class.

Many of the genres and much of the music terminology still in use originated in the Baroque period: opera, oratorio, cantata, sonata, concerto, suite, allegro, adagio, and countless other terms. Of the greatest importance were the emergence of theatrical music and of **concertato** style in Italy, since these firmly entrenched Italian composers and performers in a position of leadership. New elements of style that provided the foundation for Baroque music were: (1) dominance of the melody and bass voices in a four-voice texture, in which the inner parts might well be indicated, if at all, simply by numbers or symbols above the **basso continuo** part rather than written in the score (as opposed to the Renaissance ideal of equal-voice counterpoint); (2) the use of a limited number of basic and regularly stressed meters (rather than a constant, unstressed tactus); (3) functional **tonality** in one of two modes, major or minor (in contrast to Renaissance modality). After about 1675, the free and expressive treatment of dissonance and the use of contrasting rhythms and themes gave way to a more stable and homogeneous practice based upon functional harmony, tonal sequence, **belcanto** lyricism, and commonly accepted principles of form.

Baroque theorists and critics wrote of three principal musical styles, appropriate respectively to the chamber, the church, and the theater. **Monody**, for example, was adapted to suit each of its large-scale applications: in the theater, opera; in the church, oratorio and church cantata; and in the chamber or salon, secular cantata.

OPERA served as the crucible in which the new Baroque style was forged. Not only was it a proving ground for the free dissonance treatment and the speech rhythms of monody that were so important for MONTEVERDI, but with the opening of the first public opera house in Venice in 1637 it became the first genre to be transformed by the need to entertain a public audience. Court opera, which was born in Florence about the turn of the century, was characterized by subordination of musical to textual and dramatic values, and emphasis upon scenic and balletic display. In contrast, public opera came to be dominated by virtuoso singing in *opera seria* and by expression of character and comic values in *opera buffa*. Operatic features soon appeared in other Baroque genres; they included a new emphasis upon the creative role of the soloist (as expressed in ornamentation); the increasing importance of the orchestra; the development of larger, tonally-basic musical structures; and the establishment of a wider range of emotional expression. From opera composers such as ALESSANDRO SCARLATTI, the late Baroque masters—VIVALDI, RAMEAU, J.S.BACH, and HANDEL—inherited a rich musical language full of potential for further use in all genres.

With some modifications, Baroque ORATORIO composed to Italian texts followed the development of style in opera, and in fact was composed by Alessandro Scarlatti and other composers of opera. Latin oratorio readily assimilated monody, but perhaps because of its roots in the motet it did not remain significant in Italy after the early masterpieces by Giacomo Carissimi. Oratorio reached its peak in the late Baroque works of Handel. Having mastered Italian oratorio and opera, he created English oratorio as a Protestant entertainment of a dramatic nature. Much of the power of the Handelian oratorio stems from the composer's expansion of regular operatic resources by the addition of choral numbers, contrapuntal writing, and an increased role for the orchestra. With the further addition of chorale settings and a narrator, the great Passions by J.S.Bach constitute essentially a German equivalent of Handel's English oratorios.

Following the example of Alessandro Scarlatti, the young Handel also cultivated the Italian secular CANTATA. A direct descendant of monody, it became the leading form of vocal chamber music in the Baroque. Its significance lay particularly in its refinement of style, harmonic adventurousness, and freedom from dramatic and virtuosic concerns. The German cantata evolved from the motet. Unlike the Italian oratorio, its closest relative, it was a functional church genre; it employed chorus, orchestra, contrapuntal elements, and the chorales of the Lutheran church. The initial transformation of the motet into a small-scale sacred concerto (concertato) took place in the works of Johann Hermann Schein and HEINRICH SCHÜTZ; its culmination is represented by the magnificent cantatas of Dietrich Buxtehude and J.S. Bach.

Whereas Baroque vocal music sounds revolutionary because of its reliance upon monody, instrumental music of the period reveals an unbroken evolution from Renaissance prototypes. With early seventeenth-century composers such as Giovanni Gabrieli, Jan Sweelinck, and GIROLAMO FRESCOBALDI, the Renaissance ricercare continued to flourish, leading ultimately to the Baroque fugues of Buxtehude and Bach. The canzona (properly the *canzona di sonar*) underwent a greater transformation into the multi-movement trio SONATA of CORELLI, PURCELL, COUPERIN, and HANDEL, and the solo sonata of such violinists as Corelli, Tartini, Leclair, and Geminiani. The keyboard sonata reached its peak with the works of DOMENICO SCARLATTI. Genres whose names remained the same from Renaissance to Baroque, such as the toccata, the fantasia, and the chorale prelude, also adopted the new Baroque style traits, including its emphasis on emotional expression. Finally, the highly stylized Baroque SUITE of Froberger, Couperin, and Bach evolved from the dance-pairs of the Renaissance. Although rhythmic and motivic contrast characterized early Baroque style, the Renaissance principles of imitative counterpoint and variation remained alive, and ultimately formed the foundation of the spun-out rhythmic style of the late Baroque.

Overview 1600–1685

GENRE	ITALY	GERMANY	FRANCE	ENGLAND
Opera	Monteverdi		Lully	Purcell
Oratorio	Carissimi	Schütz	Du Mont (dialogues)	Purcell (anthems)
Cantata	L. Rossi	Schütz	Du Mont (motets)	Purcell (odes and songs)
Organ Music	Frescobaldi	Buxtehude	L. Couperin	Blow
Suite	Corelli	Froberger	Chambonnières	Purcell
Sonata	Corelli	Biber		Purcell
Concerto	Corelli			

Overview 1685–1750

GENRE	ITALY	GERMANY	FRANCE	ENGLAND
Opera	A. Scarlatti	Keiser	Rameau	Handel
Oratorio	A. Scarlatti	Telemann	Charpentier	Handel
Cantata	A. Scarlatti	J. S. Bach	Clérambault	Handel
Organ Music	Pasquini	J. S. Bach	Grigny	Handel
Suite	G. M. Bononcini	J. S. Bach	F. Couperin	Handel
Sonata	D. Scarlatti	Telemann	F. Couperin, (trio) Leclair, (solo)	Handel
Concerto	Vivaldi	J. S. Bach	Leclair	Handel

The CONCERTO was the most significant truly new genre of the period; as the instrumental equivalent of the virtuoso aria for voice, it was particularly suited for large performance halls. Instrumental virtuosity and a style idiomatic for each instrument became important features of the Baroque. As the principal instrument of the Italians, the violin dominated the era, but the adoption of equal temperament and of new fingering techniques raised keyboard instruments to an equal level in Germany. Instrumental virtuosity and the concerto became especially popular in the academies and **collegia musica** of the late Baroque, an indication that the middle-class audience that was to make public concerts possible had begun to form.

The development of most genres over the course of the Baroque period was from a continuous structure containing small sections evolved into large-scale forms composed of standard sequences of discrete movements. The process of expansion in instrumental music was based upon the development of autonomous principles of form. Together with the adoption of the doctrine of the affections from the realm of vocal music, these formal principles made possible the dramatic rise in importance of instrumental genres in the late Baroque. The **ritornello** principle evolved in the concerto, and Baroque **binary form** in the suite and the sonata. After further changes, the rondo and the sonata principles emerged becoming the dominant structures of the Classical period.

PRINCIPAL BAROQUE GENRES

Opera

Opera (originally, *dramma per musica*) is sung drama. Normally structured in several acts, it employs soloists, chorus (usually), ballet (sometimes), and orchestra in a musical representation of a dramatic story, as set forth in the libretto. The forerunners of opera were the lavish musical intermezzi and ballets that served as court entertainments in the late Renaissance. The formal beginning of opera came with the invention of monody in Florence and Rome about 1600. In his *Euridice* of 1600, Jacopo Peri provided the best early solution to the fundamental problem of opera—a flexible and expressive style for the dialogue and the declamatory passages. The attraction of lyrical singing, however, proved irresistible for both composers and the larger audiences of the first public theaters in Venice in the 1630's, and an emphasis on virtuoso singing and highly stylized musical expression of the affections in the *da capo* aria soon replaced the early concern for declamation as expressed in monody. Led by an exotic race of male sopranos (the *castrati*), Italian opera became the rage all over the civilized Western world by the end of the eighteenth century, flourishing particularly in Vienna and London.

Whereas royal patronage enabled French opera to maintain its integrity in the works of Lully and Rameau, German opera adopted first an Italianate structure, then the Italian language, and finally full-fledged Italian opera composed by Italians. Like Reinhard Keiser (1674–1739) in Germany, HENRY PURCELL (1659–1695) could not create an enduring operatic tradition in England; despite the genius revealed in his music for fifty or so stage works (at least ten with considerable music), he composed only one complete opera and that on a small scale. In the Baroque period, Italian opera served as a focus for and bearer of new elements of style, first in a basically serious manner with some comic characters and scenes, then in opera seria, and finally in opera buffa. The dramatic

Important Baroque Opera Composers

ITALIAN OPERA

Claudio Monteverdi (1567–1643)
c. 10 operas (*L'Orfeo*, 1607)

Pier Francesco Cavalli (1602–1676)
c. 30 (*L'Ormindo*, 1644)

Agostino Steffani (1654–1728)
18? (*Tassilone*, 1709)

Alessandro Scarlatti (1660–1725)
c. 100 (*La Griselda*, 1721)

Antonio Vivaldi (1678–1741)
c. 50 (*Orlando furioso*, 1727)

George Frideric Handel (1685–1759)
c. 40 (*Giulio Cesare*, 1724)

Giovanni Battista Pergolesi (1710–1736)
c. 10 (*L'Olimpiade*, 1735)

Johann Adolf Hasse (1699–1783)
c. 60 (*Attilio Regolo*, 1750)

FRENCH OPERA

Comédie-ballet was succeeded by the highly aristocratic form termed *tragédie lyrique*, comprising elements from classical tragedy, ballet, and pastorale; **opéra-ballet** returns in the works of Campra. Indigenous recitative style created by Lully. French opera emphasized drama and spectacle rather than virtuoso singing.

Jean-Baptiste Lully (1632–1687)
c. 18 operas (*Adamis de Gaule*, 1684)

André Campra (1660–1744)
c. 12 operas (*L'Europe galante*, 1697)

Jean-Philippe Rameau (1683–1764)
c. 20 operas (*Castor et Pollux*, 1737)

approach and exemplary expression of the affections in opera engaged the attention of every major composer, though not always in the same genre.

Oratorio

Oratorio is sung drama on a religious or moral story, but without action, scenery, and costumes. Like opera, it employs soloists to personify the characters of the drama, chorus (generally), and orchestra; in addition, there may be a narrator. Oratorio began as part of extraliturgical religious services in Roman prayer halls (oratories), where it served partly to entice music-lovers back into the Counter-Reformation fold. From their beginnings in the lauda and the spiritual **dialogue**, oratorio in both Italian (*oratorio volgare*) and Latin (*oratorio latino*) flourished in Italy and in such Italian musical satellites as Vienna, but after about 1650 its very success drew it even closer to opera. In Italy, oratorio became more or less a Lenten substitute for opera; it gradually dispensed with its narrator and chorus, until it became musically distinguishable from opera only by its two-part form, shorter time span, and reduced amount of recitative between arias.

Like opera, oratorio spread from Italy across Europe, but—apparently because of its religious purpose—vernacular languages and a more conservative style were generally adhered to, and native composers played a larger role in its history. In France, oratorio was cultivated (in Latin) under the term *histoire sacrée* by Marc-Antoine Charpentier after the model of his teacher, Carissimi. Many

---

Important Baroque Oratorio Composers

ITALY	OTHER COUNTRIES
Domenico Mazzocchi (1592–1665) 7 Latin dialogues (1630s)	Heinrich Schütz (1585–1672) 6 (*Die Geburt unsers Herren Jesu Christi*, 1664)
Giacomo Carissimi (1605–1674) c. 15 Latin oratorios (*Jephte*, before 1650)	Antonio Draghi (1635–1700) 13 oratorios, 29 *sepolcri*
Giovanni Legrenzi (1626–1690) 7 (*Il Sedecia*, 1676)	Marc-Antoine Charpentier (c. 1636–1704) c. 35 (*Judicium Salomonis*, 1702)
Alessandro Stradella (1644–1682) 7 (*San Giovanni Battista*, 1675)	Reinhard Keiser (1674–1739) 6 (*Der blutige und sterbende Jesus*, 1704)
Alessandro Scarlatti (1660–1725) c. 40 (*La Vergine addolorata*, 1717)	Georg Philipp Telemann (1681–1767) 9 (*Der Tag des Gerichts*, 1762)
Antonio Caldara (1670–1736) c. 40 (*David umiliato*, 1731)	George Frideric Handel (1685–1759) c. 30 (*Belshazzar*, 1745)
Antonio Vivaldi (1678–1741) 3 Latin (*Juditha triumphans*, 1716)	Johann Adolf Hasse (1699–1783) c. 10 (*La conversione di San Agostino*, 1750)

German Protestant oratorios, often concerned with the death of Christ, achieved a nonoperatic spirit by retention of the narrator and the chorus, use of chorale melodies, and the heavier German contrapuntal manner.

Although he embraced a wider range of subjects and types than did the Italians, Handel's oratorios generally reflect a truly Italian dramatic character and actually constitute religious or simply moral entertainments not designed for church performance. Because of his complete mastery of Italian opera and acquaintance with the English masque and the German Protestant oratorio, his enhanced choral and orchestral resources, and his remarkable musical and dramatic gifts, Handel's oratorios represent perhaps even better than opera the quintessential values of Baroque sung drama.

Cantata

The cantata began as a small-scale Italian secular genre; its origins lie in early Baroque monody, as may be seen clearly in that kind of secular cantata consisting basically of a single aria. The frequent subject of the early cantata is unhappy love, but comic subjects were also treated, and one variety of cantata used religious texts. The cantata came to the same leading role in vocal chamber music as did the sonata in instrumental chamber music. Continuo-accompanied solo singing in the contrasting styles of **recitative, arioso**, and **aria** characterizes the archetypal secular cantata. Sometimes the accompaniment is augmented by strings or **obbligato** instruments, and sometimes two soloists are required, the texture thus becoming that of the trio sonata. The form of the cantata evolved from a relatively free juxtaposition of contrasting sections in various small-scale forms, including that of variations over a strophic bass, to a standard sequence of two or three large da-capo arias, each one preceded by recitative, arioso, or accompanied recitative. From a center of activity in Rome, the cantata flowered all over Italy, though it did not find the general acceptance of opera elsewhere in Europe.

During the first half of the eighteenth century, the secular cantata suddenly bloomed in the academies and salons of France after the model of Alessandro Scarlatti. Although it adopted the French language and the French love for dance-like rhythms, Italian influence may be seen in such features as the da-capo aria and virtuoso vocal writing. From its inception in the works of Jean-Baptiste Morin (1677–1754; 18 cantatas), the French cantata characteristically consisted of a threefold alternation of recitative and aria. Among Morin's contemporaries, the most important for the cantata were Nicholas Bernier (1664–1734; 39 cantatas), André Campra (1660–1774; c. 20) and Louis-Nicholas Clérambault (1676–1749; 25). After 1730 a shorter form of the cantata known as the *cantatille* became common and served as a vehicle for the transition to Classical style.

The German church cantata was usually composed for soloists, chorus, and orchestra on a reflective, non-dramatic text. (In the Baroque period the genre went under such names as *Kirchenstück*, concerto, and motet rather than cantata.) Smaller than the oratorio, it served as the principal music of the Lutheran service, frequently making use of an appropriate chorale melody and text. Though musically dependent on Italian styles and forms, its texts—whether Latin or

Important Baroque Cantata Composers

ITALIAN	GERMAN
Luigi Rossi (1597–1653), c. 300	Heinrich Schütz (1585–1672), vocal concerti
Marco Marazzoli (1602?–1662), 379	
Giacomo Carissimi (1605–1674), c. 150	Dietrich Buxtehude (c. 1637–1707), c. 50?
Alessandro Stradella (1644–1682), c. 100	Johann Philipp Krieger (1649–1725), 2000 + but only 74 extant
Alessandro Scarlatti (1660–1725), c. 600	Johann Kuhnau (1660–1722), c. 75, but many lost
Antonio Caldara (1670–1736), c. 300	Reinhard Keiser (1674–1739), c. 25
George Frideric Handel (1685–1759), c. 100	Georg Philipp Telemann (1681–1767), c. 1300
Benedetto Marcello (1686–1739), c. 400	Christoph Graupner (1683–1760), 1418 sacred, 24 secular
	Johann Sebastian Bach (1685–1750), over 300, but only c. 200 extant

German — confirm its independent status. Changes in the nature of the texts after 1670 led to the establishment of two basic cantata types: the small-scale cantata based upon alternation of recitative and aria and the large-scale chorale cantata requiring chorus and orchestra. The new type of cantata emerged after 1700 in response to the devotional texts of Erdmann Neumeister; in them, the secular model took the leading role. The church cantata, on the other hand, reflected the increasing standardization of its structure by being gathered in large cycles covering the entire church year and occupying most of the productive capacity of church kapellmeisters. After its culmination in the works of J.S.Bach, the church cantata soon declined in importance.

Organ Music

Organ music has flourished chiefly in the church, either as part of the liturgy or as a necessary adjunct to the service. It has declined in those periods when church patronage has been limited. During the Baroque period, organ music enjoyed its golden age. Generally lacking organs with pedal keyboards, Italy (FRESCOBALDI), Spain (Juan Cabanilles), and England produced some great masters but could not maintain leading roles. The organ-builders of the Netherlands, Germany (Schnitger and Silbermann), and France (Clicquot) stimulated vast productivity of organ music by the great Netherlands teacher Sweelinck; by the Germans Scheidt, Buxtehude, Pachelbel, and Bach; and by the Frenchmen Titelouze, Louis Couperin, d'Anglebert, Grigny, and Clérambault.

In the organ music of Bach, the forms and styles of German, French, and Italian organ music reached their culmination of artistic expression. Among the major organ genres of the Baroque period are the following:

1. the *toccata*, the most idiomatic of early organ genres, comprising several sections (usually 3 or 5), some free and improvisatory and others in fugal style. It also appears as a single movement in free style, often combined with a separate fugue in the same key (Merulo, Frescobaldi, Buxtehude, Bach);

2. the **fugue**, a contrapuntal composition for a definite number of voices, generally written on one theme and consisting of an alternation of subject entries and episodes. As the second of a pair of movements for organ or harpsichord, it was a major independent Baroque genre; it also appeared in larger instrumental works such as the sonata and in larger vocal works such as the church cantata. Gradual adjustment to the structural possibilities of functional harmony resulted in expansion and greater complexity of form, as well as the standardization of expository procedures, subsequent entries of the subject, and episodic devices. Outstanding masters were many, including Frescobaldi, Buxtehude, and Bach.

3. *chorale-based pieces*, a highly varied category with three main types:

   a. the *chorale partita*, in which the chorale melody is usually given as many variations as the text has verses (for example, the partitas of Scheidt);

   b. the *chorale fantasia*, in which the melody is treated freely in all the voice-parts, either as an old-fashioned chorale motet with its successive points of imitation on the melody of each new phrase, or as a fugue on just one or two of the chorale's phrases (as in the fantasias of Buxtehude);

   c. the *chorale prelude*, a short piece in which the melody is usually in the top voice (often highly ornamented) with free accompaniment (Bach);

4. the *organ Mass*, the foremost type of liturgical organ music, usually comprising Kyrie, Gloria, Sanctus, Agnus Dei, and Deo Gratias, plus added pieces for various other parts of the Mass. It was performed alone, or in alternation with a choir. Composed after the model of vocal polyphony at first, it endured from the early fourteenth century to the early eighteenth, and was cultivated in the Baroque by such composers as Titelouze, Frescobaldi, and François Couperin.

Suite

A suite is an instrumental composition in several movements contrasting in tempo, meter, and character. Early in the Baroque period, the suite emerged as a collection of stylized dances in the same key, organized either according to the individual composer's taste (Johann Hermann Schein's *Banchetto musicale*) or arranged as a succession of similar types whose order was left to the performer's choice (collections by Chambonnières). Standard patterns emerged about 1650 in the works of Froberger: either **allemande–courante–sarabande**, or a four-movement plan with a **gigue** before or after the courante. By 1675 the most common pattern was allemande–courante–sarabande–gigue, and this order remained standard even when a prelude (or overture) was added at the beginning, and such optional dances as minuet and **gavotte** were inserted between the sarabande and gigue. Also standard for each movement was the formal plan known as Baroque

The Baroque Suite

MOVEMENT	KEY	LIKELY METER	TEMPO	DERIVATION
French Overture	I or i	1) $\frac{4}{4}$ 2) $\frac{3}{4}$	1) Slow 2) Fast	French
Allemande	I or i	quadruple	Moderate	German
Courante	I or i	$\frac{3}{2}$ or $\frac{6}{4}$	Lively	French
Sarabande	I or i	triple	Slow	Spanish
Gigue	I or i	compound duple $\frac{6}{8}$ or $\frac{6}{4}$	Fast	Anglo-Irish

binary, in which tonal unity was occasionally supplemented by thematic ties (rounded binary). Other Baroque suite-like genres were the **partita**, the Italian *sonata da camera* (usually in four or five movements), the concerto da camera (which fused elements of the suite with those of the concerto), and the **French overture** (often actually a suite of dances preceded by a French overture). Leading composers of the suite are listed in the table on pages 77-78.

Sonata

Originally, *sonata* meant simply music to be played rather than sung, as in the *canzona da sonare* (chanson for playing) and the sonatas by Giovanni Gabrieli. However, some early pieces entitled sonata have vocal parts as well as instrumen-

The Baroque Sonata

PERIOD	DESIGNATION	INSTRUMENTS	INDEPENDENT PARTS	LEADING COMPOSERS
Early	ensemble sonata	equal-voice instrumental group	4–6	Schmelzer
High	trio sonata	2 melody instruments and continuo	3	Corelli, Purcell, Couperin, Handel
Late	solo sonata	melody instrument with continuo	2	Corelli, Biber, Leclair, Bach
Late	harpsichord or organ sonata	solo keyboard instrument	1	D. Scarlatti, Pasquini
Late	unaccompanied sonata	solo violin	1	Biber, Bach

tal. During the seventeenth century the sonata became the leading genre of instrumental chamber music, spreading from northern Italy to other Italian cities and then to the major music centers of the Western world. After 1700 Venice assumed leadership in the sonata, which continued to be important both in the church (*sonata de chiesa*) and at court (*sonata da camera*).

The sonata, which flourished in a variety of types, was perhaps the most important genre for the evolution of functional harmony and tonal principles of structure. In addition, it played a major role in the ascendancy of the violin, which came to display more and more virtuosity. Serving as models for the period were the trio and solo sonatas of Corelli; the orderly arrangement displayed by his published collections should not, however, obscure the fact that many style traits are shared by both his chamber and church sonatas. Later sonata composers came to use the title trio or solo sonata without indication of the place of performance. Significant style changes that took place in the sonata included the growth of sections into movements through greater use of sequence and repetition, a trend towards greater homophony and slower harmonic rhythm, and the declining importance of the continuo in the late Baroque.

The form of the Baroque sonata depended upon contrast of tempo, meter, and style. Its general course, as seen below, was from serious, freely contrapuntal movements to lighter, more homophonic ones.

MOVE-MENT	TEMPO	METER	DESCRIPTION	FORM	KEY
1	Slow	4 4	freely imitative with dotted rhythms and chains of suspensions	through-composed; binary	tonic
2	Fast	duple	freely fugal	through-composed; binary	tonic
3	Slow	triple	freely motivic and lyrical	fantasia-like; binary	tonic (or other)
4	Fast	12 8	homophonic (lightly imitative)	binary	tonic

This outline of the sonata da chiesa could be amplified by the addition of another fast movement and more dancelike elements to produce the sonata da camera. In the late Baroque, the virtuosic solo sonata dominates; its form is normally either Slow–Fast–Fast or Fast–Slow–Fast.

Concerto

Conceived in the concertato contrast between opposing vocal and instrumental groups in the works of Giovanni Gabrieli, the concerto concept took more definite form in the seventeenth-century sonatas and **sinfonias** for divided orchestra. Throughout the early Baroque period, however, the term was commonly used for Italian and German church music for voices accompanied by instruments, as in the *geistliche Konzerte* of Schein and the *Symphoniae sacrae* of Schütz. The history of the concerto proper begins with the concerti grossi of Corelli and the solo concerti of Torelli and is outlined below. The solo concerto may be defined as a work for solo instrument with orchestral accompaniment, the concerto grosso as a work for several soloists (often forming a concertino in the texture of a trio sonata) and small orchestra. In addition, the *ripieno* concerto, a kind of concerto for orchestra, offers the dynamic rhythmic style and instrumental interplay of the concerto without featured soloists.

Development of the Baroque Concerto

	MOST SIGNIFICANT COMPOSERS	STYLE AND STRUCTURE
Inception: **1660-90**	Stradella (Venice) Cazzati (Bologna) T.A. Vitali (Bologna)	Concerto-grosso effects in the orchestral sinfonias and operas of Stradella foreshadow that genre, while the trumpet sonatas of the Bolognese composers point towards the solo concerto.
Maturity: **1690-1720**	Corelli (Bologna–Rome) 12 Torelli (Bologna) c. 25 Albinoni (Venice) c. 60	Within the four- or five-movement structure of the trio sonata, the Corellian concerto grosso offers dynamic (not thematic) contrast between the trio-sonata texture of the concertino and the orchestral ensemble. The solo concerto of Torelli and Albinoni adopts a fast–slow–fast plan and features virtuoso writing for the solo instrument.
Culmination: **1720-50**	Vivaldi (Venice) c. 480 J. S. Bach (Leipzig) c. 50 Handel (London) c. 35	The enormous popularity of Vivaldi firmly established the 3-movement form, the ritornello principle, the dramatic rhythmic and thematic style, the lyrical mood and ternary form of the slow movement, and the brilliant virtuosity of the solo concerto. Bach follows the example of Vivaldi, Handel that of Corelli; both contribute to the creation of the solo keyboard concerto, Bach for harpsichord and Handel for organ.

MAJOR COMPOSERS AND SELECTED COMPOSITIONS

Claudio Monteverdi   Italian   1567–1643

Achievement

1. Without sacrificing such traditional practices as tone painting, Monteverdi led the madrigal away from Renaissance contrapuntal and harmonic practice towards continuo-accompanied monody with freer dissonance treatment and some use of instrumental ritornelli as well as of **stile concitato**. He was among the first consciously and successfully to compose in two such disparate styles or practices as those of the traditional madrigal and the new monody, although his historical importance may rest more on his mastery than on his direct influence.

2. With *Orfeo* (1607), the composer established opera as the leading musical genre through his extraordinary gift for expressing the emotions, a point confirmed with greater refinement in the much later *L'incoronazione di Poppea* (1642).

3. The composer contributed to the development of the orchestra through the number and selection of instruments in his operas as well as by employing such devices as string tremolo and pizzicato.

4. In his church music Monteverdi made use of his new secular style, one of the earliest major composers to do so.

Works and Style Summary

Chamber music: c. 250 pieces, including nine books of madrigals spanning his entire career, 1 of canzonettas, and 2 of *scherzi musicali*

Operas: at least 12, of which only 3 are completely preserved, and 1 dramatic scene (*Il combattimento di Tancredi e Clorinda*)

Church music: 3 Masses, Vesper psalms, Magnificats, many motets

The composer was a master of the late Renaissance contrapuntal style he called the "first practice," employing it with dramatic aptness in his early madrigals. Gradually, his belief in the primary importance of the text and his desire to move the emotions of his listeners led to a new freedom of voice-leading and an expressive and much freer treatment of rhythm and dissonance (including the use of seventh and ninth chords) — the so-called "second practice." The traditional madrigal gave way to the new Baroque genres about 1600, and Monteverdi turned to ostinato bases, strophic variations, and the contrasts of concertato style. Less dependent on theory than on musical intuition, Monteverdi raised the early Baroque theatrical styles of recitative and aria to a higher artistic level, and integrated them with choral music, dance, and instrumental sinfonias and ritornelli to create the new mixture of styles that was to culminate in the brilliant psychological drama of Nero and Poppea.

Career   Monteverdi, who played the organ and the viol, studied with Marc' Antonio Ingegneri in Cremona. Remarkably, his first book of motets (for three voices) was published in 1582 when he was no more than fifteen, a book of madrigals in 1583, and one of canzonettas in 1584. The composer served the Duke of Mantua from about 1590 as a violist, and was his *maestro di musica* from

1601 to 1612. His next position was that of choirmaster at St. Mark's in Venice, a highly prestigious post that nevertheless allowed him to compose for Venetian confraternities and to undertake commissions for Mantua and elsewhere. He took holy orders about 1630, a time of lessened activity as a composer, but the opening of the public opera house in 1637 brought forth his last three stage masterpieces.

Girolamo Frescobaldi   Italian   1583–1643

Achievement

1. Perhaps the most significant of early Baroque composers of keyboard music, Frescobaldi brought to a lofty culmination such Renaissance genres as the toccata, canzona, and ricercare within the advanced rhythmic and harmonic idioms of the early Baroque.
2. During his lifetime Frescobaldi was famed as a virtuoso organist with an extraordinary gift for improvisation and also as a teacher, his pupils including Froberger and Franz Tunder and his influence extending to such later composers as Buxtehude and Bach.

Works and Style Summary

Organ (keyboard) music: 6 books, including toccatas, canzonas, ricercares, fantasias, partitas, capriccios, dance movements

Chamber music: 1 collection of canzonas for instrumental ensemble, 2 for any kind of instrument(s), 1 in full score

Church music: 3 organ Masses, toccatas, ricercares, canzonas

Vocal music: 2 books of arias for 1 or more voices, 1 book of 5-voice madrigals

Frescobaldi created an individual style of great expressivity and improvisatory boldness, while at the same time maintaining strict and masterful control. In his fidelity to counterpoint and his madrigalian harmonic vocabulary, he revealed his Renaissance heritage: the fantasias (1608) and the early ricercares depend upon imitation and variation, as do the early toccatas (which reveal in their expressive and forward-looking use of ornamentation and harmony his most personal and most influential tone of inspired improvisation). His mature style, on the other hand, not only explores the middle ground between modality and tonality, but his irregular rhythmic flow and greater use of textural, metrical, and tempo contrast bespeak his progressive Baroque orientation. The capriccios (1624) use variation on a larger scale, while combining elements from the other keyboard genres. Few late works are known. The intimate, even mystical, toccatas from the famous *Fiori musicali* (1635) seem to represent a new style in that genre.

Career   Born in Ferrara during the reign of the music-loving Duke Alfonso II, Frescobaldi grew up under the musical influence of Luzzasco Luzzaschi, Gesualdo, and various Neapolitan keyboard composers. He may have become organist of the Ferrarese Accademia della Morte in 1597. From 1604, or perhaps earlier, he worked in Rome, where he became organist at St. Peter's in 1608. Except for a period as court organist in Florence from 1628 to 1634, he retained his prestigious post at St. Peter's for the rest of his life, gradually earning an international reputation as both an organist and harpsichordist, and also fulfilled commissions for the Barberini family, Cardinal Aldrovandini, and Cardinal d'Este, among others.

TOCCATA PER L'ELEVAZIONE

Edited by Pierre Pidoux in *Girolamo Frescobaldi: Orgel-und Klavierwerke*, Vol. 5, pp. 42–43 (Kassel: Bärenreiter, 1953).

Historical Perspective This toccata was published in Frescobaldi's famous *Fiori musicali*, a collection of liturgical music from 1635. It is not a brilliant showpiece, but rather meditative in mood and rhapsodic in structure. It was composed to be performed in the Mass during the elevation of the Host.

Description of Style Frescobaldi adapted the short-breathed motives of the Baroque—with their contrasting rhythms, chromatic alterations, and striking dissonance—to the linear style of the Renaissance. His approach to rhythm, as stated in the preface to this collection of music, was to alter the tempo according to the affection of a passage, which results in a highly characteristic rhythmic discontinuity. The harmonic idiom reflects the transitional style period: chromaticism has nullified the church modes, but the listener accustomed to the highly directional progressions of functional harmony encounters harmonic surprises at every turn. Frescobaldi's basically conjunct lines create a rich variety of suspensions and other dissonances.

Analysis of Structure The toccata unfolds rhapsodically in a series of loosely joined, modulating episodes that are made a cohesive whole by the recurrence of prominent rhythmic patterns. Although each episode emphasizes different thematic materials, sections with motion in like note-values (mm. 1–9 and 18–23)

SECTION	MEASURES	NATURE OF RHYTHMIC MOTION OR MOTIVE	KEY
1	1–9	Even motion in half-note harmonic rhythm	e (with raised 3rd) to V of G
2	10–17	Uneven motion with motive of ♪♩	G to a
3	18–23	Even motion in eighth-notes	d Dorian (with leading tone) to V of a
4	24–33	Uneven, in quarters and sixteenths	a/C to G
5	34–42	Uneven, with new motive of ♫♫	a to V of e
6	43–48	Basically even, with half-note harmonic rhythm	e (with raised 3rd)

clearly alternate with those in uneven motion (mm. 10–17 and 24–33) until the penultimate episode (mm. 34–42). Here, the dotted-note rhythm of measures 10–17 and sixteenth-note motion of measures 24–33 both return briefly and take their place alongside an important new pattern of one eighth-note and two sixteenths. The return at the end (mm. 43–48) of several earlier motives and of the slower harmonic rhythm of the opening section helps round off the piece. Several of the sections are articulated by augmentation of note-values at closing cadences. Seldom has improvisatory freedom been more artistically controlled than in the music of Frescobaldi.

Heinrich Schütz   German   1585–1672

Achievement   Schütz was the leading German composer of the early Baroque and one of the greatest composers of music history. He remains significant (1) for introducing the new Italian monodic and concertato styles in Germany, (2) for the excellence of his treatment of the German language, (3) for his importance as a teacher, and (4) for his active part in creating a new musical flowering in Germany after the Thirty Years War.

Works and Style Summary   All of the Schütz's works are vocal, and most of those extant were written for the Lutheran church. Unfortunately, at least half of all Schütz's compositions have either been lost or they still await rediscovery:

> *German motets:* small-scale works for one or several soloists with limited accompaniment (55 *Kleine geistliche Konzerte* in two sets, and *Symphoniae Sacrae* II), medium-sized choral works (*Musikalische Exequien* and *Geistliche Chormusik*), and large-scale works for soloists, chorus(es), and instruments (*Psalmen Davids* and *Symphoniae Sacrae* III), as well as his last extant work, a German *Magnificat*
>
> *Latin motets:* the *Cantiones Sacrae*, *Symphoniae Sacrae* I (in monodic style), among others
>
> *Oratorio-like works:* an Easter oratorio, *Die sieben Worte Jesu Christi am Kreuz*, a Christmas oratorio, 3 Passions (Luke, John, and Matthew)
>
> *Psalm harmonizations:* the *Becker Psalter*
>
> *Madrigals:* one Italian collection (his Opus 1) and some lost German pieces
>
> *Operatic works:* at least 4 lost (among them, *Daphne* [1627], the first German opera)

Schütz's music represents a masterful fusion of various elements — motet-like imitative writing, madrigalian tone-painting (with chromaticism and expressive dissonance), and a keen sense of the dramatic possibilities of monody and the concertato style. In short, he brought the passion and color of Venetian music to the austere belief and linear discipline of the Germans. He even went beyond Gabrieli by differentiating clearly between solo parts and choral parts. At an advanced age, in his Passions, he explored a new, plainsong-like, unaccompanied style of recitative.

Career   Landgrave Moritz the Learned of Kassel brought the young Schütz to his court as a choirboy. In 1609 a scholarship from Moritz caused Schütz to leave his study of law at the University of Marburg in order to study with Giovanni Gabrieli in Venice. On his return to Kassel in 1612, he was again induced to drop law, now to be an organist in the Chapel Royal. In 1615 he moved to the Elector's chapel in Dresden, becoming Hofkapellmeister in 1617. With the exception of leaves of absence, one of them in order to study with Monteverdi in Venice (1628–29), Schütz held this important post for the rest of his life.

Arcangelo Corelli Italian 1653–1713

Achievement

1. During a period dominated by vocal music, Corelli achieved enormous fame entirely through instrumental composition, the first composer to do so. His trio sonatas, solo sonatas, and concerti grossi served as models of form, style, and technique for succeeding generations of European composers and laid the foundation for the magnificent flowering of instrumental music in the eighteenth century.
2. Corelli is commonly regarded as the founder of modern violin technique, particularly for his manner of bowing and his use of double stops. As a director of instrumental ensembles, he required each player of the same part to bow alike.
3. The most important violin teacher of his era, Corelli had both foreign and Italian pupils, foremost among the latter being Francesco Geminiani.

Works and Style Summary
 All of Corelli's works were for instruments, and all — or nearly all — for strings. Dating them is difficult because the composer gathered and published them in six collections of twelve pieces each, as summarized below, long after many of them were written. No composer until Haydn enjoyed the number of reprinted editions achieved by Corelli.

> *Trio sonatas:* 48, organized in four books, two for the church and two for the chamber
>
> *Solo sonatas:* 12, published in one book, six of them *da chiesa* and six *da camera* (the last being a set of variations)
>
> *concerti grossi:* 12, published in one book, eight being *da chiesa* and four *da camera*

Viewed historically, Corelli seems more a consolidator and craftsman than innovator, perhaps because his originality has been obscured by assiduous imitation on the part of other composers. In keeping with his serene and conservative character, his music avoids extremes of mood, range, and technical difficulty, depending rather upon judicious use of occasional imitation and fugue, ostinatos, and cantabile melody as well as on such characteristic devices as sequence, constantly moving (or "walking") bass lines, chains of suspensions, and cadential clashes of a second (early in his career). He helped establish the new harmonic world of functional tonality, giving preference to a more or less homophonic texture within a highly diatonic idiom. Despite purported examples of his own, it is unknown to what extent he relied on improvised embellishment by performers to fill out the texture of his music. The church sonatas maintain a Slow–Fast–Slow–Fast structure, whereas the chamber sonatas are less predictable. The solo sonatas and concerti grossi often follow a five-movement pattern, the added movement being in fast tempo and featuring some display by the solo violinist. The concerti grossi were more significant for their style than for their conservative structure, which lacks differentiation between the concertino (a string trio) and the optional concerto grosso (generally made up of four violins, two violas, violoncello, and two double basses), which merely doubles the concertino.

Career   Corelli may have studied violin with G.B.Bassani or perhaps with Benvenuti and Brugnoli. He was elected to the prestigious Arcademia Filarmonica in Bologna at the age of 17. He settled in Rome about 1675 and spent his very prosperous life as a renowned violinist and composer, fulfilling commissions for compositions, performing for the many music-loving cardinals in Rome, and directing instrumental ensembles and operatic as well as oratorio performances. Perhaps his greatest public appearance took place in 1687 at a papal reception where he led an orchestra of 150 strings. In 1706, with Alessandro Scarlatti and Bernardo Pasquini, Corelli was admitted to the famous Arcadian Academy of Rome.

Henry Purcell   English   1659–1695

Achievement

1. Purcell was the leading English composer of the Baroque period and among the greatest of all English composers. On the number and variety of his vocal works, and especially on his mastery in setting words to music, rests the greater part of his reputation.
2. Fewer in number but fully equal in expression and effortless technique are his instrumental works, in particular the trio sonatas and the fantasias.
3. His outstanding technical achievements were his mastery of a personal musical language that represents a fusion of Italian, French, and English elements, and, perhaps uniquely his, exceptional skill in writing on a ground bass.

Works and Style Summary

Songs: more than 100, most of them published in *Orpheus Britannicus* (1698 and 1702)

Chamber music: much instrumental music, some works with continuo (for example, two collections of trio sonatas) and some without (viol fantasias for from 3 to 7 parts)

Dramatic music: one chamber opera (*Dido and Aeneas*, 1689) and incidental music for about 50 stage works (*The Fairy Queen*)

Miscellaneous music: about 25 court odes and welcome songs; much sacred music, primarily verse anthems; some sacred songs; some harpsichord suites and organ music

The composer's style represents a fusion of Italian and French elements with such native English traits as simultaneous cross-relations, and a singular mastery of declamation, tone-painting, and composition on a **ground bass**. He achieved a personal melodic style, one given to disjunct motion, syncopation, and various augmented and diminished intervals. His harmonic daring and characteristically English love for rich harmonic sonorities were more and more directed towards functional harmony, which made possible the large-scale works of his later years.

Career   Purcell was a choirboy in the Chapel Royal under Captain Cooke and Pelham Humfrey, and later studied with John Blow. From 1673 he served the English court in a variety of roles, including composer, singer (countertenor), and organist, and succeeded John Blow as organist at Westminster Abbey in 1679.

Alessandro Scarlatti   Italian   1660–1725

Achievement

1. Alessandro Scarlatti was the leading Italian composer of vocal music in the late seventeenth and early eighteenth centuries and among the greatest masters of any age of opera, cantata, and oratorio. His greater depth of expression and more subtle and varied musical language brought to its peak the Italian Baroque vocal tradition.

2. Although not famous or very active as a teacher, Alessandro certainly taught his son Domenico and perhaps the important German composer Johann Adolph Hasse.

Works and Style Summary

Operas: c. 100, all except one being *opere serie*, although many have comic scenes within their serious plots (for instance, *Tigrane* and *Griselda*)

Cantatas: at least 600, ranging from continuo-accompanied secular solo cantatas on texts dealing with love to orchestrally-accompanied Christmas cantatas

Oratorios: c. 40, all composed to Italian texts (*San Filippo Neri* and *La Vergine addolorata*) except for six in Latin

Serenatas: c. 25, most more elaborate than the operas, in keeping with their character as special commissions

Church music: several Masses (one in neo-Palestrina style), a St. John Passion, some sacred vocal concerti among other works

Instrumental works: concerti grossi, chamber sonatas, toccatas, and other works

Scarlatti's vocal style underwent a remarkable improvement from journeyman imitation in a musically limited idiom to sovereign mastery of the principal form of his time — the da-capo aria. In his hands the aria became no less expressive (if somewhat more limited structurally) than the later sonata form. This development rested primarily upon his shift away from an emphasis upon the text to a music first and foremost emphasis, with a central concern for expressing the meaning or the affection of the text. After about 1700 the composer transformed his previously contrapuntal bass part into harmonic support for a liberated vocal line; he also increased the role of the orchestra as a foil for the voice. The eloquently refined chamber style of the later cantatas displays the full range of

Scarlatti's harmonic daring, one of his most characteristic traits. Once regarded as the founder of the eighteenth-century school of Neapolitan opera, Scarlatti now appears to have fallen out of fashion before that more virtuosic style swept Europe.

Career   As a youth, Scarlatti studied music in Rome (perhaps with Carissimi), where he was exposed to the music of Corelli and other fine composers. His instrument was the harpischord. His career was spent as an opera composer and chamber musician in Rome (as *maestro di cappella* in various courts and churches) and in Naples (as *maestro di cappella* in the royal chapel). The composer's first and longest stay in the employ of the Viceroy of Naples (1685–1702) helped initiate that city's long period of widespread musical influence. He returned there from 1708 to 1718, and retired there in 1722. Two indications of his fame were his election to the Arcadian Academy in Rome (1706) and his elevation to the noble title of *Cavaliere* by the Pope in 1716.

LONTAN' DALLA SUA CLORI

The score appears in *Concerto vocale,* ed. Malcolm Boyd (Kassel: Bärenreiter, 1972).

Historical Perspective   Alessandro Scarlatti composed more than six hundred secular cantatas (perhaps more than eight hundred), many of them for courtly entertainment. Not surprisingly, considering the amazing number and prevailing high quality of his cantatas, the composer soon established a standard approach to the genre and thereafter concentrated his efforts on deepening his musical expression. It is this quality that brings the secular cantata to the peak of its historical development in his works.

"Lontan' dalla sua Clori" is written for soprano voice (ranging from d' to g″) with continuo accompaniment. The text of "Far from his Clori" relates the plaint of a shepherd who, far from his beloved, expresses his torments to the rocks and the trees. The opening recitative is followed by an aria, "Where are you, my dear sweet treasure? If you don't answer, I will languish and die." In the second recitative, the shepherd describes nature itself as saddened by Clori's absence, as evidenced by the withered flowers, the birds' laments, and the muddied brook. In the second aria he calls for her hasty return, unless she wishes him to die.

Description of Style   By the time of Scarlatti, the styles of recitative and aria had diverged to the extent that—as in this cantata—recitative approached the repeated-note style of *recitativo secco*, while aria spun out its eloquent melody in typical da-capo fashion. Opening the cantata with the leap of a minor seventh gives notice of the composer's boldness, a trait also reflected in the several measures of arioso (setting the words "il pianto mio") that close the second recitative. The melodies of the arias invoke a gentle melancholy, the first by its minor mode and chromatic inflections, the second by its pastoral *siciliano* character and frequent turns to minor mode. In contrast to its melodic role in Scarlatti's early works, the bass line functions here primarily as harmonic support for the voice. A

masterful harmonist, the composer expresses the shepherd's lament with supporting dominant and nondominant sevenths, secondary dominants, diminished
sevenths, Neapolitan sixths, borrowed chords from the parallel minor, and affective use of nonharmonic tones.

Analysis of Structure The cantata follows a pattern frequently employed
by the composer: recitative–aria plus recitative–aria. A tonal link is forged between the two halves by beginning and closing the cantata in B-flat major and by
employing G minor prominently within. The first recitative modulates from B-
flat major to D minor. G minor is the key of the first aria, with a secondary emphasis upon its relative major (B-flat). The second recitative begins in E-flat major (the subdominant), modulates far afield, and closes in G minor. B-flat major
returns as the tonic of the second aria, whose middle part begins strongly in G
minor. Despite his mature allegiance to the da-capo aria, Scarlatti achieved considerable variety by diversifying the proportions of the parts as well as those of the
sections, as may be seen in the chart below.

Aria 1 (G Minor)

Part:	A (70 mm.)			B (37 mm.)		A
Section:	a¹	a²	a³	b¹	b²	
No. of measures:	22	19	29	15	22	da-
Text lines:	1–2	1–2	1–2	3–4	3–4	capo
Keys:	g–B♭	B♭–g	g	g-f	f–B♭	

Aria 2 (B-Flat Major)

Part:	A (22 mm.)			B (20 mm.)			A
Section:	a¹	a²	a³	b¹	b²	b³	
No. of measures:	6	7	9	5	6	9	da-
Text lines:	1–2	1–2	1–2	3–4	3–4	3–4	capo
Keys:	B♭–F	F	B♭	g	c–E♭	c–d	

François Couperin   French   1668–1733

Achievement

1. Couperin was the leading French composer of the early eighteenth century,
his fame resting largely upon his suites for harpsichord and his instrumental
chamber music.

2. He was a master of the trio sonata, which he apparently introduced into
France and which, in his hands, represented a masterful fusion of the Italian and
French chamber music traditions.

3. The composer was a distinguished teacher of harpsichord and organ. Among
his pedagogical contributions was an important treatise entitled *The Art of Playing
the Harpsichord* (1716), which advocated a modern system of fingering and emphasized the correct realization of ornaments.

Works and Style Summary

Harpsichord music: 4 collections of *Pièces de clavecin* (1713-30), comprising 27 suites (more than 200 pieces) of perhaps his most characteristic music

Chamber music: trio sonatas (*Les Nations*), suitelike solo sonatas (*Concerts royaux*), and other genres

Church music: organ music (including 2 organ Masses) and motets in concertato style (3 *Leçons de ténèbres*, 1714)

Secular vocal music: chiefly the *airs de cour* published in *Recueils d'airs sérieux*

Couperin's style is an aristocratic one grounded in highly stylized dance rhythms and forms, characterized by a great deal of refined ornamentation, and firmly linked to the High Baroque by the contrapuntal integrity of his outer voices and his free treatment of imitation. Among such keen harpsichord competition as that offered by Clérambault, Dandrieu, and Marchand, Couperin established his leadership by the intensity of his expressive harmony (including chromatic dissonance), the richness of his melodic invention, the aptness and scope of his descriptive tone-painting, and his mastery of iodiomatic harpsichord expression (including frequent use of the broken-chord style found in lute music). Among the vocal works, his *Leçons de ténèbres* also found him at his most eloquent, even approaching the character of opera. In his chamber music Couperin frankly borrowed Italian elements of style, ultimately succeeding in integrating the best of Corelli's style with the best qualities of music in the French, especially the Lullian, tradition.

Career   Scion of a renowned musical family, François was a student of his father and uncle, both organists, and later of the famous organist Jacques Thomelin. He served as organist at the church of St. Gervais from 1685 to 1733. In addition, he succeeded Thomelin as organist and *maître de chappelle* of the Chappelle Royale in 1693, a very important event for his career, and in 1694 he became royal harpsichordist as well as music teacher for the royal family. His quiet and faithful service was eventually rewarded with the rank of Chevalier.

HUITIÈME ORDRE, IN B MINOR (PIÈCES DE CLAVECIN, BOOK II)

The score is found in Couperin's *Oeuvres Complètes*, Vol. 3 (Paris: Éditions de l'Oiseau-Lyre, 1932).

Historical Perspective   The Eighth Ordre (or suite) was published in 1717 as the third *ordre* in the second book of four entitled *Pièces de clavecin*. Shortly before its publication, the long and glorious reign of Louis XIV (1643–1715) had come to an end, and it is the classical, highly refined, and rigorously rational approach of the *grand siècle* that is mirrored in Couperin's music. An *ordre* is a stylized set of dances loosely grouped in varying numbers around the traditional sequence of allemande, courante, sarabande, and gigue. Many of Couperin's pieces bear interesting subtitles, a popular custom of the time, but seldom does there seem to be any meaningful connection with the music. The Eighth Suite is generally regarded as one of his finest works.

Couperin, Huitième Ordre (Pièces de clavecin, Book II)

MOVEMENT	TITLE	METER	FORM	LENGTH OF SECTIONS (IN MEAS.)	SECONDARY KEY
1 (Allemande)	La Raphaéle (The Raphael)	4/4	binary	10/20	V
2 Allemande	L'Ausoniéne (The Italian, after Ausonius)	4/8	binary	18/30	V
3 Courante I	– – –	3/2	binary	9/9	III
4 Courante II	– – –	3/2	binary	8/19	V
5 Sarabande	L'Unique (The Unique One)	3	binary	8/16	III
6 Gavotte	– – –	2	binary	8/12	V
7 Rondeau	– – –	3	rondeau	–	–
8 Gigue	– – –	6/4	binary	16/35	V
9 Passacaille-Rondeau	– – –	3	rondeau	–	–
10 (Gigue)	La Morinéte (The Daughter of the Musician Morin)	12/8	binary	5/17	V

Description of Style   Each dance has its own rhythm and character, the prevailing tendency being towards short-breathed but highly ornamented themes in balancing phrases. A serious mood predominates, whether in simple, straightforward dances (such as No. 7), complex ones with various subdivisions of the beat (No. 1), or unique ones with extreme changes of tempo (No. 5). Like Bach, Couperin effected a balance between chordal richness and linear vitality. The climactic *passacaille* achieves its high tension through a concentration of suspensions and seventh chords.

Analysis of Structure   All movements share the same minor tonic. Couperin employed only two forms in the suite, the principal one being Baroque binary, a two-part form with each part immediately repeated. The two sections vary considerably in length. Tonally, movement is from the minor tonic to either the dominant or the relative major. Rondeau form appears twice in the suite, in each case offering a refrain that alternates with contrasting material. In the magnificent *passacaille en rondeau*, the highpoint of the suite, the refrain is built on a bass that ascends by step from tonic to mediant and then by half-step to the dominant, followed by a **V–I** cadence. Rather than playing through the entire *ordre* as it stands, the performer was intended to shape his own suite by choosing from among the alternative allemandes, courantes, and gigues, and by including extra dances of his choice.

Antonio Vivaldi   Italian   1678–1741

Achievement

1. The leading Italian composer of the late Baroque, Vivaldi was above all a master of the concerto. The driving rhythmic style he developed and his use of the ritornello principle, his three-movement structure, and his standard use of the cadenza were widely admired and imitated by his contemporaries, among them J. S. Bach, who arranged many of Vivaldi's violin concertos for keyboard.

2. Vivaldi figured prominently in the early eighteenth-century development towards the homophonic emphasis and contrasting textures of the Classical period.

3. A virtuoso violinist, the composer contributed greatly to the development of violin technique. His special delights seem to have been high hand positions, wide leaps, cadenzas and other improvisatory passages, and a love for double- and even triple-stopping.

Works and Style Summary   Vivaldi's large and varied output, much of which remained unpublished, has provided considerable difficulty to his catalogers: the pioneer work of Pincherle (P), Fanna (F), and Rinaldi (R) has now been superseded by the *Verzeichmis der Werke Antonio Vivaldis* of Peter Ryom, (Copenhagen: Engstrom & Sodong, 1974).

Concertos: 500 or so, including 350 solo string concertos, c. 40 double concertos, 30 concerti grossi, nearly 60 string orchestra concerti (*L'estro armonico, The Seasons, La cetra*)

Operas: nearly 50, of which at least 21 are extant (among them *Orlando furioso* and *La fida ninfa*)

Cantatas (c. 40) and *serenatas*

Church music: a great deal, including two oratorios, motets, psalms, a celebrated *Gloria*

Miscellaneous instrumental works: among them about 90 sonatas (both trio and solo) and about 60 sinfonias

Early in his career Vivaldi's style was not unlike that of Corelli's, but it was soon transformed by concerto and operatic writing into a dramatic and progressive idiom founded upon strikingly memorable themes and boundless rhythmic vitality. Vivaldi stressed wide leaps, syncopation, Lombardic (♪♫) rhythms, sudden large shifts of harmonic rhythm, ostinati, frequent use of seventh chords in a variety of homophonic textures, and juxtaposition of major and minor modes. A more or less improvisatory character emerges from his frequent re-use of vivid thematic material, his propensity for assymmetrical and irregular phrasing, his many colorful orchestral violinistic effects, and, of course, his increased level of violin technique, featuring arpeggios, scales, **bariolage**, and a rich variety of embellishment. In his vocal music Vivaldi apparently relied far more upon convention than in his concertos.

Career Vivaldi studied with his father, a violinist, and with Giovanni Legrenzi. Although he took holy orders in 1703, his career was spent in music. For many years (1703–09, 1711–18, and 1735–38) he worked as a composer, violinist, harpsichordist, teacher, and administrator at the Conservatory of the Pietà in Venice. In the years 1714–17, 1726–28, and 1733–35 he was composer and opera impresario at the Theater of San Angelo in Venice. Between operatic ventures, he settled briefly in Mantua, Rome, and possibly Prague. Despite his enormous success, the vicissitudes of operatic life found him dying as a foreigner in Vienna and being buried in a pauper's grave.

CONCERTO IN A MINOR FOR TWO VIOLINS (L'ESTRO ARMONICO, OP. 3, NO. 8)

The score is in CSM II.

Historical Perspective *L'estro armonico*, a collection of twelve concertos, was published in 1712 in a Dutch edition with a dedication to Ferdinando III, Grand Duke of Tuscany. This publication was Vivaldi's first collection of concertos, and it established his European reputation. The solo concertos in the group, which number six if the two works for two solo violins are included, usher in a new era of virtuosity and freedom for solo players. At least ten of Vivaldi's concertos, this one among them, were transcribed for other instrumental media by J.S.Bach; the present concerto was transcribed for organ.

Description of Style Rhythmic drive lies at the heart of Vivaldi's style. Short motives, usually scalar or triadic, are the rule. These unfold by repetition or sequence in a spun-out manner, with the downbeat of a new section overlapping the cadence of the old. Phrasing, which is often irregular, is normally articulated clearly. The music of Vivaldi relies heavily upon harmonic as well as melodic sequence in a clearly functional tonal idiom. Modulations take place through secondary dominants, and movement through the circle of fifths is common. Although homophony prevails, it can take many guises: unison, block chords, broken chords in all parts, melody with accompaniment, melody in parallel thirds with accompaniment. When imitation does take place, it is ordinarily between the soloists, and sometimes, as in the second movement, linked in a chain of suspensions.

Op. 3, No. 8 calls for two solo violins and four-part strings with continuo. Vivaldi specified a wide variety of dynamics with great care, and he achieved some magnificent string sonorities. Texture is varied constantly, with soloists combined or set against the ripieno group in a multitude of ways, among them dramatic unison tutti. The soloists display their abilities in dazzling arpeggiation and virtuoso passagework.

Analysis of Structure   The concerto unfolds in three movements: Allegro, Larghetto e spiritoso, and Allegro. Each movement employs a ritornello, but each application of the ritornello principle works out quite differently. In all three cases the ritornello opens and closes the movement in the tonic key. In the first movement, however, the closing statement is expanded by solo insertions. More significantly, there is a strong statement of the first portion of the ritornello in the subdominant key precisely in the middle of the movement. The tonal plan of the movement — tonic, subdominant, tonic — reflects in microcosm the tonal plan of the entire concerto. The second movement finds the ritornello being treated as a frame; it appears only at the beginning and end, each time in exactly the same form. In the third movement Vivaldi turned to an asymmetrical arrangement in which the soloists are given much more freedom to indulge in improvisatory episodes that expand in length as the movement unfolds. At the high point of the movement (mm. 86–113) stands the largest episode — an accompanied solo marked *cantabile*. In this instance Vivaldi reduced the ritornello for its last appearance to its bare essentials, a descending scale in eighth-notes and a twice-stated unison cadence in quarter-notes.

Jean-Philippe Rameau   French   1683–1764

Achievement

1. Rameau was the leading French composer of the mid-eighteenth century, primarily for his operas and ballets but also for his outstanding harpsichord music.
2. He was the leading theorist of the Baroque period, the author of a famous *Treatise on Harmony* (1722) and many other treatises. Particularly significant were his emphasis upon the common chords and his establishment of functional harmony.

Works and Style Summary

Operas and opéra-ballets: c. 20, among them the operas *Hippolyte et Aricie* (1733) and *Castor et Pollux* (1737)

Harpsichord music: 3 collections

Miscellaneous works: among them, trio sonatas, cantatas, church motets

Rameau's style is especially noteworthy for its varied and masterful treatment of rhythm, which is seen mainly in his ballet writing, in the descriptive instrumental music in his operas, and in his suites for keyboard. Harmonically, his music is expressive and as rich as could be expected from the composer's theoretical studies, with much use of secondary dominants and very skillful use of modulation. His melodies are often triadic and always have a clear harmonic basis. Rameau's orchestration is often strikingly original and, like his choral writing, always effective.

Career   The composer was a violinist as well as a famous organist and harpsichordist. He learned music from his father, an organist. Rameau began his career as an organist in Avignon and then in Clermont-Ferrand (1702–05), where he returned after 1715 (having failed to establish himself in Paris and taken several other organ posts). After making his name known by his famous *Treatise on Harmony*, he returned to Paris in 1723, publishing cantatas and keyboard pieces and gaining a reputation as a teacher and organist. He became composer, organist, and conductor to the greatest music patron in France, La Pouplinière, who supported the composer's rise to dominance in French opera from 1731 to 1753. Known for his irascible temperament, Rameau was a leading figure in the controversy between his followers and those of Lully in the 1730s and in the War of the Buffonists in the 1750s. He was given a pension and an honorary appointment as royal chamber music composer in 1745.

Johann Sebastian Bach   German   1685–1750

Achievement

1. The composer is commonly regarded as the consummate master of Baroque styles, genres, and structural principles, which he fused into a style of unmistakable individuality, great expressive intensity, and unique craftsmanship.
2. He had great impact upon succeeding generations of composers from Haydn to Bartok and beyond, mainly through his example as a master of counterpoint but also as teacher of his sons and many others.
3. Bach was known during his lifetime primarily as a great organ virtuoso and consultant on organ construction as well as a great contrapuntist.

Works and Style Summary

Church cantatas: over 300 (c. 200 extant), arranged in 5 complete cycles for the church year (composed mainly from 1723 to 1730)

Other choral works: several Masses, a Magnificat, two Passions, oratorios, motets

Organ music: chorale preludes, preludes and fugues, toccatas and other works

Keyboard music: preludes and fugues, suites, variations, fantasias, among other genres

Unaccompanied works: 6 sonatas and 6 partitas for violin, 6 suites for violoncello, sonata for flute

Ensemble pieces: among them sonatas, 6 Brandenburg concertos, harpsichord concertos

Orchestral works: including 4 suites

Works in which a didactic purpose seems evident include *The Well-Tempered Clavier* (48 preludes and fugues), *A Musical Offering*, and *The Art of Fugue*.

The music of J. S. Bach constitutes a remarkable fusion of national styles. The rhythmic and thematic vitality of the Italians, the style and dance forms of the French, and the contrapuntal tradition of the Germans are all thoroughly assimilated within an idiom unique for its harmonic richness, linear integrity, expressive intensity, timbral diversity, structural grandeur, and technical mastery. Fundamentally instrumental in character (including the vocal works) and rigorously contrapuntal, it reveals his genius for inventing themes that lend themselves to fugal treatment or to combination with sharply contrasting counterthemes. Bach's comprehensiveness in the working-out of a basic theme or motive brought about its fullest possible realization and led him to create movements and compositions of unprecedented length and cogency. He achieved unity by endowing each movement or piece with totally consistent development of a specific technique and character, and created diversity by combining several contrasting movements in one composition. By fusing traditional and contemporaneous styles and forms, Bach brought to a grand culmination the manifold variety of the Baroque period.

Career   The composer came from a family that was remarkable for producing six generations of professional musicians. He learned music from his father and older brother and also by copying and arranging the works of other composers. In addition to keyboard instruments, he played the violin. After serving as a boy soprano in Eisenach and Lüneburg, he became organist and cantor at Arnstadt (1703–07) and Mühlhausen (1707–08), court organist and then concertmaster at Weimar (1708–17), kapellmeister at the court of Cöthen (1717–23), cantor at the Thomasschule and kapellmeister at Leipzig (1723–50) and also director of the Leipzig **Collegium musicum** (1729–37, 1739–41). After the status, appreciation, and freedom granted him in his court positions, the Leipzig experience confined and embittered Bach. Perhaps the most noteworthy event of his life was his visit to the court of Frederick the Great of Prussia in 1747, which resulted in his *Musical Offering*.

CANTATA NO. 80, EIN' FESTE BURG IST UNSER GOTT
The score can be found in MSO I and CSM II.

Historical Perspective   To create *Ein' feste Burg*, Bach adapted a cantata from 1715 entitled *Alles was von Gott geboren* to his purpose by adding two choral movements, one at the beginning and one as No. 5, these being composed on the first and third verses of Luther's famous hymn. Nos. 2 and 8 also use verses of the hymn, the remainder of the text being by Salomon Franck. The first performance probably took place during the Reformation festival of either 1724 or 1730.

Description of Style   Clothed in various melodic and rhythmic guises, the chorale tune "Ein' feste Burg" permeates four of the cantata's eight movements (excluding the recitatives, the soprano solo, and the alto-tenor duet). Its sturdy frame and generally large note-values stand out clearly against the spun-out eighth- or sixteenth-note motion of the other thematic materials. Linear and chordal elements stand in perfect balance, the former being represented by independent obbligato parts (No. 2), free imitation (No. 7), elaborate fugal writing (No. 1), and by the striking canonic treatment of the main theme in No. 1. A noteworthy example of tone-painting occurs where the struggle against the devil is twice depicted by repeated sixteenth-notes (Nos. 2 and 5).

Apart from the singers, the cantata is scored for two oboes and strings in four parts, to which are added — apparently by W.F. Bach — three trumpets, two oboes d'amore, and timpani. The full complement of instruments is employed in the two great choral movements and presumably also to double the voices in the closing chorale; the two duets both feature obbligato parts, oboe and unison strings in the first, oboe da caccia and violin in the second. The soprano solo is accompanied by continuo only.

Analysis of Structure   The cantata comprises eight symmetrically balanced movements. Three employ SATB chorus: No. 1, which depicts God as man's fortress, is a grand chorale fantasia; No. 5, in which the chorus unites in octaves against the devil, is a ritornello form with the phrases of the chorale tune framed by full statements of the ritornello and separated by orchestral interludes; No. 8 is an unadorned four-voice setting of the tune, whose form is AAB. Nos. 2 and 7 are duets: the first, which depicts Christ as man's Savior, offers both a unifying ritornello and the chorale tune as cantus firmus; No. 7, also a ritornello movement, holds promise of reward after death for faith in God. Nos. 3 and 6 are recitatives, both ending in arioso. Standing in the middle of the cantata are Nos. 4 and 5; the soprano aria (No. 4), a plea for freedom from sin, is in ternary form.

NUMBER:	1	2	3	4	5	6	7	8
Kind:	Chorus	Soprano-Bass Duet	Bass Recit.	Soprano Aria	Chorus	Tenor Recit.	Alto-Tenor Duet	Chorus
Chorale:	Yes	Yes	No	No	Yes	No	No	Yes
Key:	D	D	to f♯	b	D	to D	G	D

PRELUDE AND FUGUE IN C MINOR (THE WELL-TEMPERED CLAVIER, BOOK I) The score is in MSO I, first ed., p. 184.

Historical Perspective   Bach's first collection of twenty-four preludes and fugues covering every major and minor key bears the date 1722. (A second collection of the same size followed in 1744.) Many of the pieces in this first book of *The Well-Tempered Clavier* were conceived as technical studies for the keyboard, the pedagogical intent being clear from the prefatory remark that the collection was intended "for the use and profit of the musical youth desirous of learning as well as for the pastime of those already skilled." C.P.E. Bach once recalled how, on hearing a fugue, his father could tell in a moment "what contrapuntal devices it would be possible to apply, and which of them the composer by rights ought to apply and . . . he would joyfully nudge me when his expectations were fulfilled."[1]

Description of Style   Continuous motion in regular sixteenth-note patterns occupies most of the prelude, though both pattern and pace are altered as the final cadence approaches. In the fugue, contrasting rhythmic motion differentiates the subject from its countersubjects. The subject features uneven motion in eighths and sixteenths; its melody offers three turns around an intermittent pedal-point C, against which the line descends by step. By way of contrast, the principal countersubject unfolds its basically descending scales in even motion, first in eighths and then in sixteenths. Once underway, motion is constant until the characteristic penultimate pause, followed here by one last entry of the subject over a tonic pedal point.

As in character, so in texture the prelude and fugue complement one another. The former is chordal and seems improvisatory, whereas the latter is rigorously contrapuntal. Unusual in the fugue are the ascending cycle of fifths employed in episode 2, the close juxtaposition of ascending and descending forms of the minor scale in episode 3, and the surprising manner in which two entries of the subject (mm. 11 and 20) arrive by apparent continuation of episodal sequence.

In Bach's time the term *Clavier* encompassed both large and small harpsichords as well as the clavichord and even the organ; where it was not further specified, the choice of instrument was for the performer to make. Only a few works by Bach are specifically designated as being for harpsichord, and none for clavichord.

Analysis of Structure   After asserting its tonic key by means of the progression $I–IV–vii^{7°}–I$, the prelude unfolds freely around descending scales in bass (mm. 5–10) and soprano (5–20), followed by a long dominant pedal point (21–33), a deceptive resolution (34), and a cadence over a tonic pedal point.

The fugue, on the other hand, finds every measure strictly accounted for in its basically symmetrical two-part form. In each part there are four entries of the subject, two episodes, and one transition passage. In each half, soprano (S), alto (A), and bass (B) voices play the subject in the same order: ASBA. Episodes, however, relate to one another symmetrically, the first being like the fourth in its use of both imitation and sequence, the second being like the third in its use of sequence alone. Elements of asymmetry are introduced for rhythmic variety: each phrase in the first half of the fugue is two measures in length, whereas the second half brings episodes of greater length. In both prelude and fugue may be heard Bach's extraordinary ability to work out musical ideas with unparalleled consistency and logic.

[1]Hans T. David and Arthur Mendel (eds.), *The Bach Reader.* Rev. ed. (New York: W. W. Norton, 1966), p. 277.

George Frideric Handel   German-English   1685-1759

Achievement

1. Handel was the major force in English musical life during his own time and for many years after, his influence extending to works of Haydn, Mendelssohn, and many other composers.

2. He was one of the greatest composers of dramatic music, being both the principal master of Italian opera in the late Baroque and the founder and greatest master of English oratorio.

3. Handel was internationally renowned in his time as a great composer and as an organ virtuoso with a wondrous gift for improvisation.

Works and Style Summary

Operas: more than 40 (39 extant); all are serious, some heroic (*Giulio Cesare*) and some dealing with magic and the supernatural (*Orlando*)

Oratorios: 26 English, 2 Italian; 2 Passion oratorios: 5 basic groups may be distinguished. Among the Biblical types are the dramatic-heroic (e.g., *Belshazzar*), the narrative-heroic (*Jephtha*), and the choral epic (*Israel in Egypt*). The non-Biblical types are either mythological (*Hercules*) or allegorical (*Alexander's Feast*)

Sonatas: c. 40, about half of which are solo sonatas and half trio sonatas

Concertos: many, including 18 for keyboard (the organ concerto apparently being his invention), 12 concerti grossi (all in his Op. 6, a major contribution of the period), 6 for woodwinds and strings

Cantatas: c. 100, all secular; more than 70 are for vocal soloist and continuo, about 25 are chamber duets and trios

Miscellaneous works: much choral music (the Chandos Anthems); many suites, mostly for keyboard, but also two famous suites for orchestra (*Water Music* and *Royal Fireworks Music*); some German Lieder for vocal soloist and accompaniment.

Handel was first and foremost a dramatic composer of great power and scope: his writing for voice was unsurpassed, his gift for characterization was remarkable, and his mastery of conventional Baroque forms was greatly enhanced by unexpected dramatic effects. Melodic richness, freedom, and breadth distinguish his works despite his penchant for borrowing themes from other composers and his own *oeuvre*. Dissonance was largely reserved for moments of emotional tension, as in the more frequent accompanied recitative of his later years. He seems to have written for the ear, like the Italians, being always willing to break the rules to achieve a desired effect. Handel's variety of accompanying textures and orchestration was inexhaustible, ranging from basso continuo alone to imitative counterpoint in as many as six voice-parts. Not the least of the composer's feats was to master each of the principal national styles of the Baroque, writing with consummate skill in Italian or French forms and styles and drawing freely upon the German contrapuntal style and the English choral tradition. Late in his career he even assimilated the new operatic style of Pergolesi and the Neapolitans.

Career   The composer was a student of Friedrich Wilhelm Zachow, a church organist. In addition to playing the violin at a professional level, he became an eminent keyboard virtuoso. After a brief stay as an organist at the cathedral of Halle (1702) while at the university there, he chose to make his career in opera, doing so at Hamburg (1703–1706), then in Italy (1706–1710) at Florence, Rome, and Venice. In Italy he encountered the leading genres of music and the leading composers of the age: Corelli, the two Scarlatti, Vivaldi, and Albinoni. Finally, after a brief time as kapellmeister at the court of Hanover, Handel took up the challenge of Italian opera in London (1710–37). For years he directed his own opera companies, but the London audience finally proved incapable of sustaining such ventures. From 1738, his efforts were primarily devoted to the composition and performance of his oratorios.

MESSIAH

Historical Perspective   Composed in 1741 for performance in Dublin, *Messiah* came approximately in the middle of Handel's thirty or so oratorios and was apparently writen in an astonishingly short time. In creating his unique kinds of oratorio, both Biblical and non-Biblical, Handel drew upon several sources, including the dramatic Italian oratorio, the German Passion-oratorio, and the English choral anthem. The text of *Messiah* was compiled entirely from the Bible by Charles Jennens and, although there are no characters and no action, it aims to present in a dramatic way the redemption that man achieved through the Messiah. In its theme and its reliance upon the chorus, *Messiah* is an oratorio of the anthem type, perhaps the least common of Handel's five basic types.

Description of Style   Handel's music is noteworthy for its expression of human emotions or, in Baroque terminology, "affections." Ranging from the greatest joy ("Rejoice Greatly") to the most abject sorrow ("He Was Despised") and including consolation ("He Shall Feed His Flock"), faith ("I Know That My Redeemer Liveth"), lack of belief ("He Trusted in God"), rage ("Why Do the Nations"), and praise ("Hallelujah"), the extraordinary scope and depth of his music stem from his long experience with opera. The opening theme of an aria or chorus usually consists of several striking motives that represent in musical guise the affection expressed by the text. Handel makes each theme memorable by its rhythm, its pitch contour, and, generally, its reiterated use as a ritornello. After its first statement by the instruments, a ritornello theme is taken up by the voice(s) and generally extended by motivic spinning-out into phrases of varying lengths, between and during which there recur various motives from the ritornello theme.

The arias, even those with an obbligato line against the voice, employ essentially a texture of melody with accompaniment. Choruses, on the other hand, present a wide range of textures: contrapuntal, including fugue ("He Trusted in God"); chordal ("The Lord Gave the Word"); varying textures that include both of the above ("Worthy Is the Lamb"); and antiphonal ("Lift Up Your Heads"). Some choruses ("His Yoke Is Easy") were shaped from chamber duets composed to Italian texts shortly before the oratorio. One of Handel's favorite techniques was to contrast a melody in large note-values in one voice with chordal declamation in the other voices, as in the "Hallelujah Chorus." The composer's harmonic language was simple functional harmony, with use of the secondary dominant and a great deal of sequence. Chromaticism seldom appears, but when it does ("The People That Walked in Darkness") it is used with maximum effect.

Analysis of Structure   *Messiah* unfolds in three large parts: The Prophecy and the Coming of the Messiah, The Redemption of Man, and Thanksgiving for Victory over Death. The texts of Parts I and III share a basically objective approach, while Part II offers a more direct and subjective attitude. Each part is organized by the layout of the text, and each is made up of several groups of numbers consisting generally of a recitative–aria–chorus sequence, though sometimes merely of recitative and chorus. Although the expressive language derives from the doctrine of the affections, which was developed in opera, the extensive use of choruses (which outnumber arias) and the nature of the forms employed differentiate *Messiah* very clearly from opera of the period. Only two arias (four, in one of Handel's many revisions) are da capo, most of the others being either two- or three-part forms without exact return of sections.

Discussion of Part I in some detail will illustrate the composer's approach to form. After the opening French overture, there are no fewer than six groups of numbers: (1) accompanied recitative, aria in two-part form ("Every Valley"), chorus, these three being linked by key (E major–E major–A major); (2) accompanied recitative, aria in four parts (ABA'B') with tempo change ("But Who May Abide"), and chorus, these three also being linked tonally (d–d–g); (3) recitative and ternary aria ("O Thou That Tellest") with chorus (D–D); (4) accompanied recitative, aria in two subdivided parts ("The People That Walked in Darkness"), and chorus (b–b–G); this last chorus ("For unto Us a Child Is Born") brings the Prophecy section to a close, and its powerful contrast of imitative opening with ensuing chordal section is repeated with increasing force four times; (5) the Coming of the Messiah begins with an orchestral **pastorale** in siciliano rhythm ($^{12}_8$), continues with two alternations of recitative and accompanied recitative, and closes with a chorus ("Glory to God"), this group revealing a looser tonal unity (C–C–F–d–D–D); (6) ternary aria ("Rejoice Greatly"), recitative, two-part aria in siciliano rhythm ("He Shall Feed His Flock"), and closing chorus (B♭–a–F/B♭–B♭). The use of increasing textural complexity and of unifying tonal relationships bind the small groups together, while the development of the plot links several groups (1–4 and 5–6) within the larger frame of Part I. *Messiah* represents Handel at the height of his powers and, despite its overweening popularity, offers rich rewards for detailed study.

Domenico Scarlatti   Italian   1685–1757

Achievement   Little known during his lifetime, Domenico Scarlatti was perhaps the finest harpsichordist and harpsichord composer of his generation, and among the first to employ the thematic contrast and free homophonic textures of the early Classical period. Few composers of any age can match the originality and fecundity the composer displayed after he reached the age of 50.

Works and Style Summary   The composer's works were cataloged first by Longo (the source of L. numbers), later (and more accurately) by Ralph Kirkpatrick (the source of K. numbers).

> *Harpsichord music:* c. 600 pieces, mostly sonatas (published as *Esercizi*, the first collection appearing in 1738)
>
> *Miscellaneous works:* among them operas, cantatas, and church music (including a *Stabat Mater* and a *Salve Regina*)

Scarlatti's harpsichord music is wholly idiomatic, frequently virtuosic, and, within the standard Baroque binary form, inexhaustibly varied. Its rhythmic élan is matched by a masterful use of contrast in texture, thematic material, mood or character, and figuration. Hand-crossings, wide leaps, passages in parallel thirds and sixths—these are some of the technical difficulties. Just as demanding are the musical and aesthetic challenges, such as that posed by the large amount of repetition (of both themes and sections).

Career   Domenico was a pupil of his father, Alessandro, as well as of Francesco Gasparini. At 16 he was organist and composer at the royal chapel in Naples. After further study in Venice, he became *maestro di cappella* in Rome to the Polish Queen Maria Casimira (1709–14) and later at the Vatican (1714–19). About 1720 he entered the service of Princess Maria Barbara of Portugal. He followed his royal pupil and patroness to Madrid, becoming *maestro de cámara* when she became Queen of Spain in 1746.

GLOSSARY

acciaccatura   (It.)   a keyboard ornament formed by simultaneously striking neighboring harmonic and nonharmonic tones, immediately releasing the latter.

agréments   (Fr.)   melodic ornaments, generally indicated by signs or abbreviations.

allemande   (Fr.)   a stylized dance movement in moderate quadruple time, generally the first movement (after the overture) in a Baroque suite.

appoggiatura   (It.)   a nonharmonic or embellishing tone (normally preceded by a leap) that occurs on a strong beat and usually resolves downward by step.

aria   (It.)   a formal song used in opera, oratorio, and cantata; generally distinguished from ordinary song by its greater length and its emphasis upon musical rather than textual factors.

arioso   (It.)   a type of solo vocal writing, more songlike than recitative and less formal than aria.

arpeggio   (It.)   a chord whose tones are sounded separately; a broken chord.

bariolage   (Fr.)   shifting back and forth quickly between two or more violin strings while playing a repeated tone.

basso continuo   (It.)   a continuing bass part indigenous to Baroque music and requiring realization by a keyboard instrument and, usually, a low string instrument; it may be figured (with numbers and accidentals) or it may not. (See **thoroughbass**.)

bel canto (It.) "beautiful singing," as exemplified in Italian vocal music and vocal technique of the seventeenth and eighteenth centuries, including the works of Carissimi, A. Scarlatti, Hasse, and Mozart.

binary form a two-part form (with each part repeated) having one main theme or motive, the first part moving from tonic to dominant and the second from dominant back to tonic (or, in minor, from tonic to relative major and then back to tonic.)

bourrée (Fr.) a dance movement, usually duple and rather fast; optional in the Baroque suite.

cadenza (It.) an improvised or improvisatory passage, normally a decoration of the final cadence (before the coda) in a solo concerto; cadenzas frequently provide the soloist an opportunity for virtuosic display.

camerata (It.) a small Renaissance **academy**, the most famous of which met in Florence about 1580 at the palace of Count Giovanni de' Bardi; seeking to rediscover the expressive power of Greek music led the group to experiment with Baroque monody.

castrato (It.) a male soprano or contralto whose vocal quality was the result of early castration; an exotic manifestation of Baroque opera.

chaconne (Fr.) a set of variations based upon a repeated harmonic scheme.

circle of fifths progression harmonic movement in a sequence of descending fifths, a common scheme in Baroque and Classical music.

clavecin (Fr.) a harpsichord.

clavier French or German term for the keyboard or keyboard instruments.

collegium musicum (Lat.) originally a music society formed by a group of amateurs for the performance of art music; now usually connected with a university and playing music composed before the Classical period upon appropriate instruments.

comédie-ballet (Fr.) a form created in 1664 by Lully and the playwright Moliere in order to fuse their musical and dramatic talents.

concertato (It.) a term derived from concerto and used as an adjective to mean concerto-like with reference to the contrasting instrumental and/or vocal groups in music of the late sixteenth and seventeenth centuries (as in works by G. Gabrieli, Monteverdi, and Schütz). Used as a noun in connection with vocal works, it is a forerunner of the church cantata.

courante (Fr.) a "running" dance normally in triple time; it follows the **allemande** in the standard Baroque suite.

da capo aria (It.) an aria at whose close is placed the term *da capo* (meaning to repeat the movement from the beginning to the place marked *fine*, which is the end); thus, a ternary aria with an exact but unwritten repeat.

dialogue (It., *dialogo*) a form that preceded oratorio and cantata in which two singers (or two small groups of singers) exchange conversation in music.

doctrine of affections (Ger., Affektenlehre) an attempt by Baroque theorists and composers (prominent among them Johann Mattheson) to codify the means of expressing emotions in music by imparting conventional meanings to certain keys, tempi, rhythmic patterns, and even to intervals. Once created, melodic figures or motives were then spun-out throughout a movement or section of a piece in accordance with the Baroque musico-dramatic practice of presenting one affection at a time.

double (Fr.) an ornamented repetition of a Baroque dance movement.

French overture (Fr.)   a standard type of Baroque opera overture consisting of a slow section in dotted rhythms followed by an allegro in imitative style; if such a movement precedes a suite instead, the entire suite may be titled a French overture.

fugue   See **organ music**. Three basic terms require definition to study a fugue. The *subject* is the main theme of the fugue and might well consist of a distinct head, middle, and tail. (A double fugue would have two subjects.) The *countersubjects* (there are probably more than one) are the lines sung against the subject. *Episodes* take place between entries of the subject, and their thematic material may either be new or drawn from the subject or the countersubject.

gavotte (Fr.)   a popular dance type of the Baroque period, usually in a moderate quadruple meter; an optional movement in the Baroque suite.

gigue (Fr.)   a dance movement, the last in a typical Baroque suite; characterized by a lively compound duple meter and, often, an imitative texture.

ground bass   a concise theme heard over and over in the bass part against a melody that often does not repeat.

harmonic rhythm   the rate or pattern of harmonic change.

harpsichord   a keyboard instrument whose strings are plucked. It became the leading continuo instrument of the Baroque period, taking the name of *cembalo* in Italy, *clavecin* in France, and virginal or spinet in England.

hemiola (Greek)   a rhythmic device found in all periods of Western music; alternation of triple meter at two different metrical levels; as in juxtaposition or coincidence of 6/8 and 3/4. (See Ch. 2, Ex. 1, m. 14.)

libretto (It.)   the text (or book) of an opera or oratorio.

masque   an English form of staged entertainment of the late sixteenth and seventeenth centuries, employing poetry, dancing, and music, as well as scenery and costumes.

monody   expressive accompanied solo song of the early Baroque period.

number opera   an opera made up of relatively independent individual "numbers" (arias, duets, ensembles), generally separated by recitatives.

obbligato (It.)   reference to the fact that a certain instrumental part is necessary (obligatory); often used in connection with Bach arias in which a solo instrument is obliged to play in counterpoint with the voice.

opéra-ballet (Fr.)   a hybrid form of opera in which the dramatic portion was greatly reduced to permit emphasis on dancing, choral, and scenic elements. It was created very late in the seventeenth century by André Campra, a successor to Lully.

opus (Lat.; plural, *opera*)   a term given by composers to their published works along with a number indicating the order of publication; normally abbreviated as Op. (singular) and Opp. (plural).

ordre (Fr.)   a suitelike collection of dance movements from which the performer selects several for a given performance.

ornamentation   addition of mostly stereotyped melodic figures (such as the trill and the appoggiatura) to a line of music, either during the performance by way of improvisation or by the composer or an editor. In the Baroque period, as in early music in general, improvised ornamentation was expected of the performer. In French music, composers marked their scores with symbols to call for melodic ornaments.

ostinato (It.) a melodic motive or phrase that is persistently (obstinately) repeated by the composer. It is a favorite technique of Baroque and Twentieth-
Century composers.

overture (Fr.) properly, an introductory instrumental movement played at the
beginning of an opera, stage play, oratorio, or suite. A concert overture, on the
other hand, is an independent composition.

partita (It.) in early terminology, a set of variations; in modern usage, a suite.

passacaglia (It.) a variation form based upon an ostinato theme usually heard in
the bass.

pastorale either an idyllic nature piece, usually instrumental and invoking ideal-
ized shepherds (with reference to the Nativity), or a dramatic scene composed in
the Renaissance or early Baroque (a forerunner of opera).

recitative (It., *recitativo*) a stylized kind of solo vocal writing that aims at imitat-
ing the inflections and rhythms of speech; found in opera, oratorio, and cantata. In
a rapid, nonmelodic style accompanied by continuo, it is called *recitativo secco* (dry),
while in an expressive and orchestrally-accompanied style it is called *recitativo accom-
pagnato*.

ritornello (It.) a recurring instrumental theme that serves to unify a composition, whether instrumental or vocal.

sarabande (Fr.) a dance type characterized by a slow triple meter with stress on
the second beat; the third movement in the standard Baroque suite.

scordatura (It.) any non-standard tuning of a stringed instrument.

serenata (It.) a short Baroque dramatic composition performed in the usual setting of a secular Italian cantata, but having costumes and some scenery.

sinfonia (It.) an instrumental piece that serves to introduce an opera (or operatic
scene), cantata, or orchestral suite.

stile concitato (It.) a style of dramatic expression in which excitement is conveyed by rapid reiteration of single notes, generally in string tremolos.

stretto (It.) overlapping of subject entries in a fugue.

ternary form three-part form, normally ABA.

thoroughbass a system whereby a keyboard player improvises chords over a
given bass line by means of symbols (numbers for intervals or accidentals for
altered notes) placed beneath the staff. Baroque keyboard players were expected to
realize the bass line at sight, however sparsely figured.

tonality a system of pitch organization that—in common practice—emphasizes
one central tone and chord and gives functional importance to the subdominant
(**IV**) and the dominant (**V**). Just as the pitches of the scale relate to a central tonic,
so the keys emphasized in a movement or a composition are bound in a functional
relationship, beginning with the dominant key (as opposed to chord) and subdominant key and extending to include relative major and minor keys (in the Baroque
period), parallel major and minor modes (Classical period), and, among others,
third relationships (Romantic period).

Chapter Four

Classical Music

The period from about 1740 to 1825 coincides largely with the so-called Age of Enlightenment, a time of devotion to reason and knowledge in France (Voltaire and the Encyclopedists), of rediscovery of Greek thought in Germany (Winckelmann), and of empirical philosophy in England (Locke). Academies of arts and sciences, universities, and the arts and letters flourished under a more benevolent guise of political despotism, and the increasing affluence of the bourgeoisie made it increasingly necessary for the nobles to share the burden of patronage of the fine arts. Outstanding royal patrons of music still abounded, among them Frederick the Great of Prussia (also a flute-player and composer), the opera-loving Austrian rulers Maria Theresa and Emperor Joseph II, Duke Carl Eugen of Stuttgart (also an opera-lover), and, above all, Carl Theodor of Mannheim, Elector of the Palatinate, of whom it was said that music accompanied his entire day — waking, eating, hunting, worshiping, and falling asleep.

Although the spread of Italian *opera buffa* sparked the change to the Classical style, it was the genius of the Austro-Germans for the instrumental and the abstract that brought Classicism to its peak. With the symphonists of Mannheim, most notably Johann Stamitz (1717–1757), instrumental music began its rise to a position of undisputed leadership. Only in instrumental music, after all, could the period's ideal of a universal (or cosmopolitan) musical language be realized. So pervasively did the autonomous instrumental formal principles such as sonata form and rondo form serve as a new challenge for composers — making the SYM-PHONY, SONATA, CONCERTO, and STRING QUARTET the leading genres of the period — that their influence actually extended to large-scale vocal forms — the OPERA and even the Mass. Concern for clarity and simplicity of expression, for dynamic but objective working-out of thematic and tonal contrasts, for universality of language, and for a classic balance between structure and expression of emotion came to characterize most of the era's composers, who generally demonstrated their craft and versatility by writing in all major genres, both instrumental and vocal. Melody became more prominent, and now was generally stated in discrete, balancing phrases over a wide variety of homophonic accompanying textures. Increased rhythmic activity at the ends of phrases, periods, and sections broke the continuous spunout motion of the Baroque. Finally, freely-taken dynamic and orchestral changes also contributed to the new variety of means. The rational Baroque concern for expression through monumental exposition of a single emotion according to the doctrine of affections was replaced by a more fluid and abstract sense of beauty, which nevertheless still conveyed meaning through its use of a vocabulary developed in vocal music. Perhaps the Classical composer's most remarkable feat was to assuage the veritable passion for musical novelty that characterized the late eighteenth century by a new sense of drama achieved through the eminently rational techniques of thematic development and dynamic tonal relationships. In the words of the great German poet-philosopher Johann Wolfgang von Goethe regarding chamber music, "One listens to four intelligent people conversing with each other; one expects to gain from their discourse and to learn to know the peculiarities of the instruments."[1]

Art music continued to serve a variety of roles in the Classical period. In the church and at court, it remained necessary and functional. Through its abstract nature and the intentionally broad scope of its appeal, it attracted a widely disparate body of music-lovers. In addition to providing entertainment for the upper classes, its disciplined logic and universal validity challenged the intellectual elite, as represented by Goethe. Its inherent expressiveness lured adherents of naturalism, a movement led by Rousseau, to its support; at the same time, its ability to proceed from a simple folk tune basis and raise man above the worldly to the realm of the spirit and a higher morality led many (including the philosopher Herder) to deem it the highest of all the arts.[2]

Among the first to employ the thematic contrast and freely-conceived homophonic textures of the early Classical period was the great harpsichordist-composer DOMENICO SCARLATTI. (See Chapter Three.) More conventional and more widely popular was the **style galant**. But after music had begun to appeal to a larger audience through public concerts and increased music publication for domestic use, the less elegant and more expressive *empfindsamer Stil* (sometimes termed the *style bourgeois*) also became popular. A composite of Baroque and Classical elements, this style was principally cultivated by C. P. E. Bach. Along with the gallant style, it was to serve as one of the major sources for the High Classical synthesis achieved by HAYDN and MOZART.

Despite his achievement and assertion of artistic individuality, Carl Philipp Emanuel did not enjoy independence until he left the service of Frederick the Great for the free city of Hamburg in 1768. Indeed, Haydn himself, generally recognized as the greatest composer of his period by his contemporaries, humbly wore his patron's livery and dined with the servants at Esterháza until his retire-

---

[1]Translated by A. D. Coleridge (ed.) in *Goethe's Letters to Zelter* (London, 1892), p. 369.
[2]Friedrich Blume, *Classic and Romantic Music* (New York: W. W. Norton, 1970), p. 14.

ment to Vienna. Mozart, on the other hand, was too proud and too sensitive to remain in the service of the Archbishop of Salzburg. When he chose to strive for economic independence in Vienna as a composer of operas and concertos, he could not achieve it. Still, he did not suffer the fate of several noteworthy Italian contemporaries; certain of their operas on politically sensitive themes resulted in their temporary imprisonment. After Mozart's death, Haydn glimpsed the nature of future patronage during his London sojourns.

Despite their awareness of audiences' demands, the music of Haydn and Mozart revealed on the whole an intrinsic capacity to be beautiful in an abstract manner for its own sake apart from any need to please specific noble patrons or accompany their activities. Whereas Haydn excelled in the symphony and the string quartet, establishing the principle of thematic development and laying the groundwork for Beethoven, Mozart made his chief contributions in the more dramatic genres of piano concerto and opera. Despite the excellence of his old-fashioned serious operas (*Idomeneo* may be seen as the culmination of the *opera seria*) and his creation of the incomparable *sui generis* operas *Le nozze di Figaro* and *Don Giovanni*, Mozart could not wrest leadership of opera from the Italians. It remained for BEETHOVEN to establish a lifestyle that was as independent as his basically Classical music, a feat accomplished by eschewing Italian opera and concentrating upon composing instrumental music for concert performance and for publication. When he began to overload the delicate sense of proportion, the basically formal manner, and the limited system of tonal relationships of the Classical style, he did so as much in the service of self-expression as in the need for music to fulfill its inherent purposes. Composers of the nineteenth century looked back upon Beethoven's cyclic and programmatic elements and his expansion of compositional resources as the beginning of Romanticism.

PRINCIPAL CLASSICAL GENRES

Opera

Italian opera continued to be dominant in the Classical period, but Austrian and German composers began to exert strong influence, especially in the form of symphonic elements of the new and more dynamic Classical style. New style traits appeared first in the two-part **intermezzo** of Pergolesi and his successors. They were retained in *opera buffa*, an independent comic genre that arose to challenge the popularity of traditional *opera seria* in the first half of the eighteenth century. By the end of the century emphasis on ensemble singing, more realistic characterization, and concerted ensemble finales had produced a new operatic type with plots of a fairly serious nature being balanced by comic elements and characters—the *dramma giocoso*. At the same time that Gluck, Jommelli, and Traetta were transforming traditional *opera seria* and French *tragédie lyrique* to reflect the Classical preference for balance between music and drama, the greater flexibility of *dramma giocoso* made possible the sharper dramatic contrasts, deeper characterization, and immeasurably broadened emotional range of Mozart, whose *Nozze di Figaro* (*Marriage of Figaro*, 1786) achieved a synthesis of the best elements from each of the standard Italian operatic types. As in Italian

ITALIAN OPERA

The **Metastasian** *opera seria* ideal refines but institutionalizes a lyric type of opera that features constant alternation of action (recitative) and reflection (aria), with emphasis on virtuoso singing and little or no use of chorus. *Opera buffa* rises to importance, emphasizing characterization and ensemble finales.

FRENCH OPERA

Continuance of previous emphasis upon drama and spectacle on a large scale, with use of large choral and ballet scenes connected with the action. More amenable to "reform," that is, to subordination of virtuosity and spectacle to drama, than *opera seria*.

GERMAN OPERA

Rise of the indigenous *Singspiel*, a popular folk-based genre with spoken dialogue.

Classical Opera Composers

	ITALIAN	FRENCH	GERMAN
1725 to 1740	Giovanni Battista Pergolesi, 8 (2 buffe) Baldassare Galuppi, c. 100 (31 giocosi)		
1740 to 1780	Nicolò Jommelli c. 75 (64 serie) Christoph Willibald von Gluck (27 serie) Tommaso Traetta c. 40 (29 serie) Nicola Piccinni c. 90 (27 buffe) Franz Joseph Haydn c. 15 (6 giocosi) Johann Christian Bach 10 serie	Christoph Willibald von Gluck 12 (4 tragédies) André-Danican Philidor c. 30 (22 comiques) Nicolò Piccinni 12 (10 tragédies) Pierre-Alexandre Monsigny 13 comiques Francois-Joseph Gossec 10 (8 comiques) André-Modeste Grétry c. 60 (46 comiques)	Johann Adam Hiller 14 Singspieler Georg Anton Benda 10 (5 Singspieler) Franz Joseph Haydn 6 Singspieler Karl Ditters von Dittersdorf 29 Singspieler
1780 to 1810	Giovanni Paisiello c. 75 (13 giocosi) Domenico Cimarosa c. 60 (10 giocosi) Wolfgang Amadeus Mozart 13 (3 giocosi)	Luigi Cherubini 12 (6 rescue) Étienne-Nicolas Méhul c. 30 (rescue or comiques)	Johann Abraham Peter Schulz 3 Singspieler Johann Friedrich Reichardt 15 (9 Singspieler) Wolfgang Amadeus Mozart 5 Singspieler Ludwig van Beethoven 1 rescue-Singspiel

opera, the comic genres led to exciting new developments in France and Germany. In both *opéra comique* and *Singspiel*, which differ from *opera buffa* in their use of spoken dialogue and emphasis on folklike songs, elements of a serious nature transformed tradition from within. Mozart's *Zauberflöte* (*Magic Flute*, 1791) represents the Classical culmination of *Singspiel*; the concern for social issues evident in *Le nozze di Figaro*, and, in particular, the events of the French Revolution engendered the rescue drama of Grétry and Cherubini. In Beethoven's only opera, *Fidelio* (1805), rescue drama and *Singspiel* reached the zenith of their Classical expression.

Concerto

On the whole, traditional Baroque elements such as ritornello passages, dynamic contrast between soloist and orchestra, virtuosity and improvised cadenzas, and a three-movement form were adapted with considerable success to the new elements of style and the thematic and tonal relationships of the Classical period, principally those associated with sonata form and the rondo. In discussing the concerto, the contemporaneous theorist Heinrich Christoph Koch wrote that the first movement of the concerto had the main structural sections of the sonata form (assigned to the soloist accompanied by orchestra), each of them set off distinctly by the orchestral texture of four ritornello sections. Since virtuosic display was a principal concern, the concerto lacked much thematic development. Noteworthy High Classical features include the double exposition of the modified sonata first movement and the typical rondo finale. Haydn and Mozart, the latter a renowned concert pianist, were very much steeped in the Early Classical idiom and did not disturb the balance between soloist and orchestra. In the piano concertos of Mozart the genre reached a height seldom touched since then. For the most part, Beethoven also preserved the basic Classical tradition, following firmly after Mozart until introducing some progressive elements into his last pair of piano concertos.

Important Concerto Composers

Carl Philipp Emanuel Bach	Ger. (1714-1788)	c. 50 (keyboard)
Franz Joseph Haydn	Aus. (1732-1809)	c. 30
Johann Christian Bach	Ger. (1735-1782)	c. 30
Carl Stamitz	Czech (1745-1801)	60 +
Wolfgang Amadeus Mozart	Aus. (1756-1791)	33 (21 solo piano)
Ludwig van Beethoven	Ger. (1770-1827)	7 (5 piano)

Sonata

The Classical sonata was commonly an instrumental composition in several movements for soloist (usually violin) with accompaniment or for solo keyboard. The style change from Baroque to early Classical coincided with the rise of the keyboard sonata after 1730 in the harpsichord *essercizi* of Domenico Scarlatti, the

Important Sonata Composers

(Domenico Scarlatti)	It. (1685–1757)	c. 600
Baldassare Galuppi	It. (1706–1785)	90 +
J.-J. Mondonville	Fr. (1711–1772)	25 +
C. P. E. Bach	Ger. (1714–1788)	c. 265
Franz Joseph Haydn	Aus. (1732–1809)	c. 285 (c. 50 piano)
Johann Baptist Vanhal	Czech (1739–1813)	c. 50
Leopold Kozeluch	Czech (1747–1818)	c. 50
Muzio Clementi	It. (1752–1832)	79
Wolfgang Amadeus Mozart	Aus. (1756–1791)	c. 90 (19 piano)
Ludwig van Beethoven	Ger. (1770–1827)	55 + (37 piano)

sonatas of Galuppi and other Italians, those of Vanhal and the Austrians, and, especially, the clavichord sonatas of C. P. E. Bach in Germany. Unlike the Italians with their liking for paired movements, the Germans nearly always wrote in three movements: Fast (sonata-allegro), Slow (a simplified sonata form, a partite one, or perhaps variations), Fast (rondo or minuet). Not until the 1760s did the piano sonata become common, ushering in the high Classical style of Haydn and Mozart and completing the transformation of Baroque binary into sonata form. As numerous as the piano sonata was the violin sonata, but many of these keep the violin subservient to the piano. In the Classical period the sonata became the province of the piano student and music-loving amateur, rather than a regular feature of public concert life.

String Quartet

Not until the last third of the eighteenth century — when the last vestige of the basso continuo and the traditional trio sonata had disappeared — was the string quartet free to follow the lead of the principal Classical instrumental genres. Even then, with the emergence of two violins, viola, and violoncello as the players, entertaining forms such as the divertimento had undue influence on the genre, since it was much cultivated by amateur chamber musicians. Finally, Haydn raised it to a high artistic level, indeed to leadership among the Classical chamber genres. Important steps in its evolution include equalization of the parts, a four-movement form, and use of thematic development and counterpoint

Important String Quartet Composers

Franz Joseph Haydn	Aus. (1732-1809)	c. 80
Johann Baptist Vanhal	Czech (1739-1813)	c. 100
Luigi Boccherini	It. (1743-1805)	c. 100
Wolfgang Amadeus Mozart	Aus. (1756-1791)	c. 25
Ludwig van Beethoven	Ger. (1770-1827)	16

in place of the *style galant*. Mozart, a rapt student of Haydn in the string quartet, brought to the genre his love of the dramatic. It remained for Beethoven to cross traditional boundaries of length, manner of expression, and sonority, creating serious problems for his Romantic successors.

Symphony

A Classical symphony is generally composed in four movements for a mixed orchestra of strings in four parts, pairs of woodwinds and (sometimes) brasses, plus timpani. A popular related genre was the *symphonie concertante*, a concerto-like work with two or more soloists. The symphony represents an amalgamation of elements from the Baroque sinfonia (its name, pattern of instrumentation, and its Fast-Slow-Fast basic form with the weightiest movement first), suite (the minuet, which became the third movement), and sonata (its rounded binary form as precursor of the sonata-allegro form). Just as it served to fuse heterogeneous Baroque elements into a new unity, so the symphony brought into synthesis such leading Early Classical styles as the *style galant* (J. C. Bach) and the *empfindsamer Stil* (C. P. E. Bach), thus increasing its diversity and range of expression. Given the Classical precepts of emphasis upon melody with accompaniment, balanced phrasing, dynamic tonal contrast, and thematic development (Haydn) as opposed to Baroque spinning-out of motives, there gradually emerged a view of the symphony as an organic whole with emphasis upon the finale and even of overarching cyclic unity through the recurring use of a basic motive (Beethoven). The symphony ranks as the most prominent genre of the Classical period by its sheer numbers (over 12,000 from 1720 to 1810), its dominant place in musical life, and its uninterrupted development of the procedures that defined Classical style and challenged its greatest composers.

Significant Composers of the Symphony

Giovanni Battista Sammartini	Italian 1701–1775	c. 70
Carl Philipp Emanuel Bach	German 1714–1788	c. 20
Johann Wenzel Anton Stamitz	Czech 1717–1757	c. 60
Florian Leopold Gassmann	Czech 1729–1774	c. 30
Franz Joseph Haydn	Austrian 1732–1809	100+
Francois-Joseph Gossec	Belgian 1734–1829	c. 100
Johann Christian Bach	German 1735–1782	c. 75 (15 *concertantes*)
Carl Ditters von Dittersdorf	Austrian 1739–1799	over 100
Luigi Boccherini	Italian 1743–1805	c. 25
Carl Stamitz	Czech 1745–1801	c. 90 (38 *concertantes*)
Wolfgang Amadeus Mozart	Austrian 1756–1791	c. 50
Ludwig van Beethoven	German 1770–1827	9

MAJOR COMPOSERS AND SELECTED COMPOSITIONS

Christoph Willibald Gluck   German   1714–1787

Achievement

1. Gluck was an important opera composer who won fame as a reformer by (a) attempting to subordinate musical to dramatic values, (b) increasing the role of the orchestra, in particular by making the overture an integral part of the opera, (c) narrowing the distance between the styles of recitative and aria, especially by reducing vocal virtuosity and the number of da-capo arias. In fact, most of the foregoing were already part of French operatic theory, which Gluck and his librettist Calzabigi applied to Italian opera; he succeeded, however, in establishing a better balance between music and drama than had the French.

2. He is the earliest opera composer whose works have maintained a fairly firm place in the repertory, a tribute to his dramatic genius and to his ability to express the essence of a text in a unique way.

Works and Style Summary

Italian operas: 27 or so *opera serie*, many on texts by Metastasio (outstanding are *Orfeo ed Euridice*, 1762, and *Alceste*, 1767)

French operas: 12, of which 8 are comic, 4 tragic (two of the tragedies—*Iphigénie en Aulide* (1774) and *Iphigénie en Tauride* (1779)—are notable)

Miscellaneous works: several ballets, symphonies, trio sonatas, Lieder, some church music

Despite his restricted harmonic vocabulary, his lack of textural variety, and his lack of fecundity (he borrowed again and again from his previous works), Gluck created an affecting dramatic language noteworthy for its seriousness of purpose and nobility. In 1762, under the influence of the librettist Calzabigi, he brought to Italian opera the choruses, ballet, and dramatic force of French opera in a style which shows some influence from the simple and popular style of French *opéra comique* and yet is far removed from his early work in the graceful, tuneful idiom of Pergolesi. The typical complexity of *opera seria* is eschewed in the three famous reform operas—*Orfeo*, *Alceste*, and *Paride ed Elena*—in favor of concentration upon a single crucial dramatic issue. In the two French operas on the subject of Iphigenia, he brought the *tragédie lyrique* to life again, rising to his greatest heights of melodic writing and of characterization.

Career Although he was to some extent self-taught, Gluck may have studied with Sammartini in Milan from 1737 to 1741. His opera debut came with *Artaserse* in 1741 in Milan, which proved to be the first of a series of Italian successes. After failing to establish himself in London, he returned to the travelling life of a composer of Italian opera. From 1750 to 1772 he worked in Vienna (after 1754 as court composer), where he composed both Italian and French operas. He composed a series of successful operas for Paris under the patronage of Marie Antoinette, including French versions of *Orfeo* and *Alceste*, setting off a journalistic struggle between adherents of Gluckian French opera and traditional Italian opera. His last works were written in Vienna, where he spent his final years.

IPHIGÉNIE EN TAURIDE

The opera is available in miniature score, ed. Hermann Abert (Zurich: Eulenberg, n.d.).

Historical Perspective   Gluck won fame in Vienna by bringing the French respect for drama, instrumental music, and musical moderation and balance to Italian *opera seria* (with *Orfeo* of 1762 and especially *Alceste* of 1767), curbing the Italian penchant for melodic and vocal virtuosity. After the failure of *Paride ed Elena* in Vienna, Gluck achieved success in Paris with *Iphigénie en Aulide* (1774). French versions of *Orfeo* and *Alceste* followed, then *Armide* and, almost at the end of his career, on May 18, 1779, his masterpiece — *Iphigénie en Tauride*. Set to an excellent libretto by Nicolas-François Guillard, the opera is closely modelled on the tragedy of Euripides. In Act I, Iphigenia, troubled by a dream of her homeland, is reluctant to obey King Thoas's orders to perform her duties as High Priestess of Diana and sacrifice two Greek strangers. Act II finds the strangers, Orestes and his friend Pylades, in prison. Not recognizing Iphigenia as his sister, and without revealing his identity, Orestes — tormented by guilt for his mother's murder — informs Iphigenia of the deaths of Agamemnon and Clytemnestra. Act III brings Iphigenia's decision to sacrifice one stranger and to send the other as a messenger to her sister Electra. Orestes forces his friend to go, and Pylades promises to return and save Orestes. In Act IV, just as she is about to carry out the sacrifice, Iphigenia and Orestes discover each other's identity. Thoas orders their deaths, but Pylades arrives in time to save them. The goddess Diana then descends and forgives brother and sister, and the opera concludes with a joyful chorus.

Description of Style   Gluck's orchestral art lay less in innovation than in his use of special effects at carefully selected dramatic moments. The piccolo shrieks during the Overture and the Act I storm; it is joined by tambourine, triangle, and cymbals to depict the barbaric Scythians. The three trombones are reserved for maximum effect at the appearance of the Furies (or Eumenides) in Act II and again in Act III.

A quality of melodic breadth and lyricism unusual for the composer permeates *Iphigenia in Tauris*. Despite his reputation for subordinating aria to drama, it is Gluck's arias that dwell in the memory. Although the melodies often seem to be hewn from simple broken chords, they do express character (Thoas's "De noir presentiments," Act I) as well as emotion (Iphigenia's "Je t'implore et je tremble," Act IV) and their range of expression is wide and varied. As in most music of the period, drama is generally created by harmonic and rhythmic means. Despite striking use of the diminished-seventh chord, Gluck's harmonic vocabulary was relatively limited. He did cultivate a wide variety of homophonic textures, and his control of harmonic rhythm and large-scale tonal relationships was secure. Dance music constitutes some of Gluck's most characteristic and memorable work. In this opera much of the dance music occurs in Acts I and II, and some of it is sung by various choruses as well as danced.

Analysis of Structure   Over the course of its four acts *Iphigenia in Tauris* unfolds its simple but profoundly meaningful plot slowly, with no more than one situation and one action per act. Musical emotion crystallizes in the arias and choruses, which offer a considerable variety of structures. The instrumental music, on the other hand, provides in its regular forms opportunity for ballet and spectacle, so necessary in French opera. The formal numbers, which give evidence of a trend towards larger and more closely integrated musical units, are linked by orchestrally-accompanied recitative of a flexible and sometimes highly expressive nature. Altogether, the opera is among the finest representatives of French heroic opera.

A detailed discussion of Act II will serve to exemplify the composer's musical and dramatic procedures. There are six formal numbers, two of them choruses and another containing both solo and choral portions. The act opens with a very brief, atmospheric instrumental prelude of extraordinary expressive power and characteristic simplicity, consisting as it does of an unaccompanied violin "melody" (basically an ascending scale), occasional woodwind chords, and powerful repeated dynamic contrasts. In a recitative Orestes laments the trouble into which he has brought his friend. A da-capo aria (one of several in the score) follows; its insistently repeated motives and sequence depict Orestes' near-madness and torment. In a short recitative and an expanded binary aria (of the form ABB), Pylades sings soothingly of their union in death. Scene Two brings their separation, and Orestes' reaction to it constitutes Scene Three, a powerful scene of accompanied recitative and arioso ("Le calme rentre") in which Orestes' outward calm is belied by a remarkable viola part. The viola's constant syncopation and obsessively reiterated dynamic contrast (from *sf* to *p*) reveal his inner anguish. When a troubled sleep claims him, the grave dotted rhythms and theme that began the scene return, now ushering in the Furies. The tonality, which has centered on D major since the act began, changes abruptly to D minor for the chorus of the avenging Furies. Unusual and expressive are the many suspensions, the use of trombones (especially to reinforce the ascending scale motive), Orestes' intermittent cries of anguish, the augmented rhythmic values for the words "murderer of his mother," and the climactic use of the diminished-seventh chord.

From Scene Five to the end of the act, the tonality leaves the orbit of D, passes through G minor and major, and closes in C major/minor. In these scenes, Iphigenia questions Orestes and ultimately learns of the deaths of her entire family (including Orestes, so she is told) save for Electra. Iphigenia remains alone for a grand scene in which she bemoans the unfortunate fate of her homeland, her family, and herself. It begins with a short recitative, continues with a G-minor chorus of priestesses, and climaxes in a large-scale, two-part (AB) aria in G major ("O malheureusement Iphigénie"). Like some other prominent numbers in the opera, the aria was taken from one of the composer's earlier works, in this instance *La clemenza di Tito* (1752). Once again, the aria is built of the simplest materials — a harmonically conceived melody unfolding over a syncopated violin line set against a repeated eighth-note pattern in the viola and supported by an **Alberti**-like **bass** part. At the close, Gluck brings in the priestesses to augment Iphigenia's anguished cries and to end the number when she falls silent. The act closes with a ternary piece (with orchestral introductions to both A and B sections) for the priestesses and Iphigenia in which Gluck achieves a wonderfully poignant effect by constantly juxtaposing major and minor modes. He also mitigates somewhat the act's almost unbearable anguish by closing in triple meter (the only use of it in the act) and in major mode.

Franz Joseph Haydn   Austrian   1732–1809

Achievement

1. Haydn was the major contributor to the evolution of Classical style, perhaps his most important contributions being the principle of thematic development and the integration into his style of a popular (even folklike) idiom capable of pleasing a wider and generally less knowledgeable audience than the aristocratic patrons he usually served.

2. He was largely responsible for bringing the symphony and the string quartet (both, of course, manifestations of the large-scale sonata principle) to artistic maturity, adding weight to the finale in both and reintroducing counterpoint as a compositional technique.

3. Both the Mass and the oratorio found in Haydn their greatest Classical master.

Works and Style Summary

Symphonies: more than 100 (the London symphonies, Nos. 93–104)

String quartets: c. 80 (in particular the late ones from Op. 71 through Op. 103)

Operas: c. 20, not all extant (among them the *dramma giocoso La fedeltà premiata*, 1780, and the opera seria *Armida*, 1784)

Sacred works: many, including 14 Masses, several oratorios (most notably *The Creation*, 1798), a Stabat Mater

Miscellaneous instrumental music: c. 50 extant piano sonatas, c. 35 piano trios, c. 30 concertos (half for keyboard), 30 divertimenti, more than 150 solos and trios for baryton (an obsolete string instrument, similar to the bass viol)

Lieder: over 50

English folksong arrangements: more than 400

Haydn's style is noteworthy for its originality, diversity, craftsmanship, melodic simplicity, and engaging humor. From the beginning the composer was a master of surprise and unusual phrasing. Not a prodigy, it was not until the late 1760s that he broke free from his Baroque heritage and undertook the challenges of structure and expression that led to the refashioning of the symphony and the string quartet. After 1780, all technical problems were resolved and the composer brought to the inherent dynamism of sonata texture an ability to allow the thematic materials of a movement to determine its course and its shape, thus creating a wholly satisfactory artistic unity from an inexhaustible variety of form. The London symphonies, composed from 1790 to 1795, represent the pinnacle of his instrumental art, after which he raised both the Mass and the oratorio to that same lofty level.

Career   The composer began as a choirboy at St. Stephen's in Vienna from 1740 to 1748. Except for some lessons with Porpora, he was largely self-taught in composition, with the aid of books by Fux (*Gradus ad Parnassum*) and C. P. E. Bach (*Essay on the True Art of Playing Keyboard Instruments*). His abilities as a violinist and pianist were modest. Nevertheless, he played, sang, and gave music lessons wherever he could, until he gained an appointment as kapellmeister to

Count Morzin (1758–61). He became vice-kapellmeister, subsequently kapell-meister, to four successive Princes of Esterhazy. Haydn won his greatest worldly successes on two London sojourns (in 1791–92 and 1794–95), after which he returned to Austria, where he lived quietly in retirement after 1801.

SYMPHONY NO. 104, IN D MAJOR (LONDON)
The score can be found in MSO I.

Historical Perspective This symphony, the last of Haydn's career, was also the last of twelve composed for performance in London during the composer's two journeys to England. It was written for Haydn's London concerts of 1795 and performed there during the spring as part of the Opera Concerts given at King's Theatre in Haymarket.

Description of Style Symphony No. 104 features tuneful, sometimes even folklike, melodies; the principal theme of the finale may well be a Croatian folk song. Nevertheless, in Haydn's hands all themes are amenable to thematic development, especially in the first and last movements, and some to variation, as in the Andante. Balanced phrasing and regular motion frequently serve as foils for irregular phrasing (created by elision or extension) and for such unexpected events as grand pauses and (in the minuet) strongly accented third beats. Against Haydn's generally diatonic harmonic idiom and melody-with-accompaniment texture, areas of chromaticism and contrapuntal writing — usually development sections — achieve maximum effect. For the sake of surprise, modulation may be accomplished by diminished-seventh chord (I, m. 120), augmented-sixth chord (I, m. 156), enharmonicism (II, m. 114), or simply juxtaposition (III, Trio). A grand pause followed by a deceptive resolution creates one of the many surprises in the fourth movement (m. 84).

The symphony calls for a standard Classical orchestra: pairs of flutes, oboes, clarinets, and bassoons; pairs of horns, trumpets, and timpani; four-part strings (with double bass sometimes independent of violoncello). Strings are the governing sonority, with woodwinds sometimes featured as soloists, and brasses relegated to reinforcing cadences.

Analysis of Structure Haydn's movements in sonata form often depend more upon tonal than thematic contrast and, as a result, are often based on one principal theme. In both the first and fourth movements of the *London Symphony* the second tonal area begins with a restatement of the first theme, which is also the subject of the major part of the development section (and — in the fourth movement — of the coda). To lessen the chance of monotony, Haydn varies his principal theme by changing tone colors and inventing new counterpoints (IV, mm. 55 and 195), by detaching motives from the theme (I, m. 108), and even by using inversion (I, m. 88). His recapitulations are freely recomposed and by no means merely repetitions. Both second and third movements are unusual. The Menuetto has a scherzo-like character and uses the flat submediant key for its Trio. The Andante features a phrase (mm. 23–25) that receives astonishing treatment (mm. 102–17) before its ultimate resolution (mm. 128–34); it also alludes clearly to the variation principle in the B section of an obvious ternary form.

Wolfgang Amadeus Mozart   Austrian   1756–1791

Achievement

1. Perhaps the most universal genius among all composers, Mozart mastered all the genres of his time.

2. One of the greatest of opera composers, Mozart is noteworthy for his ability to delineate character, for his mastery of the ensemble and the finale, and especially for adapting the dynamic sonata style to opera. He drew the best elements from various national styles of opera and also fused features from *opera seria* and *opera buffa* with those from *dramma giocoso*.

3. He established the form and character of the Classical concerto (particularly that for piano) by incorporating symphonic, concertante, and dramatic elements in a new synthesis in which the solo instrument and the orchestra function as equals and virtuoso display is subordinated to musical expression.

Works and Style Summary   There are more than 600 compositions by Mozart, all of them being designated by Köchel (or K.) numbers (after the first cataloger of his works).

> *Operatic works*: 22 (1 unfinished), e.g., *Don Giovanni* (1787) and *Cosi fan tutte* (1790)
>
> *Concertos*: 21 for solo piano, 6 for violin, 4 for horn, among others
>
> *Chamber music*: 33 violin sonatas, 23 string quartets, 8 piano trios, 5 string quintets, 2 piano quartets, a clarinet quintet, and more
>
> *Symphonies*: c. 50, the best-known being K. 550 (G minor) and K. 551 (*Jupiter*)
>
> *Miscellaneous music*: Lieder, concert arias, organ sonatas, 19 piano sonatas

The composer was greatly influenced as a youth by his international travels and later by knowledge of the music of Haydn and J. S. Bach. He effected a synthesis of Italian and German styles that was unique in its mastery of proportion and its balance of expressive intensity with Classical restraint. Characteristic of the composer are dramatic use of contrast, expressive chromaticism, richness of part-writing, and masterful treatment of large-scale tonal relationships. Finding a plethora of styles and genres to assimilate, Mozart showed little interest in innovation or originality for its own sake, preferring to bring technical perfection and expressive intensity to existing models. In telling Mozart's father that his son was the "greatest composer known to me either in person or by name," Haydn attributed to Wolfgang "taste and, what is more, the most profound knowledge of composition."

Career   Save for some contrapuntal studies with Padre Martini in Bologna, Mozart was educated entirely by his father, a celebrated teacher. The boy became a good organist, violinist, and violist, and an eminent pianist. Mozart began composing at 4. Much of his childhood was occupied with concert tours to the great cities of Germany, Austria, France, England, and Italy, all while serving as *Konzertmeister* to the Archbishop of Salzburg. In 1781 he left Salzburg permanently to seek his fortune in Vienna, where—despite a minor appointment in 1788 as composer to the imperial court—he was unable to find a permanent position with a steady income. Beset by financial troubles and illness, and faced with a fickle Viennese public, he suffered an untimely death.

PIANO CONCERTO IN C MAJOR, K. 503

The score is available in *Norton Critical Scores*, ed. Joseph Kerman (New York: W. W. Norton, 1970).

Historical Perspective This is the twenty-first of twenty-three piano concertos by Mozart. It closed the period in which the concerto was his favorite means of expression. Its first performance apparently came in December of 1786 in Vienna with the composer at the keyboard. In his concertos Mozart established the Classical model for the genre. His contributions lay primarily in dramatic character and fusion of concertante and symphonic elements to form a perfect balance between piano and orchestra.

Description of Style March-like themes dominate the first movement, lyrical melody the second, and dancelike themes the finale. In each, the beat undergoes constantly varied subdivision, particularly in the piano part, while basic rhythmic motives recur to provide unity, as in the pervasive upbeat figure of three eighth-notes in the first movement. Characteristically, Mozart employed a succession of contrasting themes (with subtle interrelationships among them) in each movement. Recurrent emphasis upon minor mode in the outer movements darkens and restrains the exuberant spirit normally found in Mozart's concertos. The decorative chromaticism is characteristic, as is contrast of texture, ranging freely from accompanied melody and block chords to moments of extraordinary contrapuntal complexity (as in I, mm. 261–81 and III, mm. 204–20). Remarkable throughout are the changing relationships between piano and orchestra: full orchestral power (reinforced by horns and trumpets) and then piano accompaniment for an expressive woodwind theme, the customary virtuoso passages for the solo piano and then woodwind soloists over accompanying strings.

Analysis of Structure The three movements fulfill the usual Fast (tonic) – Slow (subdominant) – Fast (tonic) pattern of the concerto, the first and second being modified sonata-forms, the third a rondo. But outward observance of convention in Mozart usually encloses unique and unexpected departures within, and the piano concertos are perhaps the least predictable of his works. This first movement begins with a large orchestral ritornello, one theme of which (m. 51) returns as the main subject of the development section and again in the recapitulation, making this section a reprise of both the opening ritornello and the solo exposition. Another portion of the ritornello (m. 66) is withheld until after the cadenza to round off the movement. Of interest is the lengthy transition from tonic to dominant in the solo exposition, which contains an E-flat theme (m. 148) among its modulatory passages, and becomes especially striking when it returns in the recapitulation (m. 326).

The second and third movements are more sectional and simpler in form than the first, although no more conventional or regular in detail, and certainly no less affecting. The closing rondo, which draws its principal theme from a gavotte composed for the opera seria *Idomeneo* (1781), is more serious than the usual concerto finale.

Ludwig van Beethoven   German   1770–1827

Achievement

1. Beethoven was "one of the great disruptive forces in the history of music" (Grout, *A History of Western Music*); he opened new pathways that were followed by Romantic composers, among them the use of cyclic and programmatic elements, expansion of the orchestra, introduction of chorus and text into the symphony, and writing out the concerto cadenza.

2. He brought new status to musicians by his proud independence and his ability to earn his own way through publication.

3. He expanded the underlying sonata structure of a single movement and of whole works, although never abrogating Classical principles, ultimately integrating all movements of a composition in one unified conception. In his works he embraced greater contrasts, changed the traditional number and order of movements, spanned wider tonal relationships, added a coda as a major element of structure, and successfully introduced many other innovations.

Works and Style Summary   There are about 250 compositions, many without opus numbers:

> *Sonatas*: more than 32 for piano, 10 for violin, 5 for violoncello
>
> *Chamber music*: 16 string quartets, 3 string quintets, a septet, 9 piano trios
>
> *Orchestral music*: 9 symphonies, 11 overtures
>
> *Concertos*: 5 for piano, 1 for violin, and 1 for piano, violin, and violoncello
>
> *Miscellaneous works*: 1 opera, 2 Masses, 1 oratorio, 4 cantatas, c. 70 Lieder, a song cycle, 20 sets of piano variations, over 150 folksong arrangements

Even as Beethoven strove for mastery of the Classical style in his early works (c. 1796–1802), the best of which are the piano sonatas, he asserted his individuality through a powerful rhythmic drive and by placing more weight on the closing movements of large-scale pieces. Having adopted Haydn's principle of thematic development, Beethoven carried it further in his middle period (c. 1803–1815), rigorously working out the possibilities of his material and, in addition, forging a closer relationship between the basic motives and the overall structure. His emphasis shifted to achieving an organic four-movement unity in symphonic works — as in Symphony No. 5, with its cyclic rhythmic motive. After a time of great emotional turmoil and little composition, the composer's late period (c. 1816–27) found him reconciling ever greater extremes of expression. The heroic manner of the middle period was replaced by a more intimate tone. A transfiguring lyricism becomes important as one extreme in a style given more and more to subtlety and uniqueness. Beethoven gradually came to disregard traditional performance restrictions of medium and genre; in these later years, he was drawn to the most austere media (piano sonata and string quartet) and to the most concentrated principles of form (variations and fugue, both of which he reconciled with the dynamic sonata style).

Career   The composer was educated musically by his father, a professional singer, and by the court organist C. G. Neefe, later studying with Haydn (1792–94). J. G. Albrechtsberger, and Antonio Salieri. He served as deputy organist at the court in Bonn (1782), rehearsal cembalist in the theater (1783), then assistant organist (1784–92) as well as violist (1788–92) in the theater orchestra. He launched his career in Vienna as a brilliant concert pianist (noted particularly for improvisation) in private salons and in public, especially from 1792 to 1796. Soon thereafter deafness began to manifest itself, eventually terminating his performances, then isolating him from society (after 1814), and ultimately (by about 1820) leaving him in a world of total silence. Through his success at selling his music to publishers and by generous subsidies from various noble friends, he did not have to accept any musical posts and was able to live independently in Vienna.

SYMPHONY NO. 3 (EROICA)
The score is in LS.

Historical Perspective   Begun in 1802 and first performed in 1804, the *Eroica* was among the composer's first works that unmistakably took a new direction. Admiration for Napoleon apparently inspired the *Eroica*, an admiration that did not survive that hero's self-coronation as Emperor. The revolutionary breadth and intensity of the symphony make it perhaps the most influential and daring of Beethoven's works.

Description of Style   Beethoven's principal building blocks for this immense symphony are the simplest of triadic and scalar motives, these forming powerful themes and yet leaving enough flexibility for the extensive thematic development that takes place throughout. Broadly conceived chordal passages or melody-with-accompaniment textures (with the melody roving freely among the parts) are set in greater contrast by Beethoven's increasing reliance upon counterpoint, most notably in a double-fugue episode (II, mm. 114ff.) and a fugato section in whose second appearance the subject is inverted (IV, mm. 119f. and 279f.). The work's tension and climactic surges, so characteristic of the composer, are the products of his use of rhythm and dynamics; for example, the triple meter of the first movement is momentarily opposed by the powerful *sforzando* chords of measures 25–34 and by the shift of rhythmic accent in measures 109–16 and 252–83.
   To the standard Classical orchestra Beethoven here added only one French horn; the three-part harmony this made possible among the horns is employed frequently (for example, in the trio of the third movement). The composer also granted the violoncello part a larger measure of independence from the string basses, even an occasional role as melodist.

Analysis of Structure   Without breaking with Classical tradition, the *Eroica* offers many innovative features. The sonata-form of the first movement employs a novel treatment of the first theme: its unexpected C-sharp (m. 7) resolves in the recapitulation (m. 406) as if it were D-flat, setting up the dramatic statement of the theme in D-flat that begins the coda (m. 561). Other unusual features are an important new theme in the development section (heard again in the unprecedentedly large coda) and the famous anticipatory horn entrance before the recapitulation (mm. 298–99). In the Funeral March, a rondo with two contrasting episodes (ABACA), two moments stand out—the dramatic interruption of the principal theme (m. 158), and its final statement, broken with poignant rests (m. 239). The ternary Scherzo and Trio feature contrast between staccato articulation in the former and legato in the latter, while strong crescendi play a role in both parts. The symphony closes with a unique movement constructed mainly on the principle of theme and variations, but with important themes in both bass and soprano, and including a fugal episode as well. The coda of this movement triumphantly culminates the entire symphony, a work without precedent in instrumental music for its scope and grandeur, and for the way in which it raises music to—in his own words—"a higher revelation than all wisdom and philosophy."

PIANO SONATA IN B-FLAT MAJOR, OP. 106 (HAMMERKLAVIER)

One source for the score is Beethoven, *Piano Sonatas for Pianoforte*, Vol. III (Ed. Harold Craxton). Notes by Donald Tovey (London: Associated Board, 1931).

Historical Perspective   The *Hammerklavier* Sonata was composed in 1817 and 1818 and published by Artaria in 1819 with a dedication to Archduke Rudolph of Austria. It stands twenty-ninth among Beethoven's thirty-two major piano sonatas. In this composition, which purposefully required piano technique beyond the grasp of the amateur performer, Beethoven self-consciously set his sights on a great and original masterpiece. That it should be his largest piano sonata (the only one of the last five piano sonatas in four movements) and that it "brought the details and the larger structure together more intimately than in the music of any other composer"[3] indicate that he succeeded.

Description of Style   The seeds from which the sonata grows are a melodic and harmonic use of the third (or tenth) and the opposition of the tonic B-flat to B-natural (Rosen). All of the principal themes employed in the sonata derive from the rising and descending third. Along with stress upon melodic and harmonic movement in thirds, which takes place at varying rates of harmonic rhythm, there is a shift in the sonata from traditional tonic-dominant relationships to tonic-mediant (or submediant) ones. So the harmonic form, like the melodic, also derives from the unifying interval of the third. On the other hand, many of the large-scale tonal motions are based upon the interval of the semitone (Rosen), which brings into play the second of the unifying factors. Having conceived a form generated so largely by such small details, Beethoven was careful to maintain rhythmic tension and to create a unity of rhythmic motion. Contrast stems from the chromatic idiom of the slow movement being set against the prevailing diatonic idiom of the rest of the sonata. In addition, contrapuntal textures, especially the great fugue of the finale, offer contrast to the basic homophonic quality of the Classical language.

Analysis of Structure   Although the content of the piece is revolutionary in its identity with structure, the outward forms of the individual movements are quite conventional (Rosen). The first movement unfolds clearly in sonata form,

---

[3]Charles Rosen, *The Classical Style* (New York: W. W. Norton, 1972), p. 406.

the second tonal area being G major, the major submediant (beginning in m. 63). The Scherzo stands second in this sonata; after an unexpected section in B-flat minor and duple meter, it fulfills the expected ternary design (but without internal repetitions). The slow movement is set in the key of F-sharp minor, a third relationship disguised enharmonically. Not surprisingly, its sonata form also uses the major submediant as a secondary key. After an introductory section during which the tempo gradually increases and the tonality moves—through a chain of thirds—to F major as dominant, the great fugue of the last movement begins. Beethoven describes it in the score as a "fugue in three voices, with some freedom." The freedom results essentially in "a dramatic set of variations . . . . With this movement the fugue is at last transformed into a Classical shape."[4] With this sonata Beethoven explored new frontiers by a powerful and deliberate act of the will.

GLOSSARY

Alberti bass broken-chord patterns used as accompaniment for a melody; generally written for keyboard instrument.

augmented-sixth chord a chord whose outer pitches are the flat submediant and the raised subdominant, both of which normally resolve to the dominant. (See Ex. 3, mm. 170–71.)

coda (It.) generally found as the closing section of a movement in large-scale works of the Classical and Romantic periods; harmonically, a final prolongation of the tonic harmony.

development the section in a sonata form that follows the exposition; its purpose is to modulate back to the tonic for the recapitulation, but its name derives from fragmenting, altering, treating in various keys, in short, "developing" themes from the exposition. Development also may take place on a smaller scale in the other sections of sonata form.

diapason the main foundation timbre of the organ.

diminished-seventh chord a four-note chord built of minor thirds, usually found either on the leading tone or a semitone below the dominant; although it can be treated like a dominant-ninth chord without a root, the ambiguity of its sound makes it a useful chord for modulation. (See Ex. 1, m. 142.)

divertimento (It.) an eighteenth-century instrumental piece in several relatively short movements for small ensemble; intended primarily to entertain, thus containing many dances, marches, and variations.

empfindsamer Stil (Ger.) an expressive German style of the early Classical period which relies strongly on changes of mood and dynamics.

episode a section of a fugue or ritornello movement that does not (generally) include the main theme; modulation and a lighter texture through use of sequences often characterize an episode.

exposition the opening section in a sonata form, featuring tonal contrast (usually modulation from a tonic area to a dominant area) and generally thematic contrast as well.

figured music in its Baroque meaning, florid polyphony using Baroque affective language, as opposed to a simple style (for instance, a chorale setting for the congregation).

[4]Charles Rosen, *The Classical Style*, p. 433.

finale (It.)   the closing movement of a large-scale composition.

intermezzo (It.)   a seventeenth- and eighteenth-century type of comic opera in two parts inserted between the acts of an *opera seria* (for example, Pergolesi's *La serva padrona*).

Metastasian   a reference to the outstanding opera librettist of the eighteenth century, Pietro Metastasio, whose 27 opera texts were set more than 800 times.

minuet   an elegant French dance in moderate triple meter; optional in the Baroque suite, it became the standard third movement of the Classical symphony.

motive   a short, characteristic thematic building block that is smaller than a theme and flexible enough to serve in development sections or transitions; a theme may well be built upon several motives.

recapitulation   the third section of a sonata form, in which the tonic returns and with it the principal themes (transposed to the tonic, where necessary).

reeds/reed pipes   organ stops of considerable power named for such orchestral reed instruments as the oboe and clarinet; generally used as solo stops.

rondo-form   a sectional form featuring one prominent theme set off by contrasting episodes, as in the following pattern: ABACABA. Often found as the closing movement of a sonata or concerto.

scena (It.)   a vocal scene of a dramatic character in Italian opera, often consisting of **recitative**, **arioso**, and **aria** for a solo singer. (See Chapter 3 Glossary.)

scherzo (It.)   literally, "joke"; a movement in triple meter; faster, more characterful, and less predictable than the typical **minuet**, whose place it takes in the typical Classical symphony and sonata.

sforzando (It.)   a strong accent on a note or chord.

sonata-form   the standard form employed by composers in first movements of symphonies, sonatas, string quartets, and (modified) concertos. It features tonal contrast, thematic contrast (usually, but not always), and a true **development section**. The early Classical sonata form reveals its heritage in that it remains **binary** (actually, rounded binary); in the High Classical period it soon adopts a three-part form: **exposition**, **development**, and **recapitulation**. Finally, with the usual occurrence of a **coda** in the works of Beethoven, it becomes a four-part form. (Study the compositions in Chapter 4 by Haydn, Mozart, and Beethoven.)

sonatina (It.)   a short, simple sonata; a modification of the **sonata-form** in which there is no development.

stopped pipes   organ pipes that are covered at the top, producing pitches an octave lower than voiced and altering the harmonics.

stops   on the organ, handles or levers above the manuals that enable an organist to change the registration (the actual pipes that are sounding).

style galant (Fr.)   a light-textured, elegant style of the early Classical period.

UNIDENTIFIED MUSICAL EXAMPLES

Reading scores helps train both the eye and the ear. Study of a Baroque and a Classical music anthology from those listed in the bibliography is highly recommended. The analytical notes for the compositions listed in Chapters 3 and 4 should be heard several times with score at hand. In addition, the Comparative Style Table that follows should be studied thoroughly before attempting to identify the music examples below. For those requiring still more assistance with a specific example, a list of hints is given below. The following questions should be answered in detail and in writing for each of the unidentified score pages:

1. What is the style period of the excerpt, and what musical (and historical) factors — specifically, which elements of tone color, of melody and rhythm, and of harmony and texture — support your answer? Consult the Comparative Style Table for choices.
2. What kind of composition is it — opera, oratorio, secular or church cantata, solo or trio sonata, concerto or concerto grosso, chorale prelude or toccata, suite, fugue, symphony, string quartet — and what musical, historical, and textual factors support your choice?
3. Who among the major composers of the periods in question is the most likely composer, and why?

Hints for Score Examples

Ex. 1. Identify the solo instrument in this concerto and determine the nature of its part.

Ex. 2. Note the entrance of each vocal part and describe the texture as well as the nature of the vocal lines themselves (whether syllabic or melismatic, etc.).

Ex. 3. What is the genre? (See especially mm. 72–74.) The predominant texture? In whose hands did this genre flourish?

Ex. 4. Identify the genre by the two groups of instruments involved, the period by the bass line.

Ex. 5. The pitch materials — key, chords, progressions — and the sustained note-values offer the major clues.

Ex. 6. What do juxtaposition of contrasting tempi, *sforzandi* on weak beats, the melodic character of measures 144 and 155, and hand-crossings add up to in this genre?

Ex. 7. Observe the instrumentation, the nature of the themes, and the dynamic markings.

UNIDENTIFIED HISTORICAL SOURCES

After studying the opening essays and entries in Chapters 3 and 4, mark the clues in the following sources and answer the questions below. Hints are given after the sources.

1. What kind of source is it and what is your evidence?
2. What is the style period (Early Baroque, High Baroque, Early Classical, High Classical) and what is your proof?
3. Summarize the message of the source as briefly as you can.
4. What composers might be the authors of Nos. 3 and 4? the subject of No. 6?
5. How might you interpret or apply what you have learned from the historical source?

Consult the chapter glossaries for definitions of unfamiliar terms.

PERIOD	TONE COLOR	TEXTURE	HARMONY
Early Baroque Period: 1600–1685	Continuo-based textures with preference for mixed consort; wide variety of instrumental and vocal sonorities, use of violin family and cornetto, greater dynamic range. Omnipresent harpsichord (or organ).	Melody-bass polarity in monodic, concertato, and polychoral styles; melody with accompaniment (with improvised inner voices), chordal, or imitative texture. Growing preference for trio-sonata texture.	Harmonic idiom between modal and tonal (with many chromatic changes); striking use of more frequent dissonance (some unprepared), fast harmonic rhythm, **V–I** cadences but still many step progressions.
High Baroque Period: 1685–1750	Wide variety of instrumental and vocal sonorities with parts present throughout; preference for trio-sonata texture, then for concerto sound; 4-part strings and continuo usual, with frequent obbligato parts; terraced dynamics with wider contrasts, equal temperament, greater virtuosity (clarino trumpeters and castrato singers).	Standardized textures of melody-with-accompaniment (inner parts improvised), SATB homophony, or contrapuntal voices in imitation as in fugue. Grandest achievement — perfect balance between the vertical and the horizontal dimensions of music.	Functional harmony based on central tonic with much tonal sequence and strong harmonic flow (circle of fifths frequent); larger harmonic vocabulary and more dissonance for expression (but fully regulated). Fast to moderate harmonic rhythm, with relatively few but very strong **V–I** cadences (often with trill on upper neighbor).
Early Classical Period: 1725–1775	Establishment of modern orchestra: pairs of winds, 4-part strings, timpani. Gradual decline of continuo and rise of modern chamber ensembles; wide variety of timbres, occasional use of piano, dynamics gradual as well as terraced and used to articulate thematic contrast.	Contrasting textures as the rule, with melody-with-accompaniment as the foremost type among basically homophonic textures. Much use of 2-voice texture. *Empfindsamer Stil* characterized by richer and more varied textures.	Limited harmonic vocabulary (strongly diatonic wth major mode preferred); modulations sometimes surprising but limited in number and range of related keys. Slower harmonic rhythm with much Alberti bass; **V–I** cadences (some feminine).
High Classical Period: 1775–1825	Timbre and dynamics important thematically, at times structurally; beginning of modern art of instrumentation. Varying orchestral timbres based on 4-part strings, pairs of woodwinds, pairs of reinforcing brasses (sometimes), plus timpani. Much contrast of full and light orchestral textures; gradual dynamics, more idiomatic use of instruments.	Contrasting textures remain standard, from light and episodic to full and cadential with emphasis still on homophonic varieties of texture. Noteworthy integration of counterpoint with Classical style; much 3-voice and then 4-voice writing.	Larger harmonic vocabulary with freer (unprepared and chordal) treatment of dissonance; more use of minor keys and of mode changes; greater use of modulation (including third relationships), especially in building bigger cycles of tension and release. Harmonic rhythm variable and used to build climaxes.

RHYTHM	MELODY	FORM
Metrical rhythm with varied motion, often uneven or discontinuous with marked contrasts of pace and irregular phrasing, except in dance or dancelike movements. Formal song usually in triple meter. Hemiola.	In monody, circumscribed range and frequent use of stylized speech-rhythms; relatively short phrases, affective and dramatic quality, improvised ornamentation required at performer's discretion; bel canto style begins.	Music built in short sections with much contrast and unsystematic use of imitation at phrase beginnings; much use of ground bass, ostinato, strophic form, variations, and expanded binary (AAB).
Motion more regular and continuous, culminating in constant motor rhythm within unchanging beat in the energetic, driving concerto style; asymmetrical phrasing common save in dancelike movements, much syncopation, wide range of tempi; discontinuous recitative style.	Development of longer, spun-out melodic phrases with striking motives, clearly-articulated themes (with more and wider leaps), expanded range, more ornate figuration; diatonic idiom increasingly invaded by harmonically-inspired chromaticism; words subordinated to more melismatic style (improvised embellishment required); recitative styles more varied, from near-patter to highly disjunct & expressive.	Development of tonal architecture and emergence of standard multi-movement genres with conventional sequences of movements (SFSF and FSF) and formal principles: Baroque binary, ternary (da capo aria), fugue, ritornello, variations. Fundamental structural process based on motivic "play," or "spinning-out."
Variable rhythmic motion (themes contrasted by rhythm) within basically moderate tempi. Articulation of short phrases by frequent rests and cadences. Simple meters accented on first beats of measures.	Greater emphasis on melody, featuring contrasting themes of simple character (triadic and scalar). Periodic structure with clearly articulated and balanced phrases of a short-breathed nature. Expressive use of ornamentation.	Dynamic tonal and thematic processes, principally in a binary sonata form with or without coincidence of tonal and thematic recapitulation; later in 3-part sonata-form, rondo, variations, etc. Basic structural process — creation and grouping of more or less balancing phrases.
Highly differentiated rhythms over a basically regular periodic structure; tempi more extreme, longer phrases (now often unbalanced by overlapping and elision as well as by generally greater subtlety, sforzandi, and syncopation). Development of highly original rhythmic motives common. Harmonic rhythm used to articulate large-scale forms.	Thematic differentiation between primary, transitional, secondary, and closing themes. Trend towards more characteristic motives, antecedent-consequent phrasing (also extension and contraction of balancing phrases), more chromaticism, use of buffa elements as well as seria, use of folklike melodies.	Thematic development. 3 and 4-part sonata-forms, rondo, sonata-rondo, ternary forms, variations, and even fugue. Increasing complexity and enlargement of scale, with three or four movements as conventional norms, founded on large-scale tonal relationships.

Ex. 1

Ex. 2

Ex. 3

Ex. 4

Ex. 5

Ex. 6

Ex. 7

HISTORICAL SOURCE NO. 1

When Carl Eugen came to Stuttgart as a paragon among adolescent princes, he inherited a Kapelle of eight singers and thirteen instrumentalists with an obscure Italian, Brescianello, as Kapellmeister; he also inherited a constitution guaranteed by Frederick the Great and the Emperor, and a regulation limiting the
5   amount of money which could be spent on court music to 5000 gulden a year.

Carl Eugen did not immediately concentrate on music . . . . When he married in 1748, he was content with the services of a touring company of French actors for the festivities. In 1750, he spent 35,000 gulden on the conversion of Eberhard Ludwig's court opera house into a theater holding 4000 people, and
10   opened it with an opera by Graun. In the following February, Nicolò Jommelli's *Ezio* was produced, and in the following April came Jommelli's *Didone abbandonata*. Two years later he engaged Jommelli as Ober-Kapellmeister at a salary of 3000 florins, which by 1767 had increased to 6100 florins; he had found the composer he needed . . . . At the same time, Ignaz Holzbauer, later to find fame in Mannheim,
15   was engaged as Kapellmeister and Carl Eugen, apparently eager to have a concert orchestra as brilliant as his opera, did all he could to entice Johann Stamitz from Mannheim. He would accept nobody less than Gaetano Vestris, the greatest available choreographer, to direct his ballet, although Vestris could only spend three months of every year in Stuttgart.
20   Money was spent in the theater as though for several years Carl Eugen had lost all touch with reality. When he decided that he would live permanently in his summer palace at Ludwigsburg, an opera house had to be built for him there; the building progressed too slowly to satisfy his plans and he employed his grenadiers as builders' laborers while sending out his cavalry to conscript peasants to join in
25   the work. A theater was built at his new palace, The Solitude, but simply destroyed when it was complete because its acoustics were unsatisfactory. In 1767, opera and ballet productions cost 22,000 florins and the wages of the Kapelle, the ballet, and the theater staff added another 100,000 florins to this; more than a third of the duke's own income and more than a tenth of the entire revenue of the state were
30   spent in the theater. 6000 infantry were lent to France for 400,000 florins a year; monopolies of tobacco, salt, and the right to mint coins were sold; taxation was increased threefold; cities were compelled to pay tribute to avoid having troops billeted on their citizens; by ceaseless bullying, Carl Eugen forced up his civil list payment from less than 25,000 gulden in 1750 to more than 1,500,000 in 1762 . . . .
35   For six years he turned a deaf ear to the demands of the Imperial authorities, which Frederick the Great was ready to implement by force if necessary, . . . but little by little the duke returned to common sense. In 1767 he dismissed his French actors and half his ballet company. In 1768, he cut down the size of the opera company and the orchestra. In 1769, Jommelli left Stuttgart, realizing that the days of
40   glory there were over; he tried by correspondence to establish his right to the scores of the works he had composed for Carl Eugen, but unsuccessfully. In 1770, the duke acceded and cut down his Kapelle to 46 singers and players . . . . In 1776, he was satisfied with a Kapelle of 16 musicians augmented by his students, and he lived to 1793, constructively occupied with educational and social reforms, dutiful-
45   ly attending the performances of opera buffa, French opéra comique, and Singspiel, which appealed to his citizens.

HISTORICAL SOURCE NO. 2

This style of music should not be subjected to ordinary time any more than are the newer madrigals, in which the time changes, and which are sung sometimes faster, sometimes slower, according to the sense of the words.

Toccatas of the day are rich in various kinds of passages, and manifold ex-
5   pressions, to which the measure should be adapted. The beginning must be played
slowly in arpeggios, whereupon a faster measure can be taken at will. Understand
me, reader, if you can.

HISTORICAL SOURCE NO. 3

It is not surprising that _____ should, occasionally, have entertained
blasé notions of his art; that he should have mistaken noise for grandeur, extravagance for originality, and have supposed that the interest of his compositions would
be in proportion to their duration. That he gave little time to reflection is proved
5   most clearly by the extraordinary length of some movements in his later symphonies . . . . His great qualities are frequently alloyed by a morbid desire for novelty;
by extravagance, and by a disdain of rule . . . . The effect which the writings of
_____ have had on the art must, I fear, be considered as injurious. Led away
by the force of his genius and dazzled by its creations, a crowd of imitators has
10   arisen, who have displayed as much harshness, as much extravagance, and as
much obscurity, with little or none of his beauty and grandeur. Thus music is no
longer intended to soothe, to delight, to "wrap the senses in Elysium"; it is absorbed
in one principle — to astonish.

HISTORICAL SOURCE NO. 4

Wed., Oct. 31. This morning I went with young Oliver to his Conservatorio
of St. Onofrio, and visited all the rooms where the boys practice, sleep, and eat. On
the first flight of stairs was a trumpeter, screaming upon his instrument till he was
ready to burst; on the second was a French horn, bellowing in the same manner.
5   In the common practicing room there was a Dutch concert, consisting of seven or
eight harpsichords, more than as many violins, and several voices, all performing
different things, and in different keys; other boys were writing in the same room;
but it being holiday time, many were absent who usually study and practice there
together.
10   The jumbling them all together in this manner may be convenient for the
house, and may teach the boys to attend to their own parts with firmness, whatever
else may be going forward at the same time; it may likewise give them force, by
obliging them to play loud in order to hear themselves; but in the midst of such
jargon, and continued dissonance, it is wholly impossible to give any kind of polish
15   or finishing to their performance; hence the slovenly coarseness so remarkable in
their public exhibitions; and the total want of taste, neatness, and expression in all
these young musicians, till they have acquired them elsewhere.
The beds, which are in the same room, serve as seats for the harpsichords
and other instruments. Out of thirty or forty boys who were practicing, I could
20   discover but two that were playing the same piece: some of those who were practicing on the violin seemed to have a great deal of hand. The violoncellos practice in
another room; and the flutes, hautbois, and other wind instruments, in a third, except the trumpets and horns, which are obliged to fag, either on the stairs, or on the
top of the house.
25   There are in this college sixteen young castrati, and these live upstairs, by
themselves, in warmer apartments than the other boys, for fear of colds, which
might not only render their delicate voices unfit for exercise at present, but hazard
the entire loss of them forever.

The only vacation in these schools, in the whole year, is in autumn, and that
30   for a few days only; during winter, the boys rise two hours before it is light, from
which time they continue their exercise, an hour and a half at dinner excepted, till
eight o'clock at night; and this constant perseverance, for a number of years, with
genius and good teaching, must produce great musicians.

HISTORICAL SOURCE NO. 5

Friday the 15th. At 11 o'clock in the morning there was a grand *concert* by
_____ in the auditorium of the National Playhouse. It began with that fine
(1) *Symphony* by _____ which I have long possessed. (2) Then came a superb
Italian scena, "Non so di chi," which Madame Schick sang with infinite expressive-
5   ness. (3) _____ played a Concerto composed by him which was of an extraordinary prettiness and charm . . . . _____'s playing is a little like that of the
late Klöffer but infinitely more perfect. Monsieur _____ is a small man of
rather a pleasant appearance; he had a coat of brown marine satin nicely embroi-
dered, he is engaged at the Imperial Court. (4) The soprano Cecarelli sang a beau-
10   tiful scena and rondeau, for bravura airs do not appear to be his forte; he has grace
and a perfect method, an excellent singer but his tone is a little on the decline, that
and his ugly Physiognomy, for the rest his passages, ornaments and trills are admirable . . . .
In the second Act (5) another concerto by _____, which however did
15   not please me like the first. (6) A duet which we possess and I recognized the passage "Per te, per te" with the ascending notes . . . . It was a real pleasure to hear
two people although la Schick lost by comparison with the soprano in the matter of
voice and ornaments, but she scored in the passages at least. (7) A Fantasy without
the music by _____ very charming *in which he shone infinitely exhibiting all the*
20   *power of his talent.* (8) The last Symphony was not given for it was almost two o'clock
and everybody was sighing for dinner. The music thus lasted three hours which
was due to the fact that between all the Pieces there were very long pauses. The orchestra was no more than rather weak with 5 or 6 violins but apart from that very
accurate; there was only one accursed thing that displeased me very much. There
25   were not many people.

HISTORICAL SOURCE NO. 6

Finally, Mr. _____ is the most eminent of the Musikanten in
_____. He is an extraordinary artist on the clavier and on the organ, and he
has until now encountered only one person with whom he can dispute the palm of
superiority. I have heard this great man play on various occasions. One is amazed
5   at his ability and one can hardly conceive how it is possible for him to achieve
such agility, with his fingers and his feet, in the crossings, extensions, and extreme
jumps that he manages, without mixing in a single wrong tone, or displacing his
body by any violent movement.
This great man would be the admiration of whole nations if he had more
10   amenity (*Annehmlichkeit*), if he did not take away the natural element in his pieces
by giving them a turgid (*schwülstig*) and confused style, and if he did not darken
their beauty by an excess of art. Since he judges according to his own fingers, his
pieces are extremely difficult to play; for he demands that the singers and instrumentalists should be able to do with their throats and instruments whatever he can

15   play on the clavier. But this is impossible. Every ornament, every little grace, and everything that one thinks of as belonging to the method of playing, he expresses completely in notes; and this not only takes away from his pieces the beauty of harmony but completely covers the melody throughout. All the voices must work with each other and be of equal difficulty, and none of them can be recognized as the
20   principal voice. In short, he is in music what Mr. von Lohenstein was in poetry. Turgidity has led them both from the natural to the artificial, and from the lofty to the sombre; and in both one admires the onerous labor and uncommon effort — which, however, are vainly employed since they conflict with Nature.

Hints for Historical Sources

1 Of what value is all this information about a noble's infatuation with music, particularly with opera? Ponder the changing nature of patronage through music history, and consider the decline of opera seria.

2 In which period does rhythmic freedom — as in the "newer madrigals" — come to rest upon the individual player as never before? Whose fame rests squarely upon his keyboard music, in particular upon his toccatas?

3 Could this composer's revolutionary originality and extraordinarily long symphonies actually have been injurious to his art? (Such would today be an unusual view of one of the greatest of composers.) Note particularly lines 4 to 7.

4 The instruments of the so-called Dutch concert (lines 5-6), those practiced on the stairs (lines 3-4), and the nature of the singers (line 25) all point to one historical period. What does the scene suggest about performances of the period?

5 Consider first the problem of period, using as primary evidence the information in lines 3-5 and 9-10. The multi-talented performer-composer's identity may be deduced from clues found in lines 3-5, 9, 19-20.

6 The period of the "great man" in question may be deduced in part from his instruments (line 2) and his style of composition (lines 18-20). His preemption of the creative role of the performer (lines 15-18) is particularly significant.

Chapter Five

Romantic Music

The Romantic period (c. 1800–c. 1910) began amid the glories and agonies of the years following the French Revolution, the socioeconomic and political repercussions of which resounded throughout the century. Napoleonic ideas and exploits inspired artistic and patriotic fervor across Europe, spurring the creators of the fine arts to comment and to act directly upon the burning Romantic libertarian, egalitarian, and humanitarian issues — Schiller and Hugo in their stage dramas, Pushkin and Manzoni in their prose and poetry, Delacroix and Goya in their paintings. The revolutionary activities of Wagner in Germany and the patriotic sentiments of Verdi in Milan contributed in no small measure to the successful movements of national unification in those countries. Standing as a formidable bulwark against these liberal attitudes, however, were the conservative interests of militarism and imperialism. Soon to be arrayed with them there loomed a new force, redolent with significance for Western society — industrialism.

During the nineteenth century, art music became bourgeois by economic necessity as well as by public demand. Privileges of rank and noble fortunes passed gradually into the possession of a new and less cultured aristocracy of money. Even court composers, not insignificant in their number notwithstanding the popular image of Beethoven, turned regularly to the public concert hall and the opera house. Publication of his music (an important factor even before encroaching deafness terminated his career as a virtuoso) was, after all, what enabled Beethoven to maintain his attitude of fierce independence. Unfortunately, most musicians and composers did not possess his genius; the story of the suffering caused by the Romantic transition to public patronage remains to be told. Recognition of musical genius by an admiring but untrained and materialistic public must have seemed small compensation for the loss of the security of courtly service.

Compositional genius, concern for relevance to contemporary ideals and issues, and emphasis upon self-expression contributed greatly to the Romantic composer's self-imposed search for greater originality. Together with the lessened demand for his art, the compulsion for originality also contributed to his lower level of productivity and to a greater dependence upon extra-musical inspiration. To an extent apparently unknown before the Romantic period, composers seem to have been drawn to nature and, especially, to the other fine arts, whose leading figures they encountered regularly in the salons of the gifted and monied élite. Magical was the effect of literature upon BERLIOZ (Shakespeare and Virgil), SCHUMANN (Jean Paul and Heine), Wolf (Goethe and Eichendorff), LISZT (Lamartine and Goethe), and RICHARD STRAUSS (Nietzsche), of painting upon Mussorgsky, and of nature upon many, among them Mendelssohn and Smetana. For the first time, composers such as Schumann, Berlioz, and WAGNER wrote literary essays themselves. Some, like E.T.A. Hoffman, divided their gifts among several arts.

The goal of creating a higher art by combining more than one in a new synthesis appealed to most Romantic composers. It was realized with newborn vigor in ART SONG and in OPERA, the latter culminating in the grand so-called "universal art-work" (*Gesamtkunstwerk*) of Wagner. Program music, a term normally applied only to instrumental music, was realized best in the outstanding new Romantic genres of PIANO MUSIC (in particular the short character piece) and the SYMPHONIC POEM, as well as in the programmatic symphony and sonata. Whereas the leading composers of program music, such as Berlioz, Liszt, and Richard Strauss, constituted the progressive wing of Romanticism, the conservatives, led by SCHUBERT, Mendelssohn, and BRAHMS, cultivated the traditional genres of **absolute music**—the SYMPHONY, sonata, and string quartet. Divided in their allegiance were the nationalists—Smetana and Dvorak (Bohemian), Mussorgsky and Tchaikovsky (Russian), Grieg (Norwegian), and many others; in the traditional genres their work revealed its German influence, but they expressed their nationalistic aspirations in their operas, songs, and program music. Romantic composers' reliance upon extramusical programs also served to attract and hold the attention of their audiences in other than inherently musical ways.

Romantic music reflected an increasing preoccupation with color, both tone color (timbre) and harmonic color. The expanded orchestra, featuring complete string, woodwind, and brass families, with their seemingly limitless possibilities of blend and mixture, engaged the imaginations of most composers; among the greatest masters of orchestral writing were Berlioz, Wagner, MAHLER, and Richard Strauss. In like manner, the enhanced sonority of the piano, reinforced now by a cast-iron frame and an improved sostenuto pedal, inspired Schumann, CHOPIN, and Liszt. The harmonic vocabulary of Romantic music expanded rapidly to include much more chromaticism, more altered and borrowed chords, and new and more freely treated dissonances. In the music of Richard Strauss, both instrumental and harmonic color may be said to find their Romantic apotheosis. As in the extension of dynamic range, so in the growing preference for extreme time dimensions. The most characteristic Romantic pieces tend to be either truly small-scale and intimate in tone (as with the miniaturists Schumann and Chopin) or immensely large and dramatic (as in

Wagner and Mahler). Previously dependent upon readily perceivable tonal relationships, diatonic harmonies, and a steady rhythm, time seems all but suspended in certain late-Romantic compositions. Irregular qualities of motion stem from manifold tempo changes, frequent accelerandi and ritardandi, and, at times, subtle **cross-rhythms** and macro-rhythms, added to which is the apparently implicit demand for **rubato** from the performer. Called upon to cover a wider scope of expression, Romantic melody displays a broader range of pitch and mood, with frequent emphasis on lyrical character and asymmetrical phrase structure.

A point of crisis seems to have been reached in the early years of the twentieth century, when the most significant features of Romantic music threatened to destroy the common Western tonal language that had been established during the Baroque period. The Romantic need for self-expression, often achieved through program music, came into conflict with inherently musical needs. A progressive style conflicted at times with adherence to traditional Classical forms; the new Romantic structural devices — the cyclic principle and a dynamic kind of **thematic transformation** — might well seem arbitrary and formless, as on occasion in Wagner's remarkable attempt to build giant structures in an organic manner from tiny **leitmotifs**. Increasing harmonic and tonal complexity, greater rhythmic freedom, a larger palette of orchestral colors, and longer movements and compositions threatened aural coherence at the same time that greater demands upon performers and conductors separated many composers from their audiences through the necessity for professional performing virtuosi. All of these potential aesthetic and practical difficulties beset especially those composers heavily influenced by Wagner, and they resulted in some precocious departures into truly modern music, as in certain works by Mahler and Richard Strauss. Nevertheless, Romantic composers succeeded so well in their quest to reconcile the demands of their art with those of their new public that their works still represent the largest part of the standard art-music repertory.

PRINCIPAL ROMANTIC GENRES

Symphonic Poem

Inspired by plays, novels, poetry, paintings, legends, and historical events, Romantic composers cultivated program music with a passion: the character piece for piano, the program symphony, the concert overture, and, finally, the symphonic poem. The term refers to a programmatic composition, usually in one movement, for orchestra. It was first employed in 1854 for the first of twelve such works (among them *Orpheus* and *Hamlet*) by Franz Liszt (1811–86), the greatest pianist of the age and highly influential as a composer for such progressive style traits as thematic transformation, enharmonicism, and the use of augmented triads, diminished intervals, the whole-tone scale, parallel harmonic motion, and delayed resolutions. The culmination of the symphonic poem took place in the eight tone poems (including *Don Juan* and *Also sprach Zarathustra*) of Richard Strauss (1864–1949), who expanded the range of extramusical subjects to philosophy and even to autobiography (*Ein Heldenleben*).

Other Important Symphonic Poem Composers

Bedrich Smetana (1824–1884)	9	(*Má Vlast*, a cycle of six)
Peter Ilyich Tchaikovsky (1840–1893)	3	(*Romeo and Juliet*)
Antonin Dvořák (1841–1904)	c. 10	(*Othello*)
Henri Duparc (1848–1933)	1	(*Lénore*)
Paul Dukas (1865–1935)	2 extant	(*L'apprenti sorcier*)
Jan Sibelius (1865–1957)	c. 15	(*Tapiola*)
Alexander Scriabin (1872–1915)	3	(*Poem of Ecstasy*)
Sergi Rachmaninov (1873–1943)	3	(*Isle of the Dead*)

Because its evolution was basically confined to the Romantic period and fulfilled so well the Romantic need to express a wider general culture and national sentiments in a freely shaped, purely instrumental movement, the symphonic poem played a major role in the development of Romantic style.

Symphony

In winning the battle for the symphony, the Romantic traditionalists (principally Austro-Germans) preserved its basic four-movement structure and resisted programmatic tendencies, but they could not prevent the adoption of lyrical melody that proved inimical to thematic development or an expansion of harmonic vocabulary and time-scale that undermined the structural function of tonality. The progressives, like the traditionalists, took their inspiration from Beethoven; but they depicted their narrative and psychological dramas through brilliantly effective orchestration, and they wrought a new kind of unity through use of the cyclic principle, a program, a text and voices.

Important Symphony Composers

TRADITIONALISTS	TRADITIONALISTS ABROAD	PROGRESSIVES
Franz Schubert 8	Peter Ilyich Tchaikovsky 6	Ludwig Spohr 9
Felix Mendelssohn 5	Antonin Dvořák 9	Hector Berlioz 3
Robert Schumann 4	Carl Nielsen 6	Franz Liszt 2
Anton Bruckner 9 +	Jan Sibelius 7	César Franck 1
Johannes Brahms 4		Alexander Borodin 2
Gustav Mahler 9 +		Vincent d'Indy 3

Concerto

The Romantic concerto served primarily as a vehicle for such virtuoso "titans" of the violin and piano as Nicolo Paganini and Franz Liszt, respectively. Although they were successful in preserving the structure of the symphony, the

Important Concerto Composers

TRADITIONALISTS	PROGRESSIVES
Felix Mendelssohn 2 piano, 1 violin	Niccoló Paganini 5 violin
Johannes Brahms 2 piano, 1 violin, 1 violin/cello	Ludwig Spohr 15 + violin
Camille Saint-Saëns 5 piano, 3 violin, 3 cello	Frédéric Chopin 2 piano
Antonin Dvořák 1 piano, 1 violin, 1 cello	Franz Liszt 2 piano
Sergei Rachmaninov 4 piano	Henri Vieuxtemps 7 violin, 2 cello

traditionalists could not maintain Classical balance in the concerto even outwardly, as witnessed by the dominating role of the soloist, the loss of the orchestral exposition, and the introduction of cyclic, programmatic, and other innovative or highly subjective elements. Nevertheless, composers such as Mendelssohn, Schumann, and Dvořák were able to make enduring artistic contributions to the concerto repertory. By appealing to the middle-class audience's love for virtuosity and expression, the genre remained popular throughout the century.

Piano Music

Changes in the structure of the piano contributed greatly to its leading role in Romantic music, among them the use of a cast-iron frame, increased tension on the strings, a **double-escapement** action, an improved soundboard, and **overstringing**. Now the titans of the piano could exorcise the ghost of Paganini and create the magnificent Romantic repertory for solo piano.

The major Romantic genres for piano were (1) the so-called character piece, normally a one-movement quasi-programmatic work, often gathered in

Important Composers of Piano Music

CHARACTER PIECE		ÉTUDE		SONATA	
Franz Schubert	c. 300	Carl Czerny	thousands	Franz Schubert	c. 15
Frédéric Chopin	c. 200	Frédéric Chopin	c. 25	Frédéric Chopin	3
Robert Schumann	c. 250	Robert Schumann	c. 20	Robert Schumann	3
Franz Liszt	c. 125	Franz Liszt	c. 75	Franz Liszt	2
Johannes Brahms	c. 75	Johann Brahms	c. 50	Johann Brahms	3
Alexander Scriabin	c. 185	Alexander Scriabin	c. 20	Alexander Scriabin	10

cycles or collections and including such types as nocturnes, preludes, impromptus, and ballades: (2) the étude, which could either be in the nature of a technical exercise or of a piece combining technical difficulty with artistic quality and expressive intent; (3) the sonata, an absolute piece traditionally in three movements but freely altered in structure and character by the progressive Romanticists.

The great pianists of the age—first among them Franz Liszt—developed an unprecedentedly virtuosic technique matched with an equally poetic sensitivity. In their hands the character piece flourished, charting new paths in the use of the cyclic principle, an ever-advancing harmonic vocabulary, and free treatment of dissonance. By the end of the century, few traditionalists such as Brahms remained to keep alive the Classical framework of the piano sonata.

Art Song

The flowering of German lyric poetry, the broader cultural interests of composers, and the growing emphasis on harmonic and timbral color to depict textual images and moods led to the rebirth of song in the nineteenth century, at first as a solo (or duet) form with piano accompaniment, then with the greater emotional range of the song cycle, and finally with the timbral possibilities of the Romantic orchestra. In their wide range of expression, their variety of vivid accompaniments, and their inexhaustible melodic inventiveness, the songs of Schubert set a high standard for his successors. Greater significance for the piano part, as in the songs of Schumann, characterized the development of the Lied, which reached its zenith of refinement in Wolf, whose Lieder show an extraordinary concern for the quality of his texts, for their rhythms and accents as well as their meanings. Orchestrally accompanied songs by Richard Strauss and Mahler magnify the dramatic and operatic character of the Lied and transplant it to the concert hall.

In France, the *mélodie* underwent an evolution similar to that of the Lied, but carefully adapted to the vastly different rhythms, sensuous sounds, and subtle allusions of French poetry.

Important Composers of Song

AUSTRO-GERMAN *LIED*		FRENCH *MÉLODIE*	
Franz Schubert	c. 600	Hector Berlioz	c. 40
Carl Loewe	c. 375	Franz Liszt	c. 12
Robert Schumann	c. 250	Georges Bizet	c. 50
Robert Franz	c. 285	Charles Gounod	c. 200
Franz Liszt	c. 80	Jules Massenet	c. 250
Peter Cornelius	c. 100	Edouard Lalo	c. 35
Johannes Brahms	c. 200	Henri Duparc	13
Hugo Wolf	c. 250	Gabriel Fauré	c. 100
Gustav Mahler	c. 50	Ernest Chausson	c. 40
Richard Strauss	c. 200	(Claude Debussy	c. 80)

Opera

Opera prospered both commercially and artistically in the Romantic period. Although it remained dominant in Italy and achieved an indigenous vernacular character in Germany, Paris served as the operatic capital well into the century, drawing all the leading Italian and German composers into the orbit of commercial grand opera. Librettists drew on historical subjects closer to their time and liberally spiced them with sex, murder, and religion, while composers met the challenge with a chromatically expanded harmony, freer treatment of dissonance, and the manifold timbral possibilities of the greatly enlarged Romantic orchestra. Structurally, composers sought greater musical continuity by eliminating *secco* recitative, enhancing the expressive use and melodic character of orchestrally accompanied recitative, and building composite arias and larger scenes, or even avoiding strong cadences altogether. One quintessential Romantic ideal was realized in Wagner's "universal artwork" (*Gesamtkunstwerk*), a kind of symphonic drama in which the orchestra often carries the main themes or motives (*Leitmotiven*) while the singer declaims the text. By writing his own libretti, building his own opera house, choosing and training his singers and conductor, and directing the action, Wagner assumed nearly complete control of a genre historically beset by the need for greater artistic collaboration. He not only extended the time-scale of the individual music drama, but also created a monumental unified cycle of four music dramas in *Der Ring des Nibelungen*. By way of contrast, Verdi preferred to modify the traditional number opera and to emphasize human tragedy, even that of everyday life. Realism (**verismo**), so far as possible in opera, gradually emerged as a focus in France and especially in Italy in the later Romantic period, resulting in streamlined plots and brief, highly charged outbursts of emotion. That the new harmonic and orchestral possibilities could match literary subtlety as well as naturalism was demonstrated in France by Debussy's return in his only completed opera to one of the earliest concepts of opera—the sung play. Romantic opera served as a significant focus for the expression of national sentiments—often against German political and cultural oppression. Nevertheless, if the symphony may be assumed to have seized musical leadership in Haydn's era, when leadership finally passed once again to opera, it was in the Germanic form of the Wagnerian and post-Wagnerian symphonic drama.

MAJOR COMPOSERS AND SELECTED COMPOSITIONS

Franz Schubert   Austrian   1797–1828

Achievement

1. Schubert was one of the most prolific and greatest of composers, his fame resting chiefly on the quality of his music rather than upon its historical significance (since only his Lieder were widely known in his lifetime).
2. He established the Lied as a major genre; his model inspired a host of successors, none of whom surpassed his scope of expression and variety of achievement.

Important Opera Composers

ITALIAN	FRENCH	GERMAN	OTHER
Clear separation between melodrama and comic opera by the intermediate *dramma semiseria*; use of thematic recurrence; singers remain dominant.	Types include spectacular grand opera, intermediary lyric drama, modest opéra comique with spoken dialogue, and a new, farcical genre — *opéra bouffe*.	Freest, because least tradition-bound, to indulge love for nature and supernatural, leading ultimately to the symphonic *Gesamtkunstwerk* of Wagner.	Often nationalistic in its use of speech-derived rhythms and melodies, ethnic plots and characters, patriotic and revolutionary sentiments.
Johann Simon Mayr 68 (34 sr/18 cm)	Daniel Francois Auber c. 45 (cmq)	Carl Maria von Weber 10 (plus opa)	Ferenc Erkel 9
Gioacchino Rossini 37 (19 sr)	Giacomo Meyerbeer 15 (4 grand)	Heinrich Marschner 15 (4 cm)	Stanislaw Moniuszko 9 (plus 9 opa)
Vincenzo Bellini 10 (8 sr)	Hector Berlioz 3 (1 grand)	Albert Lortzing 16 (13 cm)	Bedrich Smetana 8 (4 cm)
Gaetano Donizetti c. 70 (35 sr)	Charles Gounod 10 (2 cm)	Richard Wagner 13 (7 music dramas)	Modest Mussorgsky 3
Saverio Mercadante c. 60 (4 bf)	Georges Bizet 7 (5 cmq)	Peter Cornelius 2 (1 cm)	Peter Ilyich Tchaikovsky 10
Giuseppe Verdi 26 (2 cm)	Jacques Offenbach c. 100 (bff)	Engelbert Humperdinck 8	Antonín Dvořák 10
Giacomo Puccini 12 (1 cm)	César Franck 4 (1 cmq)	Hans Pfitzner 5	Nikolai Rimsky-Korsakov 16
Pietro Mascagni 16 (plus opa)	Jules Massenet 32 (6 cm)	Richard Strauss 15	Leos Janacek 10

Key to Abbreviations: sr (opera seria), cm (comic), bf (buffa), cmq (comique), bff (bouffe), opa (operetta)

Works and Style Summary   Schubert's works are identified by "D." numbers after the thematic catalog by Otto Erich Deutsch.

Art songs: more than 600, ranging from strophic ("An die Musik") to declamatory and through-composed ("Der Doppelgänger") to ballads ("Erlkönig"), and including two song cycles, *Die schöne Müllerin* (1823) and *Die Winterreise* (1827)

Orchestral works: eight symphonies (plus sketches for others); seven overtures

Chamber music: c. 35 works, among them an octet, a piano quintet (the *Trout*), a string quintet, fifteen string quartets, two piano trios, a string trio

Piano music: about fifteen piano sonatas and many character pieces (among them eight *Impromptus* and six *Moments musicaux*), variations and the famous *Wanderer Fantasie*

Miscellaneous vocal music: six Masses, much church music and choral music (including some for men's chorus), about fifteen operas, incidental theater works

Schubert's music is remarkable for its breathtaking lyricism. Just as noteworthy is its emphasis on harmonic color. His expanded harmonic vocabulary within a key is complemented by an expanded range of relationship among keys, his music being especially rich in **bi-modal** allusions and mediant relationships. He was a master of the unexpected, from astounding modulations to expressive silence. In instrumental music, Schubert began as an imitator of Mozart and Beethoven, but soon found his own voice and expanded and transformed the dramatic Classical forms to accommodate his more lyrical and introspective style.

Career   Schubert learned violin, organ, and singing as a child, played viola in chamber music, and became a good pianist, often accompanying his own songs. He studied composition with Ruzicka and Salieri. After a brief try at teaching elementary school (1814–17), he settled in Vienna, sharing a modest existence with his friends, failing to find salaried positions, and publishing about 100 works (mostly songs) for small sums from publishers. His music was known, however, and was valued by music-lovers.

DER LINDENBAUM (DIE WINTERREISE, D. 911)
The score is in CSM III, 96.

Historical Perspective   The series of poems entitled *The Winter Journey* was published in 1824 by Wilhelm Müller, and set to music by Schubert in 1827. The poetic cycle is remarkable for its unrelieved lamentation, Schubert's music for the depth of its world-weariness. "Der Lindenbaum," the fifth song in the cycle, offers what Richard Capell called "a midwinter glimpse of the ghost of Spring." Even his much-loved linden tree's whispered message of peace cannot interrupt for more than a fleeting moment the heartsick traveller's winter journey.

Description of Style   Seldom even in the works of Schubert has folklike simplicity of melody and rhythm been employed to greater effect than in "Der Lindenbaum." The vocal range exceeds a fifth only at points of climax, while the words are set basically in syllabic fashion. Indeed, the halting dotted-note rhythm and the completely diatonic melody create a warm and pleasant mood of nostalgia that is abruptly dashed (m. 25) by a sudden change of mode. How simple and yet how moving it is to hear the now familiar melody in minor mode, and how much more lovely and meaningful is the return of the melody in the original key in the fourth strophe. Much of the folklike feeling of the song stems from its simple harmonies. Aside from a few secondary dominants in the first strophe and the change to the parallel minor in the second, virtually all nondiatonic activity in the song is limited to the third strophe, with its use of the flat submediant (m. 45), the augmented-sixth chord (m. 52), and other chromaticism. After this indulgence Schubert employs no accidentals whatsoever in the last strophe, eliminating even the expected secondary dominant in measure 67. In such austere harmonic surroundings, the reintroduction of the B-sharp in the piano postlude becomes a gesture full of expression. As so often in Schubert's songs, the piano accompaniment sets the mood of the poem. In this instance, a triplet motive in broken sixths apparently represents the sound of the wind rustling through the linden tree, a wind that turns cold and gusty with the turn to minor mode in the second and third strophes.

Analysis of Structure "Der Lindenbaum" is a modified strophic song. Whereas Müller's poem has three four-line stanzas, Schubert's song has four strophes. The composer divides the third stanza of the poem in half and treats the first pair of lines as his third strophe and the second pair as his fourth. Poetically, the last two lines of the third stanza rhyme with the last two lines of the first. Musically, Schubert's first and fourth strophes are virtually the same, their key being E major. By way of contrast, the second strophe translates the tune into E minor and then returns to E major for its second half. The third strophe offers contrast both of mode (again E minor) and thematic material. By varying the length of the piano introduction to each strophe and by adding a piano postlude after the fourth strophe, Schubert modified the square proportions of the usual strophic song into sections of 24, 20, 13, and 22 measures.

Gioacchino Rossini　　Italian　　1792–1868

Achievement

1. Rossini was the leading Italian composer of the early nineteenth century and one of the greatest of all composers of *opera buffa*.
2. The composer had considerable influence on German (Schubert and Weber) and French (Meyerbeer) music, as well as on younger Italian contemporaries.
3. By writing out vocal ornaments in full in certain of his scores (*Semiramide*, 1823), he began the trend towards curtailing improvisation by singers.

Works and Style Summary

Operas: 37 Italian operas, of which nineteen are *opere serie*, 7 *semiserie*, 9 *buffe*; of his two French operas, one is a grand opera (*William Tell*) and one is comic

Miscellaneous works: among them, many songs and piano pieces, about 20 cantatas, 5 string quartets; most notably, a *Stabat mater* (1842) and a Mass (1864)

Rossini was gifted with an incomparably spirited and evocative sense of rhythm. His melodies are often memorable, the accompanying harmonies usually simple (but with striking use of mediant relationships). Although capable of complexity, as shown by his ensemble writing in the comic operas, more in evidence are his famed crescendo and his love for contrast. His orchestra is colorful and important, often stating the principal melody while the voice declaims in recitative fashion. In some of his operas the orchestra is always present, replacing continuo accompaniment in serious operas as early as 1816. Rossini raised orchestral standards throughout Italy. Although somewhat undiscriminating in his choice of libretti and generally content with stereotyped characters, he did bring some of the greater freedom of *opera buffa* to serious opera, for which he was regarded in his time as a revolutionary.

Career   Rossini studied with Padre Mattei in Bologna, but learned more by studying Haydn and Mozart on his own. He was a fair violist and cellist, a horn player, and a good pianist and singer. He built his reputation in Italy (1810–23), following which he spent one lucrative season in London and then settled in Paris as the director of the Théatre Italien. He arranged some of his earlier works for French performance and wrote new French works as well. His abrupt retirement from opera (1829) was followed by a return to Italy (1836–55), but his last years were spent indulging his social genius and scintillating wit back in Paris.

THE BARBER OF SEVILLE

The full score is available in miniature (New York: Edwin F. Kalmus, n.d.).

Historical Perspective   The *Barber* was first performed at the Teatro di Argentina in Rome on February 20, 1816, approximately two months after Rossini signed the contract. According to the composer, its creation occupied only twelve or thirteen days. Despite a first-night fiasco, apparently the result of organized opposition, the opera soon began its triumphal and still-enduring career. Verdi said of it that "for abundance of ideas, comic verve, and truth of declamation, *Il barbiere di Siviglia* is the most beautiful opera buffa in existence." The libretto was written by Cesare Sterbini after the play *Le barbier de Seville* (1775) by Beaumarchais. The opera involves Figaro (baritone) and Rosina (mezzo-soprano), ward of the overly protective and designing Dr. Bartolo (basso buffo). A series of disguises propels the action, the first two disguises worn by the Count/Lindoro (tenor) bringing the would-be lovers together briefly and building to the fine imbroglio finale of Act I. Act II opens with yet another disguise — the Count as a student of Rosina's music teacher Don Basilio (bass) — and it climaxes in a grand compound ensemble ("Buona sera"). From the storm that begins Scene 2 to the dénouement, the marriage of the now-revealed Count and Rosina, Rossini deftly and quickly unravels the twisted thread of the plot. The opera closes with a very short and simple rondo-finale.

Description of Style   Vivacious rhythms limn with wonderful suggestiveness the characters' actions on the stage, and form a foundation for Rossini's inexhaustible melodic gift. Often, one rhythm may be maintained while the melody is altered a great deal. Character is drawn as surely as gesture. "Una voce poco fa," for example, captures both the charm and strength of Rosina. Tunes are mostly diatonic, florid in solo arias and usually syllabic in ensembles. The vocal embellishments normally consist of grace-notes before important strong beats, and passagework near or at the ends of sections, phrases, or subphrases. Frequently, the orchestra carries the principal theme while the vocalist declaims in repeated-note figures, sometimes in very rapid *parlando*. A characteristic increase in pace is often achieved by progressive subdivision of the beat, as in the opening number of Act II.

Rossini ordinarily wrote in a simple harmonic vocabulary, couched in strong functional progressions that may turn towards the relative major or minor, but seldom to the parallel key. Firmly in the Mozart mold, he was a virtuoso composer of ensembles, balancing with seeming ease the contrasting emotions of his characters and, by grouping them in different ways, obtaining grand climactic effects (as in the finale of Act I). Rossini employed a full Classical orchestra, including pairs of horns and trumpets, piccolo, three trombones, and bass drum. In the Overture, as throughout the opera, the composer makes much use of solo woodwinds. Other characteristic features are contrast (often extreme) in dynamic levels, as well as in articulation, with frequent use of staccato and pizzicato. Perhaps Rossini's most arresting trademark is the crescendo (achieved both by progressive addition of orchestral parts and by dynamic indications), which he employed with such aptness and variety that its effectiveness survives its appearance in almost every number of the opera. Tone-painting occurs in the Act II "Temporale," in which piccolo and trombone contribute to the depiction of a thunderstorm.

Analysis of Structure   Except for the finales, Rossini's operas ordinarily unfold as a series of independent and thematically unrelated arias and ensembles, with *secco* recitative as connecting tissue. Most of the arias and ensembles are composed in compound slow–fast forms. Rossini also employs a ritornello-like form in which the principal theme appears first in the orchestra and then recurs intermittently throughout. Some arias display the tonal plan of the sonata form, but without its thematic design or development. Ternary forms are few and typically unbalanced. Regardless of the large-scale structure of a number, Rossini generally builds by immediately repeating themes and by stitching together theme-groups in various ways rather than by development. To offset so much repetition, he relied upon contrast—thematic, timbral, dynamic, and articulative. Both the reliance upon repetition and the character of the themes suggest a closer relationship with the Italian opera buffa tradition than with Mozart.

Discussion of Act I, Scene 2 in some detail will serve further to exemplify the composer's methods. Rosina has set her heart upon Lindoro (who is actually the Count). Her aria "Una voce poco fa" unfolds in two parts and, as in "Ecco ridente" (Scene 1), the main theme of the second part is clearly derived from that of the first. Rosina enlists Figaro's aid, but they are interrupted by the arrival of Bartolo, soon followed by Don Basilio. The latter, in the aria "La calunnia," advises Bartolo to slander their enemy; the aria is rounded tonally but continuous thematically, with ever-new theme-groups. Here, the use of crescendi is wedded perfectly to a text depicting the cancerous growth of rumor, and it is further enhanced by onomatopoeical explosions. As the two men go off to make marriage plans for Bartolo and his ward, she and Figaro resume their plotting. The duet "Dunque io son" embodies the tonal plan of a sonata, this time including a modulatory section that is noteworthy for its parallel minor mode. With Figaro safely dispatched with her letter, Rosina is now assailed by the returning Bartolo. His grim determination not to be bested is expressed in a characterful *parlando* aria whose very form reflects his will: in a compound two-part number, Rossini causes the ritornello theme and slow tempo of the first part to recur near the end of the second, a rare and therefore striking event. The Act I finale consists of five major sections. It begins in C major with the entry of the Count disguised as a soldier, reaches a high point in A-flat major with the bewilderment of the others at the respect shown the "soldier" by the police ("Fredda ed immobile"), and closes — following an arresting unison theme for all the principals — in C major in a grand state of confusion.

Hector Berlioz   French   1803-1869

Achievement

1. Berlioz was the leader in the new programmatic symphonism of the Romantic period, a result of his wide literary culture and interests and his genius for orchestral writing.

2. A virtuoso of the orchestra, he was the first to reveal its manifold possibilities and the first composer to perform primarily as a virtuoso conductor. His *Treatise on Modern Instrumentation and Orchestration* (1844) is the first significant book on the subject and remains a classic.

3. The composer was important for applying the cyclic principle on a large scale.

4. Berlioz was a prolific and brilliant music critic and writer, whose journalistic efforts were better known to his fellow Parisians than his music.

Works and Style Summary

Orchestral music: including purely instrumental symphonies (*Symphonie fantastique*), symphonic dramas with soloists, chorus, and orchestra (*Romeo and Juliet*), and 5 concert overtures (*Roman Carnival*)

Operas: 3, including the vast epic *Les Troyens* (1856-58)

Art songs and song cycles: particularly *Les nuits d'été* (1841, orchestrated 1856)

Sacred music: several works on religious texts, among them a *Requiem* (1837), *Te Deum* (1849), and the oratorio *L'enfance du Christ* (1854)

The style of Berlioz is uniquely unconventional in its truly orchestral conception (with a linear rather than chordal approach and many striking effects), its emphasis upon continuous and irregularly phrased melody (with remarkable rhythmic vitality), its unusual dissonance treatment (avoiding the conventional passing-tones and appoggiaturas of the time), and in its later development towards greater restraint and Classical objectivity (despite his continued reliance upon literary works for inspiration). Prophetic is the importance granted the pa-

rameters of timbre and, on occasion, of space (as in the very large and the outdoor works). He tended to disregard contemporaneous categories of genre and
formal principle, preferring instead to strive freely towards his expressive goals.

Career   Deeply moved on hearing Gluck's *Iphigénie en Tauride*, Berlioz
turned from the study of medicine to music, eventually studying at the Paris
Conservatory with J. F. Le Sueur and Anton Reicha. After three unsuccessful attempts, he finally won the Prix de Rome in 1830. Although he became famous in
that same year with the premiere of the *Symphonie fantastique*, he found it difficult
to make a living; his works met with more success in Germany, England, and
even in Russia than in France, which encouraged him to tour extensively. He
held the post of assistant librarian at the Paris Conservatory from 1852 until his
death, and he wrote a great deal as a professional music critic.

SYMPHONIE FANTASTIQUE
The score appears in LS.

Historical Perspective   The *Fantastic Symphony* represents a successful blend-
ing of the French penchant for program music with the German-dominated Classical forms of instrumental music. It was completed in 1830 and first performed
on December 5th at the Paris Conservatory. It marked the beginning of Berlioz's
professional career and his influence upon other composers. Berlioz later revised
the symphony and gave it a sequel entitled *Lélio, or the Return to Life* (1832). Love
for an English actress inspired the work and its famous program, whose purpose
was — in Berlioz's words — "to fill in the gaps which the use of musical language
unavoidably leaves in the development of dramatic thought." The program deals
with a lovesick young musician whose drug-induced slumber yields strange vi-
sions in musical images of the past (I: Reveries — Passions), of an encounter with
his beloved at a party (II: A Ball), of a summer evening in the country (III: Scene
in the Country), of his own hanging (IV: March to the Scaffold), and of a dia-
bolical orgy (V: Dream of a Witches' Sabbath). Notwithstanding the program,
the composer hoped that "the symphony by itself can afford musical interest independent of any dramatic purpose."

Description of Style   Berioz unified the symphony by using one theme (the
idée fixe) in various guises in each movement, an early Romantic manifestation of
the cyclic principle. Unusual length, irregular phrasing, expression through melodic contour, and chromatic alteration of an underlying diatonic framework
characterize the *idée fixe* (which represents obsession with the beloved), as they
frequently do in Berlioz's melodies. No less characteristic is the element of melodic variation, so marked in this work as to constitute thematic transformation.
With Berlioz, harmonic development is also striking, since conventional chords
underlie melodies in unconventional ways. Third relationships, root progressions
by step, and bi-modal scales are common. A linear approach to texture permits
melodies to appear in any voice and, in the first and last movements, generates
the climax (I, m. 360 and V, m. 414).

Berlioz revolutionized orchestration by new and startling combinations of instruments and by treating all instruments as part of a mass ensemble rather than as independent entities. Harps, bells, muted horns, and muffled drums are employed in the symphony, among other unusual and noteworthy effects so numerous as to permit mention of only two: a solo cornet becomes increasingly important in the course of the Ball; an E-flat clarinet vulgarizes the *idée fixe* in the Finale. Characteristically, the full deployment of brass and percussion is reserved for greatest impact in the closing movements.

Analysis of Structure   Conventional and forward-looking traits stand side by side in the symphony. With regard to form, for example, there are conventional principles (I: sonata form; II: dance and trio; III: ternary; V: rondo) and departures from the convention (I: arch form; IV: march; V: introduction of the *Dies irae* theme), while unity is insured by a recurring theme. Similarly, with regard to the structural use of keys, there are small-scale tonic–dominant relationships (as in the sonata form of the first movement), and there are large-scale bi-modal third relationships woven into an encompassing five-movement plan: I: c/C, II: a/A, III: F, IV: g/G, V: C/c/C.

Frédéric Chopin   Polish/French   1810–1849

Achievement

1. As the Romantic composer-pianist *par excellence*, Chopin was distinguished by his originality, his technical mastery, and his almost exclusive dedication to piano music.
2. Chopin redefined the étude as a poetic as well as a technical piece, and he also apparently invented the ballade for piano.

Works and Style Summary

Small-scale piano pieces: 24 famous preludes (and a few others), 19 nocturnes, 3 impromptus, 30 études, c. 60 mazurkas, c. 20 waltzes, several dance-types
Larger piano works: 4 ballades, 4 scherzi, 16 polonaises
Large-scale works: 2 piano concertos and 3 piano sonatas
Miscellaneous works: 1 violoncello sonata and 17 Polish songs

Chopin's style is uniquely idiomatic technically for piano. It is founded largely upon melody, which is composed over inexhaustibly varied accompanimental textures. Chopin's melodies range from straightforward, even popular, tunes, to operatic cantilena with subtle use of ornamentation and rubato, to étude-like figuration. He retained a strong propensity for dance movements with distinctive rhythms: mazurka, polonaise, and waltz. Perhaps the most striking musical events are harmonic and tonal, including chromatic and enharmonic effects, remote modulations, striking use of nonharmonic tones and chordal prolongations, use of modality, linear dissonance, and even at times beginning or ending in other than the principal key. Forms are basically simple, being based on a more or less improvisatory treatment of ternary form, usually lacking thematic development. Although Polish nationalistic sentiments find expression in his music, Chopin seldom wrote program music.

Career Chopin played in public and composed from an early age, his teachers being Albert Żwyny and Joseph Elsner. He also travelled widely as a youth. After a warm reception in Paris in 1831, he made it his home, giving piano lessons to the cream of society, performing in fashionable salons, and giving a small number of exclusive concerts, until an extensive concert tour in England helped hasten his death.

BALLADE IN G MINOR, OP. 23
The score is in MSO II, p. 31.

Historical Perspective The *Ballade in G Minor* was composed between 1831 and 1835, and published in 1836 with a dedication to Baron von Stockhausen. A ballade is the musical equivalent for a narrative poem. The genre was apparently invented by Chopin and is programmatic, but he left no clues to any programmatic content in Op. 23. According to Robert Schumann, this ballade was the piece that Chopin liked best of all his works.

Description of Style Chopin's melodies remain models of Romantic lyricism, whether isolated in the top voice as quasi-operatic cantabile (m. 68) or embedded in a wide-ranging pianistic texture (m. 218). Melodies often recur with improvisatory ornamentation (compare passages beginning at mm. 38, 110, and 170). Each significant theme unfolds in its own tempo. The piece achieves a climax in the coda by rhythmic and dynamic means rather than by treatment of principal thematic materials. Chopin's firmly homophonic framework displays much variety of accompaniment, ranging from arpeggiated chords to repeated block chords. The expanded chordal vocabulary stems from extended tertian harmonies and free treatment of nonharmonic tones, as well as from such traditional sources as the Neapolitan-sixth (mm. 1–3) and diminished-seventh chords.

Analysis of Structure Seldom are Chopin's forms as subtle as that of the *Ballade in G Minor.* On the one hand, it features a rondo-like recurrence of two principal themes in the unique pattern outlined below. The rounded and lyrical nature of the themes support this scheme. On the other hand, with some imagination one can hear clearly an arch-like variant of sonata form. Chopin does, after all, dispose the principal themes in the sonata manner, and he also fulfills

RONDO FORM

Measure Nos.:		8	36	68	94	106	126	166	194	208
Themes:	Introd.	A	B	C	A′	C′	D	C	A″	Coda
Keys:		g		E♭	a	A		E♭	g	g

SONATA FORM

Sections:	Introd.	Exposition		Development		Recapitulation		Coda
Themes:	1		2	(1)	(2)	2	1	

the modulatory purpose of a development section. The arch-like pattern derives from the reversed order of themes 1 and 2 during the reprise; its symmetry is further strengthened by having each theme return in its original key.

Robert Schumann   German   1810-1856

Achievement

1. Schumann was a major composer for the piano, principally of the Romantic character piece, which he published in cycles with programmatic titles.
2. He was the major successor to Schubert as a Lied composer. Of special significance was the increasing importance of his piano parts.
3. The composer was a highly influential writer on music, chiefly in a progressive music journal (the *Neue Zeitschrift für Musik*) that he helped to found, and edited for years.

Works and Style Summary

Piano music: 36 opus numbers of solo music, plus some two-piano music; most are sets of character pieces (the cycle *Carnaval*), but there are some important larger works (*Symphonic Études*)

Art songs: 32 opus numbers, comprising more than 200 Lieder for soloists with piano accompaniment; all are in collections or cycles (*Dichterliebe*)

Orchestral music: 4 symphonies, 4 concert overtures, several concertos (especially the *Piano Concerto in A Minor*), among other works

Chamber music: most important are a piano quintet, a piano quartet, and 3 string quartets

Miscellaneous works: much choral music (some for men's chorus), a secular oratorio, an opera, some works for organ

Schumann's music offers a striking combination of Romantic and traditional traits. The former are manifested in his extra-musical inspiration, frequently intimate tone, and penchant for cyclic treatment of themes, while the latter are apparent in the echoes of the music of Beethoven and Bach, his cultivation of the symphony and chamber music, and his disdain for mere virtuosity.

Career   Schumann's career as a piano virtuoso was terminated before it began when he injured his right hand. (But Clara Wieck, his piano teacher's young daughter, finally married him over bitter parental opposition, and became the family's professional pianist.) Schumann took up composition, studying with Heinrich Dorn. His multifaceted musical interests led him to serve as editor and journalist for the *Neue Zeitschrift für Musik* (1835–1844), as a music teacher at the Leipzig Conservatory (1843) and, privately, in Dresden (1845–1850), and as a conductor of choral groups and an orchestra in Düsseldorf (1847–1853). His idealism and introspective nature made it difficult for him to make his way as a professional musician.

Franz Liszt   **Hungarian**   **1811–1886**

Achievement

1. Liszt was the greatest pianist in an age of virtuoso pianism, with immense influence on the further development of the medium both through his playing—he popularized the piano recital—and his piano compositions.

2. As the creator of the symphonic poem, Liszt was a principal leader in the field of programmatic composition. In this and other genres he proved to be a significant experimenter with revolutionary harmonic and melodic ideas, including augmented triads, delayed resolutions, the whole-tone scale, and enharmonicism.

3. The composer was a major teacher, numbering among his pupils Hans von Bülow, Carl Tausig, and Ferruccio Busoni.

Works and Style Summary

Piano music: 2 piano concertos, the great *B-Minor Sonata* (1853), many character pieces and études (*12 Transcendental Études*), transcriptions for piano of Beethoven symphonies, Schubert songs, and much more

Orchestral music: thirteen symphonic poems (*Orpheus*), and 2 programmatic symphonies (*Faust* and *Dante*)

Choral works: many, among them several Masses, 2 oratorios (*Christus*), some works for men's chorus

Miscellaneous works: art songs (c. 80), organ music, and other works

Liszt's style was eclectic in its early stages, revealing the composer's Hungarian heritage, German training, French adherence to programmatic inspiration, and Paganinian virtuosity. Later, despite some unevenness and a continuing fondness for rhetorical grandiosity, he developed a distinctive language noteworthy for its progressive use of the **cyclic principle**, **thematic transformation**, enharmonicism, parallel motion, and such striking chromatic sounds as the augmented triad and various diminished intervals.

Career   As a pianist, Liszt was a child prodigy, studying with Czerny and concertizing at the age of nine. After being refused admittance (as a foreigner) to the Paris Conservatory in 1823, he continued his travelling concert life with Paris as a home base until the triumphant climax of his pianistic career in 1847. His period as kapellmeister to the court in Weimar began in 1848, a time noteworthy for his generous help to many musicians (including Wagner) and to progressive musical causes. He took minor orders in the church in 1858, and divided his later years among Rome, Weimar, and Budapest.

PIANO SONATA IN B MINOR

The music is available in miniature score (Zurich: Eulenburg, n.d.).

Historical Perspective   Composed in 1853, during the composer's Weimar years, the sonata was published in 1854 with a dedication to Robert Schumann.

By its one-movement form and its improvisatory or fantasy character, the sonata has had much influence on subsequent composers. Indeed, it may well be the crowning achievement among the composer's piano works. For performers, it has become one of the touchstones of modern pianism.

Description of Style   Liszt used the expanded tonal and dynamic resources of the Romantic piano to their full effect. His extremes of articulation in this sonata range from the smoothest *legato* to the most powerful *marcato*. His technical demands, especially the frequent use of octaves and of the sostenuto pedal, often serve to enhance the sonority. Liszt's themes tend to be short and flexible in nature, and therefore well suited for transformation and development. Their range of character is wide; for instance, the rhetorical and dramatic *marcato* theme (m. 14) is later transformed into a lyric, *cantando* theme (m. 153). Phrasing is generally irregular, and one of the principal themes unfolds in triple meter, as opposed to the prevailing quadruple time. Without renouncing functional harmony, Liszt often approaches its limits through his freedom in treating dissonance, chromaticism, enharmonicism, and modulation. Homophonic and contrapuntal textures are employed with equal facility, the latter most noticeably in an extended fugal passage (mm. 460 ff).

Analysis of Structure   What Liszt terms a sonata bears little resemblance to the Classical genre by that name. In the words of Humphrey Searle, "the logic of a rigid framework was replaced by the cogency of an emotional argument."[1] Having ensured a degree of unity by severely limiting the thematic material of his one-movement form, Liszt drew upon every resource of imagination, skill, and passion to sustain his rhapsodical argument. Four principal themes dominate: (A) the descending scale of the slow introduction; (B) the Allegro theme in octaves, which spans a range of five octaves and introduces triplet motion; (C) the continuation of this Allegro theme, memorable for its repeated-note beginning and chromatic close; and (D) a richly homophonic theme (marked *grandioso* at its first appearance) of narrow range. Each of the four sections (as shown below) draws upon all four themes in the manner of a free fantasy, passing them through an extraordinary variety of changes in harmony, texture, register, dynamics, and thematic interrelationship. Only one thematic element is reserved from this process, an Andante theme in triple meter (E), which is used to offer contrast in the second and fourth sections.

SECTIONS	LOCATION	PRINCIPAL TEMPI	THEMES	IMPORTANT KEYS
1	mm. 1–330	Allegro	ABCD	b . . . D
2	mm. 331–459	Andante	EABCD	F# (A)
3	mm. 460–649	Allegro	ABCD	C♭ . . . B
4	mm. 650–end	Presto	EABCD	B

[1] *The Music of Liszt*. Second ed. (New York: Dover Publications, 1966), p. 61.

Richard Wagner   German   1813–1883

Achievement

1. Wagner redefined and recreated opera as "music drama," in which every aspect of a work serves the dramatic purpose, and musical unity derives from symphonic development of recurring themes or motives (leitmotifs).
2. The composer developed a revolutionary harmonic language that greatly extended and ultimately weakened the functional role of tonality through an expanded harmonic vocabulary, increased chromaticism and dissonance, and studied avoidance of cadences.
3. He expanded the orchestra to include full homogeneous groups of related instruments (with emphasis on brasses and woodwinds), required technical virtuosity from all instruments, and consistently employed a rich polyphonic texture. The orchestra is often given the task of conveying the "inner meaning" of his music dramas.
4. His writings about music were influential, particularly the treatise *Opera and Drama* (1851). His single-minded application of all his theories and extraordinary efforts in creating the music drama culminated in the construction of a personal Festspielhaus (festival theater) devoted entirely to performances of his own works, a remarkable achievement that greatly enhanced the status of the Romantic composer.

Works and Style Summary

Operas: 14 (the first incomplete), the last 7 of which are music dramas; all are written on his own librettos. The quintessential Wagner begins with *Tristan und Isolde* (1859) and *Die Meistersinger* (1861), reaches a climax with *Der Ring des Nibelungen* (consisting of four music dramas: *Das Rheingold*, 1854; *Die Walküre*, 1856; *Siegfried*, 1871; *Götterdämmerung*, 1874), and ends with *Parsifal* (1882)

Miscellaneous works: some orchestral music, choral works, piano music, many songs, some arrangements of works by other composers

Wagner's style evolved from being highly derivative (*Die Feen* shows the influence of Weber, *Das Liebesverbot* that of traditional Italian and French models, and *Rienzi* that of Meyerbeer) to an individual synthesis of traditional Romantic opera with Wagnerian elements of style and dramatic psychology (*Der fliegende Holländer, Tannhäuser, Lohengrin*). With the achievement of a continuous vocal line within a unified symphonic texture and an expanded sense of time was born the Wagnerian music drama.

In opera, up to now, the composer did not even try to achieve unity of form for his entire work. . . . The principal motives of the dramatic action, having now attained to the condition of a distinct melodic phrase that fully realizes the underlying intentions, are gathered into a unified artistic form extending as a binding medium, not merely over individual parts but over the drama as a whole. In this way not only these melodic passages, which elucidate each other and thus create a unity, but also the emotional and phenomenal motives to which they refer are transmitted to the feeling. In this context, the perfectly unified form has been accomplished and, through it, a unified content is manifested or, better still, rendered possible. (Wagner, *Opera and Drama*, 1851).

Career   Wagner, who was largely self-taught, began his career in 1833 as a chorus-master and soon became a conductor at various German theaters (1834–39). He failed in his early attempts to have his work produced in Paris (1839–42), even spending some time in debtor's prison. Through the success of *Rienzi* and *Der fliegende Holländer* he became kapellmeister at Dresden (1843–49), but revolutionary political activity brought exile from Germany until 1860. He established a reputation in London and Paris as a conductor and, upon returning to Germany, won enough friends and patrons (above all King Ludwig II of Bavaria) to live and compose as he pleased. He even succeeded in building his own opera house in Bayreuth in 1876.

TRISTAN UND ISOLDE

Historical Perspective   Composed between 1857 and 1859, interrupting his work on *Siegfried*, the third music drama in the Ring cycle, *Tristan and Isolde* was first performed in Munich under the aegis of King Ludwig of Bavaria on June 10, 1865. As was his custom, Wagner wrote his own libretto for *Tristan and Isolde*, which he apparently based on a Celtic legend. According to Joseph Kerman, "dramatically speaking *Tristan and Isolde* is Wagner's best work, the clearest in form and idea, and the most complete in realization."[2] Musically, the opera is commonly regarded as a major landmark in the history of Western music and a quintessential expression of the Romantic *Zeitgeist*. Each of the three acts moves towards one climactic moment, when the first theme of the opera's Prelude recurs in complete form: in Act I, at the drinking of the love-potion; in Act II, after King Mark's question "Why this disgrace?"; in Act III, at the moment of Tristan's death. Together, they reveal what Wagner clearly regarded as a triumphal progression from love through its ally night to an ultimate attainment of death. The love-death of Isolde, which closes the opera, thus becomes a final blessing for the lovers. The plot deals with the love story of Tristan and Isolde. The knight Tristan has won Isolde as a bride for King Mark. Aided by a love potion, the two betray the King and are discovered. Tristan returns home wounded, recounts the tale, and upon the arrival of Isolde with news of pardon, dies.

Description of Style   Wagnerian vocal melodies often unfold either in long asymmetrical phrases or in short declamatory phrases of an expressive nature. In either case, the continuous musical and dramatic flow is achieved by orchestral development of recurring leitmotifs, which serves as a foundation for the voices. Wide leaps are characteristic of the composer. Save for an occasional folklike melody associated with Kurwenal or the sailors in Act I, Wagner's vocal line is generally chromatic in character and very seldom tuneful in the conventional sense. Perhaps the most striking feature of *Tristan* is its rich chromatic texture, which is derived partly from harmonic and partly from contrapuntal means. Wagner favors full textures with much doubling, and his part-writing often leads progressions to unconventional resolutions. The prevalence of chromaticism extends almost to its limits the traditional system of functional harmony. Tonal ambiguity also results from his continual modulation, studied avoidance of cad-

[2]*Opera As Drama* (New York: Vintage Books, 1959), p. 213.

ences, frequent enharmonicism, and unusual resolutions of the half-diminished-seventh chord. In addition, Wagner occasionally uses seventh chords and even ninth chords as consonances, and he depends heavily upon suspensions, appoggiaturas, and accented passing-tones to represent the restless, yearning nature of the drama.

The increased importance of the orchestra's role underlies and makes possible the Wagnerian concept of music drama. By keeping the audience aware of deeper meanings and the relationships of dramatic events and feelings, Wagner's orchestra actually elucidates the psychological course of the drama. Rather than being sung, the all-important web of leitmotifs is generally spun by the orchestra. One of the greatest of orchestrators, Wagner was not content with the usual resources of the Romantic symphony orchestra; he expanded that body so that a chord of homogeneous timbre could be performed by each instrumental choir. For this purpose, his woodwinds section includes English horn and bass clarinet, while his brasses include bass trombone and tuba. For their part, the strings require reinforcement to balance the augmented winds. Despite its great size, however, the Wagnerian orchestra frequently achieves delicate chamber effects.

Analysis of Structure   Form in the traditional operatic sense is seldom discernible in the continuous dramatic and musical flow of *Tristan and Isolde.* Although the leading structural elements remain those of theme and tonality, they are often so obscured or fleeting in the greatly expanded dimensions of Wagnerian acts as to be almost imperceptible. Questions as to the exact relationship among similar leitmotifs or the specific key of a particular musico-dramatic "period" still produce conflicting answers more than 100 years after the opera was composed. Nevertheless, some structural points do seem fairly clear. The large-scale ternary (ABA') plan of the three acts is certainly established in the analysis of the opera by Alfred Lorenz (*Der musikalische Aufbau von Richard Wagners 'Tristan und Isolde,'* 1927). The following discussion of Act III offers the fruits of deeper structural probing by Joseph Kerman (*Opera As Drama*) as well as Lorenz.

After a long Prelude similar to that of Act I, Act III proper begins with the shepherd's melody played on the English horn. When Tristan awakens, he gradually recalls the suffering of the past, inveighs against day and life, and joyfully anticipates the coming of Isolde. Then, in an eloquent musical variation on the same themes, the same events are retraced, ending with the actual arrival of Isolde and the death of Tristan. To these two similar musical sections (called *Stollen* by Lorenz), the composer appended a different closing section (*Abgesang*) consisting of Isolde's lament for Tristan, King Mark's arrival and the death of the faithful Kurwenal, and, finally, the love-death of Isolde. The act may therefore be regarded (according to Lorenz) as being in *Bar* (AAB) form, a structure found on a much smaller scale in the Lieder of Medieval German musicians.

The following passage describes one of the aspects of Wagner's musical form in his own words:

> I should like herewith to designate the art of transition as the most subtle and profound feature of my art. I am repelled by what is abrupt and sudden. It is often unavoidable and necessary, but it should not happen without having first created a mood that, preparatory to this sudden transition, would make it seem imperative.

My masterpiece in this fine art of a gradual transition is undoubtedly the great scene in the second act of *Tristan*. The beginning of the act reveals life in its most overpowering emotional aspect: the close is filled with the most sanctified yearning for death. These are the two pillars, and note how I have combined them. This now is the secret of my musical form, and I have the temerity to affirm that its perfect harmony, its clear interpretation of every detail, has hitherto not even been dreamed of. If you could but know how this guiding precept has inspired me with musical inventions of rhythm, harmonic and melodic development, which formerly would never have occurred to me, you would fully realize how, even in the most specialized branches of art, nothing true can be invented that does not arise from prime motives.[3]

Giuseppe Verdi   Italian   1813–1901

Achievement   Verdi was the leading Italian composer of the middle and late Romantic period and one of the greatest opera composers of any period. From such traditional elements of Italian opera as closed forms separated by recitative, emphasis upon singing and melody, and commitment to direct emotional utterance, he forged an individual and powerful dramatic language that — virtually alone — stood against the Wagnerian tide. His works have been a basic part of the international operatic repertory without interruption since the premiere of *Nabucco* (1842), but perhaps most prominently in recent years, when most of his earlier operas have been successfully revived.

Works and Style Summary   From 1839 to 1893, Verdi composed 24 serious operas and two comedies. The early ones are melodramatic (*Ernani*, 1844). The middle operas have increasingly fine depiction of character as well as dramatic unity (*La Traviata*, 1853), and lead to the grand operas of vast scope which he wrote for Paris (*Don Carlos*, 1867). Near the end of his life came two transcendent masterpieces of human drama, *Otello* (1887) and *Falstaff* (1893). His Requiem Mass (1874) is also a great dramatic masterpiece in operatic style. Other compositions include *Four Sacred Pieces* (his last compositions) and several other choral works, about twenty songs, and a string quartet.

Verdi's style is voice-dominated. In his earlier works, a predominant melody is generally only thinly accompanied by the orchestra, within a simple rhythmic framework. Later, emphasis shifts to delineation of character, both by melodic means and through a much-expanded harmonic vocabulary, subtler use of rhythm, and vastly enhanced treatment of the orchestra (which is often employed innovatively). His construction of scenes and acts reveals steadily increasing skill in recitative and ensemble writing, in the handling of dramatic intensity and climax, and in the deployment of tonal relationships and leitmotifs.

Career   Verdi studied with a local organist and, as a teenager, served as a church organist. He attended the Busseto municipal school of music (1825–29) but was subsequently refused (for being too old) by the Milan Conservatory in

---

[3]As translated by Paul Nettl, *Book of Musical Documents* (New York: Philosophical Library 1948), p. 247.

1832. He studied with Vincenzo Lavigna from 1832 to 1835. Regarding orchestration and dramatic music, he was essentially self-taught. After directing the Busseto Philharmonic Society from 1836 to 1838, he became an independent opera composer, living in Milan (1839–49) and at Sant' Agata, near Busseto, (1849–1901) and travelling to Paris, London, and St. Petersburg, as well as to many Italian cities to oversee production of his operas. The immense success of *Nabucco* in 1842 firmly established his career, his identification with the movement seeking political freedom and the unity of Italy enhanced his popularity, and his gradual development as a dramatic composer elevated the taste of his audiences and brought him to the pinnacle of his profession. He was internationally acclaimed while alive and universally mourned at his death.

Johannes Brahms   German   1833–1897

Achievement

1. Brahms was the great traditionalist of the Romantic period, a major composer who wrote absolute rather than programmatic music, he succeeded in reviving chamber music, the symphony, and even Protestant church music, as well as such earlier forms as the variation.
2. Not only did he study and learn from Baroque and Classical music, but he also edited such earlier music as the works of François Couperin and Mozart.

Works and Style Summary

Chamber music: 24 works, including 3 string quartets, 3 violin sonatas, 2 violoncello sonatas, 2 clarinet sonatas, 2 string quintets, 2 string sextets, a horn trio, a clarinet quintet, a piano quintet, 3 piano quartets, 4 piano trios

Art songs: more than 200, including a song cycle, vocal duets and quartets, folksong arrangements, individual Lieder

Orchestral music: 4 symphonies, 2 concert overtures, 2 orchestral serenades, a set of orchestra variations (on a theme drawn from Haydn)

Concertos: 2 for piano, 1 for violin and violoncello, 1 for violin

Choral music: a wide variety for chorus and orchestra (*A German Requiem,* the *Song of Destiny*), and even *a cappella* motets

Keyboard music: piano music (3 sonatas, ballades, intermezzi, rhapsodies, variations, and some two-piano music), organ music (mainly chorale preludes)

Brahms' style is a remarkable synthesis of Romantic expression and Classical tradition; the latter is reflected especially in his use of Classical forms, conservative functional harmony, and avoidance of programs, while the former appears in his love for dark sonorities and the alto register (horn, viola, clarinet), for lyrical melody and folk music, and for cyclic unifying links in large-scale works. His respect for and knowledge of tradition is also evidenced by his revival of counterpoint and of the theme with variations, as well as in his subtle use of such rhythmic devices as hemiola, syncopation, and cross-rhythms.

Career   The composer was a pupil of his father, who played double bass, and later of Eduard Marxsen. He began as a pianist, first in taverns and then on a concert tour with a professional violinist. After being heralded by Schumann in 1853, he held several posts as a conductor of choral and orchestral societies and finally settled in Vienna in 1878.

Gustav Mahler   Austro-Bohemian   1860–1911

Achievement

1. Mahler was the leading "post-Romantic" symphonist and a major song composer. Virtually all of his works have entered the standard repertory.
2. The composer figured prominently in the development of new music in Austria. His path-breaking approach to orchestration had noteworthy impact upon Schoenberg and others of the younger generation.
3. He was a renowned conductor of tyrannical bent whose performances were of the highest artistic accomplishment, creating enduring standards for his successors.

Works and Style Summary

Symphonies: 10, the last unfinished; numbers 2, 3, 4, and 8 require vocal soloists and/or chorus

Art songs: c. 50, including the cycles *Lieder eines fahrenden Gesellen* and *Das Lied von der Erde*

Mahler was a brilliant master of orchestration, his effects ranging from large-scale deployment of vast performing resources to small-scale chamber textures. His melodies are noteworthy for their lyricism and, at times, for their folk-like character. March and waltz rhythms permeate his music and, occasionally, parody finds a place. Mahler retained both the strongly tonal context and the Classical structural principles of the traditional symphony; but he apparently used modulation in a symbolic rather than functional way, and he avoided literal repetition in his forms by subtle use of variation. His later works found him making more and more use of counterpoint.

Career   Mahler, who was a pianist and conductor as well as a composer, studied with Franz Krenn at the Vienna Conservatory. He served as an opera conductor in several places, most notably at the Royal Opera in Budapest (1888–91), at Hamburg (1891–97), and, at the pinnacle of his career, as director of the Vienna Court Opera (1897–1907). For a short time (1908–09) he was principal conductor of the Metropolitan Opera and then conductor of the New York Philharmonic (1909–11). Although he always sought financial security in order to compose, his composing was mostly limited to the short periods between operatic and concert seasons.

Richard Strauss   German   1864–1949

Achievement

1. Richard Strauss ranks among the outstanding composers of opera, symphonic poem, and Lied. Most of his operatic and symphonic works from 1888 to 1912 have entered and remained in the standard repertory.

2. He was a brilliant orchestrator. In 1905, he published a revised and enlarged version of Berlioz's famous treatise on instrumentation.

Works and Style Summary

Operas: 15, including *Salome* (1905), *Elektra* (1909), *Der Rosenkavalier* (1911), *Ariadne auf Naxos* (1912), *Arabella* (1933)

Symphonic poems: 9, among them *Don Juan* (1888), *Death and Transfiguration* (1890), *Till Eulenspiegel* (1895), *Also sprach Zarathustra* (1896)

Lieder: c. 200, including 4 sets with orchestra (*Vier letzte Lieder*, 1948) and 26 collections with piano accompaniment

Miscellaneous works: orchestral, chamber, piano, and choral works

Strauss used leitmotifs and thematic transformation, and he continued to stretch tonality in a post-Wagnerian idiom until after *Elektra* (1909), when he gradually turned towards a less flamboyant Romantic style within a clear, classically oriented framework, placing a new emphasis upon soloists while subduing the orchestra. His skill and craftsmanship were matched by an extraordinary melodic gift.

Career   Strauss' training was supervised from age 4 by his father, a famous horn player. The boy studied composition with F.W. Meyer from 1875 to 1880 and also studied piano and violin. In 1885 Strauss became assistant conductor to Han von Bülow. Subsequently, he held several other posts before becoming chief conductor at Munich (1896), conductor and director of the opera at Berlin (1908) and, ultimately, conductor and co-director of the Vienna State Opera (1919). In his later years he was a prominent guest conductor.

GLOSSARY

absolute music   music without extra-musical or programmatic associations.

bi-modal   a term describing music that draws upon the characteristic scale degrees of both major and minor modes on the same tonic.

cabaletta (It.)   the second part of a nineteenth-century double aria, with a faster tempo and requiring greater virtuosity from the singer.

cavatina (It.)   the first part of a nineteenth-century double aria, normally shorter and simpler than the second.

cross-rhythm   simultaneous use of conflicting rhythmic patterns or accents.

cyclic principle   unifying the movements of a large-scale composition by recurrent use of the same theme; a characteristic Romantic device.

double-escapement   a mechanism in the piano that holds the hammer at a certain height after it has struck the key, while the key returns. It can now be played again immediately, and the hammer is in position to strike the string sooner than the first time.

half-diminished-seventh chord   differs from the fully diminished-seventh chord in that its seventh is minor (not diminished)

leitmotif (Ger., *Leitmotiv*)   a theme or motive that represents a character, emotion, idea, or even object. Leitmotifs are used as short, symbolic musical building blocks in the operas of Wagner and later composers.

mazurka   a name for a number of Polish dances in triple meter with tempi ranging from slow to fast. Those of Chopin are the best-known ones.

nationalism   a term generally employed in reference to the rise of East-European national musics in the late nineteenth and early twentieth centuries. Nationalistic music is characterized by the use of folklike rhythms and melodies (or perhaps just scales), as in the works of Mussorgsky, Smetana, and many others.

nocturne (Fr.)   a lyrical character piece for piano, best represented in the works of Chopin.

overstringing (or cross-stringing)   an arrangement whereby the bass strings of the piano cross over the other strings.

parlando (It.)   a style of delivering recitative very rapidly with some approximation of speech; features many repeated pitches.

polonaise (Fr.)   a festive Polish dance in moderate triple meter; several were composed by Chopin.

rubato (It.)   a flexible treatment of tempo in which either the melody is allowed freedom over a steady accompaniment (apparently the proper historical approach to performing Classical and Romantic music), or the entire texture moves faster or slower at the player's discretion.

thematic transformation   considerable variation of a recurring theme, especially of its mood and character; a practice employed often by programmatic composers of the Romantic period. (See the discussions of Berlioz's *Symphonie fantastique* and Liszt's *Piano Sonata in B Minor* in this chapter.)

third relationship   when the roots of adjacent chords are a third apart.

verismo (It.)   realism, a movement in late nineteenth- and early twentieth-century opera, corresponding to a contemporaneous trend towards literary realism.

Chapter Six

Twentieth-Century Music

Only in an Age of Technology could music become principally a commodity; but only an Age of Anxiety careening between world wars and economic depressions would saturate its aural environment with electrically transmitted sound separated from sense. A state of *Weltschmerz* (world-weariness) inherited from the decaying Romantic world characterized many Western artists in the early twentieth century, perhaps as a result of a conflict between their humanitarian ideals and a ruthlessly profit-minded society. About mid-century, composers faced a more fundamental dilemma that threatened their relationship with an already much-diminished public: philosophical, theoretical, and stylistic developments in the realm of sound and rhythm seemed to demand redefinition of the art of music.

Music invades contemporary living spaces to an extraordinary extent—shopping malls, supermarkets, elevators, bedrooms, cemeteries, psychiatric waiting rooms. Most of it is not art music, which can claim only about five percent of the commercial music market. To describe the principal ways in which twentieth-century composers reacted to the aesthetic and musical difficulties of late Romantic music and to read of their attitudes in their own words may provide the clearest introduction to the contemporary state of affairs in the world of art music.

It is obvious that one technical fad after another has swept over Twentieth-Century music as the music of each one of its leading composers has come to be intimately known. Each fad lasted a few years, only to be discarded by the succeeding generation of composers, then by the music profession, and finally by certain parts of the interested public. . . . The tendency to fad has been greatly encouraged by the promulgation of systems, particularly harmonic systems. Many recent composers following Schoenberg, Hindemith, and Messiaen have gained renown by circulating descriptions of their systems even in places where their music was not known. This kind of intellectual publicity can lead to a dead end even more quickly than the older fads derived from the actual sound of music in styles the composer did not even bother to explain.[1]

Nationalism represents the twentieth-century style with the broadest public acceptance. More deeply colored by folk modes, rhythms, and lore than Romantic nationalism, it flowered particularly in the hands of Eastern-European composers such as Janacek and Kodaly, the Englishmen Vaughan Williams and Holst, the Spaniard de Falla, the Americans Ives and Copland, and, above all, the Hungarian BÉLA BARTÓK. The indelible effect of his field research into Hungarian folk music was described by Bartok as follows:

> The study of all this peasant music had the decisive significance for me that it led me to the possibility of a complete emancipation from the exclusive rule of the traditional major-minor system . . . and [they] moreover display extremely free and various rhythmic structures and changes of meter. . . . Returning to their use, moreover, made possible novel harmonic combinations.[2]

Orchestral suites, symphonies, operas, art songs, and piano music proved closest to the nationalists' hearts. With composers such as the Americans Gershwin and Bernstein a potentially fertile cross-fertilization seemed to be taking place between art music and popular commercial music. However, extinction under the impact of mass media threatens all of the world's indigenous folk cultures, which have been a primary source of inspiration for both popular and art music in the past.

Harmony in Western music has undergone a continuous development towards greater complexity since the establishment of functional harmony during the Baroque period. In the late nineteenth century Debussy's nonfunctional use of chords opened a new frontier of freely treated harmonic color. The leading explorer of **atonal** regions beyond the pale of tonality was ARNOLD SCHOENBERG. Impelled to justify the apparently arbitrary creative products of his high mission, he worked out a highly influential twelve-tone method of composition based on a tone row or series. Eminently gifted students such as ALBAN BERG and Anton Webern helped place his method among the foremost twentieth-century techniques, despite its inherent difficulty. Songs, operas, and symphonic poems have been favored by the serialists, but such heavy reliance upon extramusical subjects has drawn criticism. The anxiety-ridden, nightmarish texts of many atonal works (such as Schoenberg's *Erwartung* and Berg's *Wozzeck*) evoke the inner world of the psyche, as revealed by Freud and Kafka, in a manner as uncompromising as Schoenberg's own aesthetic credo:

> I believe that a real composer writes music for no other reason than that it pleases him. Those who compose because they want to please others, and have audiences

---

[1]Elliott Carter, "Shop Talk by an American Composer," *The Musical Quarterly* XLVI (1960), 190.

[2]From the composer's *Autobiography* of 1921, as translated in William Austin, *Music in the Twentieth Century* (New York: W. W. Norton, 1966), p. 226.

in mind, are not real artists. They are not the kind of men who are driven to say something whether or not there exists one person who likes it, even if they themselves dislike it. They are not creators who must open the valves in order to relieve the interior pressure of a creation ready to be born. They are merely more or less skillful entertainers. . . . [3]

A third major tendency important in the twentieth century has been Neoclassicism, the revival of techniques, forms, and style features characteristic of the Renaissance, Baroque and Classical periods. Among the neo-classical composers contributing to the large number of symphonies, concertos, sonatas, and string quartets composed after 1900 were MAURICE RAVEL, Darius Milhaud, Paul Hindemith, Sergei Prokofiev, and Dimitri Shostakovich. Greatest among those whose solution to the contemporary crisis in musical language required, in part, a return to the past was IGOR STRAVINSKY, who chose eclectically such models as Mozart, Haydn, and Gesualdo, and re-established a craftsmanlike, objective attitude towards musical creativity:

> As for myself, I experience a sort of terror when, at the moment of setting to work and finding myself before the infinitude of possibilities that present themselves, I have the feeling that everything is permissible to me. . . . I have no use for a theoretic freedom. Let me have something finite, definite — matter that can lend itself to my operation only insofar as it is commensurate with my possibilities. . . . My freedom thus consists in my moving about within the narrow frame that I have assigned myself for each one of my undertakings. [4]

A conservative response to the apparent problem of musical language in the early twentieth century produced one group of composers that perceived no crisis and simply continued writing in a rich post-Romantic vein, including Jan Sibelius and Sergei Rakhmaninov. Arrayed against them and their traditional values were the avant-garde, who sought to overcome years of relative neglect of the parameters of timbre (EDGARD VARÈSE) and rhythm (Stravinsky). Separated from much of the music-loving public by their audacity, but led nevertheless by their theoretical, philosophical, and aesthetic attitudes to redefine music in broader terms, avant-garde composers increasingly received support from arts foundations and universities after the middle of the century. New developments that led away from a large public included the Eastern philosophy and **aleatory** (or chance) methods of John Cage, the totally serialized technique of Milton Babbitt, microtonal scales and instruments (Harry Partch), the use of the electronic synthesizer (Karlheinz Stockhausen), new timbres produced by conventional instruments and voices (KRZYSZTOF PENDERECKI), computer composition (Lejaren Hiller), stochastic or mathematical techniques (Iannis Xenakis), "thirdstream" fusion of **dodecaphony** with jazz (Gunther Schuller), and theatrical music (Luciano Berio). So rapidly have styles changed after mid-century that a dynamic steady-state has been proposed within which to contain it. [5] The present

[3]From the composer's essay "Heart and Brain in Music," in *Style and Idea*, trans. Dika Newlin (New York: Philosophical Library, 1950).

[4]As translated by Arthur Knodel and Ingolf Dahl in *The Poetics of Music* (New York: Vintage Books, 1960), pp. 66–68.

[5]Leonard B. Meyer, "As It Is, and Perhaps Will Be," *Music, The Arts, and Ideas* (Chicago: The University of Chicago Press, 1967).

author theorizes that the real crisis in twentieth-century music lies in the displacement of the vocally-derived "common" musical language of the past by emphasis upon technical and acoustic properties idiomatic to instruments. It is nevertheless quite possible that the materials and techniques that will carry the glorious Western music tradition many years into the future have been created and lie waiting among the unparalleled profusion of innovative twentieth-century styles.

Twentieth-Century Styles and Genres

MAJOR STYLE TRENDS

Nationalism	Neoclassicism	Serialism	Avant-garde
Vaughan Williams (E)*	Busoni (I–G)	Schoenberg (A)	Ives (US)
Ives (US)	Roussel (F)	Webern (A)	Varèse (F)
Falla (S)	Ravel (F)	Berg (A)	Partch (US)
Bartók (H)	Falla (S)	Dallapiccola (I)	Messiaen (F)
Stravinsky (R)	Stravinsky (R)	Messiaen (F)	Cage (US)
Gershwin (US)	Prokofiev (R)	Ginastera (Ar)	Lutoslawski (P)
Copland (US)	Milhaud (F)	Babbitt (US)	Xenakis (Gr)
Lutoslawski (P)	Piston (US)	Boulez (F)	Berio (I)
Ginastera (Ar)	Hindemith (G)	Stockhausen (G)	Stockhausen (G)
Bernstein (US)	Shostakovich (R)	Stravinsky (R)	Penderecki (P)

MAJOR GENRES AND MEDIA

Opera	Art Song	Orchestral Music	Chamber Music
Puccini (I)	Schoenberg (A)	Vaughan Williams (E)	Schoenberg (A)
Schoenberg (G)	Ives (US)	Schoenberg (A)	Ravel (F)
Stravinsky (R)	Ravel (F)	Ives (US)	Bartók (H)
Berg (A)	Webern (A)	Ravel (F)	Stravinsky (R)
Prokofiev (R)	Berg (A)	Bartók (H)	Webern (A)
Hindemith (G)	Poulenc (F)	Stravinsky (R)	Hindemith (G)
Poulenc (F)	Weill (G)	Prokofiev (R)	Shostakovich (R)
Britten (E)	Barber (US)	Shostakovich (R)	Carter (US)
Ginastera (Ar)	Britten (E)	Carter (US)	Boulez (F)
Henze (G)	Crumb (US)	Lutoslawski (P)	Crumb (US)

*NATIONALITIES
A — Austrian	F — French	H — Hungarian	R — Russian
Ar — Argentinian	G — German	I — Italian	S — Spanish
E — English	Gr — Greek	P — Polish	US — American

MAJOR COMPOSERS AND SELECTED COMPOSITIONS

Claude Debussy   French   1862–1918

Achievement

1. Debussy created a unique and forward-looking style of great technical finish and poetic appeal and of wide influence, principally through his frequent non-functional use of harmony and his novel orchestration.

2. Despite his dislike for the term, the composer is generally regarded as the creator of impressionism (the realization in music of the aesthetic of the symbolist poets and impressionist painters), which constitutes one important facet of his style.

3. He was highly significant for writing in a new, coloristic manner for piano and for contributing greatly to its literature.

Works and Style Summary   A perfectionist rather than a prolific composer, Debussy left many works incomplete. The most significant genres and representative pieces are listed below:

> *Orchestral music: Prelude to the Afternoon of a Faun, Nocturnes, La mer, Images*, and several ballets (*Jeux*)
>
> *Piano music:* several sets and collections, including *Suite bergamasque*, two books each of *Préludes* and *Études*, as well as individual works.
>
> *Art songs:* c. eighty (*Chansons de Bilitis*)
>
> *Operas:* several begun, only one completed — *Pelléas et Mélisande* (1902)
>
> *Chamber music:* a string quartet and a violoncello sonata, among other works.
>
> *Several choral works*

Debussy's style is lyrical and evocative of mood or atmosphere through unconventional use of rhythm and color (both orchestral and harmonic), with chords selected for sound more than function and subordinated to the melody. Melodically, he sometimes employs **whole-tone**, pentatonic, and pseudo-modal scales. Dissonance is rich but mild, with much use of seventh and ninth chords that do not always resolve. Forms are fluid and often symmetrical. After 1915 the composer's style moved towards greater melodic and harmonic simplicity.

Career   The composer studied at the Paris Conservatory from 1872 to 1884, with some interruptions. His composition teacher was Ernest Guiraud. From 1880 to 1882 he served as pianist in the household of Nadezhda von Meck (Tchaikovsky's famous patroness). In 1884 he won the Prix de Rome. His first great success was *Pelléas*, which established him as a major composer. He played his own piano works and sometimes conducted his orchestral ones. On occasion, he wrote music criticism.

PRELUDE TO THE AFTERNOON OF A FAUN
The score appears in MSO II.

Historical Perspective The *Prelude*, a symphonic poem in one movement, was apparently begun in 1892 and completed about two months before its first performance in Paris on December 22, 1894. In words written or at least approved by Debussy, the *Prelude* is described as "a very free illustration of the beautiful poem of Mallarmé. By no means does it claim to be a synthesis of the latter. Rather there are successive scenes through which pass the desires and dreams of the faun in the heat of this afternoon. Then, tired of pursuing the fearful flight of the nymph and naiads, he succumbs to intoxicating sleep, in which he can finally realize his dreams of possession in universal Nature."

Description of Style Timbre is perhaps the work's most striking feature. To the three flutes and four horns of an otherwise standard orchestra, the composer added English horn, two harps, and antique cymbals. Not only do magical features abound (harp glissandi, evocative string accompaniments, subtle use of horns), but the flute emerges reborn as an expressive rather than merely decorative instrument, and tone color itself helps articulate musical structure. According to Debussy, melody is the primary element in his style. He described this piece as being "in a mode that tries to contain all the nuances." Allusions to the whole-tone and pentatonic scales are subsumed by the irregularity of the phrase structure and the constantly changing tempi and time signatures. An especially subtle use of pitch is seen in the treatment of the note C-sharp in manifold contexts, among them its unaccompanied appearance at the beginning, its transformation into a tonality (D-flat, m. 55), and its ultimate role as the sixth of an E-major scale (m. 94, as in m. 21).

Harmony follows the melody so closely in a free-voiced and freely changing fashion that it is difficult to separate the two. Seldom does the harmony give rise to accompanying melodies, and just as seldom to parallel motion. After the tonally ambiguous opening, an expanded E major is finally indicated (m. 21) and indirectly affirmed (m. 30), followed by a section clearly in D-flat major and a return to E. Each harmonization of the prominent opening theme is varied, the composer's harmonic vocabulary favoring seventh and ninth chords, especially full dominant ninths. As striking as its frequency is the emotional neutrality of Debussy's dissonance, which seems to be used more for color than to convey feelings.

Analysis of Structure Despite various authors' lack of agreement in detail, the *Prelude* may be said to "follow the rising movement of the poem" (Debussy) and to contain a climactic section (mm. 55–78) of obvious contrast to the beginning and end in thematic material, tonality, and regularity of motion and phrasing. Unusual in a ternary form is the appearance in the B section of subordinate themes from A (as in mm. 61 and 67) and the general feeling that the B theme (m. 55) grows out of what went before. The form seems poised in a fittingly ambiguous way between a rounded two-part shape in proportion (I:mm. 1–54; II:mm. 55–110) and a three-part structure in terms of disposition of thematic materials and keys.

Béla Bartók   Hungarian   1881–1945

Achievement

1. Bartók was probably the foremost nationalistic composer of the twentieth century; he made major contributions to the standard repertory in most genres. Since his works were not widely known until after about 1930, however, their importance lies more in their quality than in their influence upon other composers.
2. The composer did extensive research into East-European folk music, publishing five books and many articles, as well as recording and transcribing more than 9000 folksongs, largely from Roumanian, Slovak, and Hungarian sources.

Works and Style Summary

String music: including six string quartets, two concertos, two rhapsodies, four sonatas, and smaller works

Piano music: four works for piano and orchestra, a piano sonata, "Allegro barbaro," about 400 small-scale pieces (*Mikrokosmos*), suites, other works

Orchestral works: among them, 2 ballets (*The Miraculous Mandarin*, 1919), *Music for Strings, Percussion and Celesta* (1936), the *Concerto for Orchestra* (1944)

Vocal works: an opera (*Bluebeard's Castle*, 1911), a cantata, songs

Didactic works: among them, *Music for Children* (piano pieces), *Mikrokosmos*, 44 short violin duos, 27 choruses for children's or women's voices

Bartók wrought a personal synthesis from sources as disparate as Romanticism (especially aspects of style from Liszt and Debussy), Expressionism (dissonant harmonies and compelling subjects), Neo-Classicism (especially the styles of Bach and Beethoven) and, above all, Nationalism (pentatonic scales, modal harmonies, and irregular meters from folk music). The dissonant character of his expanded tonality often stems from a contrapuntal texture. Such an emphasis upon the linear may well be reinforced by his vigorous and irregular treatment of rhythm and his colorful use of orchestration. Transformation of a few germinal themes (sometimes even by inversion) often makes for a strong thematic unity within his carefully molded and frequently symmetrical forms.

Career   Bartók began to compose at 9 and gave his first piano recital at 11, subsequently learning organ as well. He studied composition with Hans Koessler and piano with István Thomán at the Budapest Academy of Music. In 1907 he began his career as a professor of piano at the Budapest Academy, a post he kept until 1934. Initial recognition as a composer came with a ballet entitled *The Wooden Prince* (1917); as a concert pianist, his reputation grew with regular tours that began after 1924. In 1940 he emigrated to the United States to escape political persecution, but encountered financial difficulty and illness. Although several of his best-known masterpieces were composed during these last years, his music did not become popular until after his death.

CONCERTO FOR ORCHESTRA

The music is available in miniature score (London: Boosey and Hawkes, 1946).

Historical Perspective   The *Concerto for Orchestra*, Bartók's last large orchestral work, was commissioned by Serge Koussevitzky and first performed by him with the Boston Symphony Orchestra in 1944. The title stems from "its tendency to treat the single instruments or instrument groups in a concertante or soloistic manner." According to the composer, "the general mood of the work represents, apart from the jesting second movement, a gradual transition from the sternness of the first movement and the lugubrious death-song of the third, to the life assertion of the last."

Description of Style   Virtuosic treatment of the instruments makes this work a touchstone of modern orchestral excellence. From the treatment of the brasses in the first-movement fugato to the pairing of woodwinds in the second and the perpetual motion of the strings in the finale, the composer seeks appropriate realization of his thematic materials rather than novelty for its own sake. Especially noteworthy in the work are folk-influenced traits: melodies of narrow range moving conjunctly, rhythms whose asymmetrical character reveals derivation from word-reliant folk rhythms, alternating meters reminiscent of Bulgarian dance music. On the other hand, the manner in which motives are spun out, varied, and transformed reflects a high degree of art. Tonal centers remain, but are expanded to include various mode and scale possibilities, among them pentatonic. Chords are built from fourths or fifths as well as from thirds, and are often colored by adding seconds or sevenths. A prominent role is played by counterpoint, as in the complex fugal section of the finale, in which the fugue subject undergoes single, double, and triple augmentation as well as diminution, inversion, and an intricate stretto in four voices.

Analysis of Structure   The five movements create a symmetrical design, with the Elegia as the centerpiece. At the center of this middle movement, surrounded by what Bartók referred to as a "misty texture of rudimentary motives," there occur several folk-like themes, one of which is derived from the introduction to the first movement. The second and fourth movements share a lighter character, and both are divided into distinct sections. The second movement, "Giuoco delle coppie" (Game of Pairs), unfolds as an ABA form, the B section containing chorale-like music for brasses and side drum, while the A section features paired bassoons, oboes, clarinets, flutes, and muted trumpets taking turns at various intervals. In the fourth movement, "Intermezzo interrotto," the alternation of song-like themes is interrupted for a parodic treatment of a theme from Shostakovich's *Seventh Symphony*. The first and fifth movements share reference to sonata form, but with significant deviations. The last movement, with its perpetual motion and complex counterpoint, is in the nature of a *tour de force*. The arch form of the first movement, with its central *tranquillo* section framed by fugal sections and its main themes reversed at the recapitulation, reflects in microcosm the symmetry of the entire composition.

Arnold Schoenberg   Austrian   1874–1951

Achievement

1. Schoenberg was an important innovator: a) he emancipated the twelve chromatic tones of the octave from their tonal roles in his atonal works (1907–15); b)

he created a composition out of changing tone colors alone, a technique called *Klangfarbenmelodie* (No. 3 of *Five Orchestra Pieces*, 1909); c) he made prominent use of a speech-like technique called *Sprechstimme* (*Pierrot Lunaire*, 1912); d) he created the 12-tone method of composition (1923).

2. The composer was a principal representative of **Expressionism** in music as well as a founder or leader of several groups that fostered new music.

3. He was a highly influential teacher and a profound thinker about music. His notable disciples included Alban Berg and Anton Webern; among his writings are numbered such well-known books as *Harmonielehre* (*Theory of Harmony*) (1911) and *Style and Idea* (1950).

4. Schoenberg was an expressionist painter of noteworthy achievement, whose works earned him the respect and friendship of Kandinsky.

Works and Style Summary

Art song sets or cycles: 12, totaling c. 50 Lieder (*Pierrot Lunaire*)

Operas: 4, including *Erwartung* (a monodrama) and *Moses and Aaron* (unfinished)

Orchestral works: 12, among them 2 chamber symphonies, a symphonic poem, concertos for violin and for piano, *Variations for Orchestra*

Chamber music: 12, including 5 string quartets, a string sextet, a wind quintet, a string trio

Piano music: 6 sets, comprising 21 pieces (*Five Piano Pieces*, 1923)

Miscellaneous works: among them, 16 choral works and a symphonic cantata (*Gurrelieder*)

All of Schoenberg's music depends upon motivic development in a contrapuntal framework whose texture and rhythm vary constantly. His early works were composed in a post-Wagnerian chromatic idiom (*Transfigured Night*, 1899). Further chromaticism led to his atonal period, from 1907 to 1915 (*Erwartung*), followed by eight years in which no works were completed. After 1923, most of his compositions employ the 12-tone method (*Suite for Piano*, Op. 25). In his later years his music occasionally used the phrase structure, regular rhythm, and forms of traditional Western music.

Career Although Schoenberg studied counterpoint with Alexander von Zemlinsky, he was largely self-taught as a composer. As a performer, he played both violin and violoncello. His father's death forced him to work as a bank clerk, then as an arranger of operettas and popular songs. He also conducted amateur choruses and light music at a cabaret; only later did he appear as a conductor of his own works. A teacher of composition for most of his life, he taught in Berlin and Vienna until 1933, when he emigrated to the United States, and then in various American universities, most notably at U.C.L.A. His compositions encountered unrelenting opposition and almost universal incomprehension throughout his life.

Maurice Ravel   French   1875–1937

Achievement

1. Ravel was one of the most famous and most accomplished composers of his time, with virtually every one of his works entering the international repertory.

2. The composer made a significant contribution to early twentieth-century piano literature, his *Jeux d'eau* (1901) opening a new era of piano sound.

Works and Style Summary   Ravel wrote about 50 compositions altogether, a small number but wide-ranging in its scope, some outstanding examples being listed below.

> *Piano music:* "Pavane pour une Infante défunte," *Jeux d'eau, Miroirs, Sonatine, Gaspard de la nuit, Valses nobles et sentimentales, Le Tombeau de Couperin*
>
> *Orchestral music: Rapsodie espagnol,* 2 piano concertos, 6 ballets (e.g., *Daphnis and Chloe*), *La Valse, Bolero*
>
> *Chamber music: String Quartet in F Major, Piano Trio,* miscellaneous sonatas
>
> *Art songs and song-cycles: Histoires naturelles, Trois Poèmes de Mallarmé, Chansons madécasses, Don Quichotte à Dulcinée* (the last three with instrumental accompaniment)

Ravel was an eclectic composer, drawing in an individual and masterful way upon elements from Impressionism (his *Jeux d'eau* was composed before the publication of Debussy's impressionistic piano works), earlier music in the Western tradition (*Le Tombeau de Couperin*), Spanish music (*Bolero*), and jazz (*Piano Concerto for the Left Hand*). He maintained a Neo-classic stance emotionally and in his use of functional harmony and clear Classical structures. On the other hand, he frequently used modality and cultivated a high degree of dissonance through use of major sevenths, minor ninths, and chords with unresolved appoggiaturas.

Career   Ravel spent sixteen years at the Paris Conservatory, where he studied composition with Fauré (among others) and became a capable pianist and conductor. Although he tried again and again, he never won the coveted Prix de Rome. He was able to devote his life almost entirely to composition, his appearances as a pianist (accompanying his own songs) and as a conductor of his own music being infrequent.

STRING QUARTET IN F MAJOR

Historical Perspective   The *String Quartet* was Ravel's first important chamber piece. It was composed in 1902–03 and enthusiastically received during its first performance on March 5, 1904. Born in conscious competition with Debussy's *String Quartet* of 1894, the *String Quartet in F Major* won more praise from Debussy than from its dedicatee, Gabriel Fauré. With characteristic modesty, Ravel said that "my Quartet . . . responds to a desire for musical construction, which undoubtedly is inadequately realized, but which emerges more clearly than in my preceding compositions."

Description of Style   All of Ravel's works reveal the composer's fascination with timbre and his penchant for exercising his performers' virtuosity. In the *Quartet* are found frequent use of pizzicato and tremolo, as well as of mutes (II and III), of harmonics (IV), of playing on the fingerboard (I and IV), and of playing near the nut of the bow (*en talon*). The instruments are treated equally, with much changing of registers and contrapuntal exchanging of thematic material. Meticulously indicated changes of dynamics occur every few measures. The composer's melodies are basically diatonic, with relatively little use of chromaticism and none of the whole-tone scale. Use of modality (II, aeolian) brings some variety of pitch materials. Except for the first movement, meters change often and are sometimes irregular (IV, 5/8). Tempo modifications, like those for dynamics, are very numerous. Dissonance reaches a high level in the *Quartet*, often being unresolved. Chords are usually built in thirds, including seventh-chords (many non-dominant), ninth-, eleventh-, and even thirteenth-chords. Frequently, they come about through rich contrapuntal writing. Despite the amount of dissonance, Ravel's harmonic rhythm and the nature of his chord progressions remain largely traditional and predictable.

Analysis of Structure   The *Quartet* unfolds in the conventional four-movement plan of the Classical period, but with the usual order of the second and third movements reversed. The first movement offers a clearly-articulated sonata form: Exposition (1st theme, mm. 1–54; 2nd theme, 55–83), Development (84–128), and Recapitulation (1st theme, 129–183; 2nd theme, 184–213). In the Recapitulation, the return of the second theme at the same pitch level but in the tonic key (as opposed to the relative minor of the Exposition) constitutes a favorite Ravel device. In the second movement, a scherzo-like ternary form (Fast–Slow–Fast), a similar device of varied repetition is found in which a theme and its accompaniment return (52–59) virtually unaltered in notation but with a different key signature and accidentals than on its first statement (13–20). At least one theme in each movement seems to grow from the same melodic or rhythmic material that begins the composition. The third movement, another ternary form (1–64, 65–80, 81–119), offers a particularly clear reference to the unifying theme in measures 19–20 and many times thereafter. For his Finale, Ravel wrote a rondo in which the unifying theme of the *Quartet* provides contrast to the movement's principal theme in 5/8 meter.

Igor Stravinsky   Russian   1882–1971

Achievement

1. Perhaps the greatest composer of the twentieth century, Stravinsky was probably the most versatile and certainly one of the most influential. His impact stemmed principally from his emancipation of rhythm, his orchestration (especially his use of instrumental soloists), his revival of traditional forms and styles, his use of folk, popular, and jazz elements, and his ultimate recourse to serial techniques. One of his most remarkable gifts was that of realizing in sound the movements of dance.

2. Stravinsky wrote copiously about his life, his aesthetics, his own music and that of others (*Chronicles of My Life*, 1936; *The Poetics of Music*, 1942; nine volumes in collaboration with Robert Craft).

Works and Style Summary

Orchestral works: c. 50, including 13 ballets (especially *The Firebird*, *Petrushka*, and *Le sacre du printemps*), 7 concertos, 3 symphonies

Chamber music: c. 30 works, including instrumental pieces (*Octet*) and vocal pieces

Operas: 4, particularly *The Rake's Progress* (1951), his only full-length opera and his longest composition, and the opera-oratorio *Oedipus Rex* (1927)

Religious works: c. 15 for voices and instruments (*Symphony of Psalms*, 1930)

Miscellaneous works: several piano pieces (2 sonatas, and 2 works for two pianos), and several songs, among other works

Stravinsky's style continually changed and yet always remained distinctive and individual, drawing upon folksong (*The Nightingale*), popular dances and the march (*The Soldier's Tale*, 1918), and jazz sonorities (*Ebony Concerto*). He also found congenial the forms and styles of earlier periods of Western music, including the Romantic (*The Fairy's Kiss*), Baroque (*Dumbarton Oaks Concerto*), Classical (*Symphony in C*), and Renaissance (*Monumentum pro Gesualdo*) periods. The closing portion of his career found him adapting to his purposes the serial technique, as in *A Sermon, a Narrative, and a Prayer* (1961). The composer's style is characterized by novel rhythmic procedures, such as irregular and changing meters, unpredictable application of accents, motoric use of rhythm, and frequent use of ostinatos. Whether large (as in the early works) or small and soloistic, his uniquely brilliant orchestration is always fully integrated into the compositional idea. His highly dissonant harmonic language, which becomes bitonal at times, is generally oriented towards unifying "poles," or central pitches. As for structure, the composer often builds in an episodic manner by fragmentation, rearrangement, and superimposition of thematic units. According to Stravinsky, his works do not indulge in the expression of emotion; the listener is perhaps the final judge on this point.

Career   Stravinsky studied with Rimsky-Korsakov from 1903 to 1908. His association with Sergei Diaghilev and the Russian ballet (mainly from 1909 to 1923) brought him recognition with *The Firebird* (1910) and international fame with *Petrushka* (1911) and *The Rite of Spring* (1913). His works eventually earned him wealth enough to be a full-time composer, doing other things when and as he desired. From 1910 to 1918 he lived mostly in Switzerland, then from 1920 to 1939 in France, beginning a concert career as a conductor and a pianist in 1924. In 1939 he emigrated to the United States, from which — as the most famous composer in the world — he often visited Europe, even Russia (1962), and did much guest conducting in his later years.

Alban Berg   Austrian   1885–1935

Achievement

1. Berg applied the twelve-tone method with freedom and frequent recourse to traditional forms, creating an individual style with a post-Romantic warmth of expression.

2. He composed two operas that are among the last that have entered the standard repertory, and his *Violin Concerto* and *Lyric Suite* have done so as well.

3. The composer was a notable apostle of dodecaphony, both as a disciple and defender of Schoenberg and as a teacher. He was one of the founders of the Society for Private Musical Performances in Vienna.

Works and Style Summary

Operas: Wozzeck (1921) and *Lulu* (1935, orchestration unfinished)
Orchestral music: Violin Concerto (1935), *Three Orchestral Pieces*
Art songs: among them, *Seven Early Songs, Four Songs* (Op. 2), *Altenberg Lieder* (Op. 4, with orchestra), *Der Wein* (concert aria)
Piano music: Piano Sonata, Op. 1
Chamber music: Chamber Concerto for piano, violin, and 13 winds, two string quartets (including the *Lyric Suite*)

Berg gradually abandoned the tonal style he derived from the late music of Wagner and Mahler (*Seven Early Songs*) in favor of atonality (in the fourth of *Four Songs*) and, ultimately, dodecaphony ("Schliesse mir die Augen beide," 1925). His twelve-tone music is noteworthy for its lyrical warmth and dramatic tension as well as for its singular use of the method. His cultivation of large-scale works, his classical approach to form, and his frequent use of tone-centers have also helped to make his works more widely accepted and performed than those of Schoenberg or Webern.

> Not a measure in this music of ours—no matter how complicated its harmonic, rhythmic, and contrapuntal texture—but has been subjected to the sharpest control of the outer and the inner ear, and for the meaning of which, in itself and in its place in the whole, we do not take the artistic responsibility.[6]

Career   Berg was self-taught until he became a student (1904–11) and friend of Schoenberg. He worked for Universal Edition, a music publishing firm (1911–1915), and taught privately in Vienna. When he became famous with *Wozzeck*, which was first performed in 1925, he subsequently devoted himself to composition. Only a fair pianist, he wrote articles and gave lectures on new music.

VIOLIN CONCERTO
The score is published by Universal Edition (Vienna, 1936).

Historical Perspective   Berg's *Violin Concerto*, his last composition, was commissioned by Louis Krasner in February of 1935 and completed in August of the same year. It was not performed until about four months after Berg's death, when Krasner played it for the International Society for Contemporary Music festival at Barcelona on April 19, 1936. The death of young Manon Gropius, daughter of Alma Mahler, in April of 1935 caused Berg to make this concerto a requiem for her. The composition is dedicated to "the memory of an angel" as well as to the violinist.

Description of Style   The orchestra required by Berg is not large, consisting of five-part strings plus harp, woodwinds basically in groups of three, brasses in

---

[6]Berg, "What Is Atonal," a radio talk given in 1930, as translated in Nicolas Slonimsky, *Music since 1900.* Fourth ed. (New York: Charles Scribner's Sons, 1971), pp. 1311–1315.

pairs plus two additional horns and a tuba, and a percussion section augmented by a deep tamtam and a high gong. Noteworthy are the imaginatively handled part for alto saxophone and the care with which the tone-row is employed for idiomatic violin passagework. The composer generally uses timbre to articulate structure and only rarely suggests *Klangfarbenmelodie*, a technique of varying the tone color of each successive pitch.

Analysis of Structure   The tone row on which the concerto is based begins with eight ascending thirds, these forming alternating minor and major triads and being identical in retrograde; it closes with three whole-tone steps, also ascending and also the same in retrograde. Other principal themes are a Carinthian folksong and a chorale melody. Although these themes offer strong contrast to those generated entirely by the row, each shares with it an important motive — a major triad in the case of the folk melody, and a series of whole-tone steps in the chorale tune. Berg alters the row by changing the order and number of intervals employed in a theme, by changing melodic contour, and by varying the rhythm (by augmentation and diminution). Climaxes are achieved by rhythmic as well as dynamic intensification, whether by progressive subdivision of the beat (including triplets, as in Part I of the concerto) or by prominent dotted rhythms (climax of Part II Allegro).

The quasi-tonal use of the row, which contains major, minor, augmented, and diminished triads as well as seventh chords, serves as a point of contact between the traditional melodies and the dodecaphonic ones. Because Berg avoids cadences and emphasizes fourths and sevenths in the harmony, however, his progressions do not normally arouse or satisfy tonal expectations. Berg's mastery of counterpoint — including inversion, stretto, pedal point, and canonic imitation — is amply demonstrated in the chorale variations of Part II.

The concerto is in two parts or movements, each of which is constructed in two sections. The opening Andante ("Preludium") is ternary (mm. 11–37, 38–83, 84–103), with a short introduction and a transition leading to the Allegretto (Scherzo). The Scherzo is symmetrical in design but asymmetrical in proportion: A (mm. 104–36), B (137–54), C (155–66), B' (167–72), A' (173–257). The last section is expanded by introduction of the Carinthian folksong (m. 213).

The second part of the concerto opens with a ternary Allegro (marked "always rubato and free like a cadenza") divided as follows: measures 1–43, 44–95, 96–135. Following a grand climax in measure 125, it leads directly into the closing Adagio. Here, after variations on the chorale melody "Es ist genug" (the initial statement being in Bach's setting for Cantata No. 60), Berg leads directly from the chorale melody to a return of the folksong (m. 202) and ultimately to a return of the row itself and of the material from the opening measures of the composition.

Edgard Varèse   French   1883–1965

Achievement

1. An important pioneer, Varèse explored new (including electronic) sources of musical sound. He was the first composer systematically to exploit percussion and to raise rhythm to an equal plane with pitch.

2. Varèse worked tirelessly on behalf of new music, including that of other composers; he founded choruses, orchestras, and concert societies for that purpose.

Works and Style Summary The composer's early works were mostly destroyed or left unpublished. His legacy comprises just 12 highly distinctive pieces, among them the following:

Amériques (1921, revised in 1927), written for an enormous orchestra including 11 percussionists

Hyperprism (1923), for 9 winds and 7 percussionists

Arcana (1927), for very large orchestra

Ionisation (1931), for 41 percussion instruments (13 percussionists) and 2 sirens

Density 21.5 (1936, rev. 1946), for unaccompanied flute

Déserts (1954), for 20 instrumentalists playing winds and percussion, plus tape

Poème électronique (1958) a tape recording with electronic sounds, noises, bells, voices, and piano

Nocturnal I (left incomplete), for solo soprano, chorus of basses, and orchestra, on Anais Nin's *House of Incest*

Varèse concentrated upon finding new means of expression in the areas of tone color and rhythm. He used new sonorities drawing from conventional instruments by using unusual combinations of timbre and density based on the laws of resonance. Rhythm was predicated upon the alternation and variation of rhythmic cells. Later he combined noise with the sounds of conventional instruments, finally employing electronic sounds. Varèse mistrusted all systems of composing.

> When new instruments will allow me to write as I conceive it, taking the place of the linear counterpoint, the movement of the sound-masses, of shifting planes, will be clearly perceived. When these sound-masses collide, the phenomena of penetration or repulsion will seem to occur. Certain transmutations taking place on certain planes will seem to be projected onto other planes, moving at different speeds and at different angles. There will no longer be the old conception of melody or interplay of melodies. The entire work will be a melodic totality. The entire work will flow as a river flows. (From a lecture given by Varèse in 1936 entitled "New Instruments and New Music.")[7]

Career Varèse studied mathematics and the natural sciences before working at the Schola Cantorum in Paris with d'Indy and Roussel in 1904 and at the Paris Conservatory with Widor in 1905. From 1906 to 1914 he composed, founded choruses, and conducted in Paris and Berlin. Moving to New York, he was active there from 1916 to 1936 (except for 1928–33 in Paris), founding the New Symphony Orchestra (1919), and the International Composers' Guild (1921). The period from 1937 to 1949 found him teaching as well as trying to develop an electronic instrument for composing. After 1950, he finally saw the appearance of some of his compositions on phonograph recordings; he continued to teach, while

[7]Benjamin Boretz and Edward T. Cone (eds.), *Perspectives on American Composers* (New York: W. W. Norton, 1971), p. 25.

working on electronic music in various studios and laboratories. In the last years of his life came some degree of recognition, perhaps still incommensurate with the achievements that had won him the respect of Debussy, Schoenberg, Stravinsky, Boulez, Cage, and Stockhausen.

Elliott Carter   American   1908-

Achievement

1. Carter has won his high reputation largely through the quality of his music alone, several works being commonly regarded as indispensable of their kind (among them, the three string quartets, *Variations for Orchestra, Double Concerto for Harpsichord and Piano,* and *Brass Quintet*).
2. He has been a leader in exploring the realm of rhythm through his treatment of simultaneous large-scale rhythmic levels and his use of metric modulation (a gradual change of tempo expressed in terms of note-values).
3. Carter has been one of the most articulate of contemporary composers, expressing his views in various writings and interviews (among them, *Flawed Words and Stubborn Sounds; a Conversation with Elliott Carter,* edited by Allen Edwards, 1971).

Works and Style Summary   The composer has written relatively little, but in virtually all genres, including songs, choruses, ballets, opera, oratorio, and symphony. He is best known for his instrumental music, especially the chamber music — 3 string quartets (1951; 1959; 1971) and a *Brass Quintet* (1974) — and a small number of large-scale works — *Variations for Orchestra* (1955), *Double Concerto for Harpsichord and Piano* (1961), *Piano Concerto* (1966), and *Concerto for Orchestra* (1969).

From modest Neo-classical beginnings, Carter forged an individual and complex contrapuntal style that eventually absorbed serialism and displayed novel elements in the realms of instrumentation and rhythm, among them metric modulation and a complex use of polyrhythms. In each work the composer seems to set specific compositional problems for himself and then work them out, or at least reconcile conflicting materials.

Career   Carter studied first at Harvard with Walter Piston, and later with Gustav Holst and Nadia Boulanger; still, he seems to have worked out his style for and by himself. After serving as musical director of the Ballet Caravan, he has spent most of his career teaching composition at such institutions as Columbia, Yale, Cornell, and Juilliard, while always reserving the time and energies necessary for his creative work.

Krzysztof Penderecki   Polish   1933-

Achievement   Penderecki has composed several works that have entered the international repertory and, through their success, he has brought avant-garde sounds before a wide and appreciative public.

Works and Style Summary   Although some of his works employ electronic (*Psalmus,* 1961) and concrete (*Fluorescences,* 1961) sound sources, Penderecki has composed mainly for conventional instruments and for voices.

> *Vocal music:* c. 15 works, among them *Psalmy Dawida* (1958) for chorus and percussion; the *St. Luke Passion* (1965) for soloists, chorus, and orchestra; *Utrenia* (1971) for 2 choruses and orchestra
>
> *Dramatic works: The Devils of Loudun* (1969) and *Paradise Lost* (1978)
>
> *Orchestral works:* c. 25, including *Anaklasis (1960),* for strings and percussion, *Threnody for the Victims of Hiroshima* (1960), for 52 strings, *Violin Concerto* (1963), *De natura sonoris* I (1966), *Symphony No. 1* (1973), *Symphony No. 2* (1980)
>
> *Chamber music:* 2 string quartets (1960, 1968)

Following a period in the 1950's as a serialist, Penderecki achieved individuality and dramatic intensity in a complex idiom that exploits and experiments with available sound resources (pitched, unpitched, microtonal, and electronic sounds); various idioms (tonal, atonal, serial); consonant and dissonant effects. He is noteworthy for the use of such string devices as **tone clusters**, glissandi, **sul ponticello** writing, and percussive effects. The chorus, too, is employed in unconventional ways. To capture his music in score, the composer adopted an optical notation with time-fields expressed in seconds. The impact of his music has been considerably abetted by his frequent use of very powerful subjects, whether religious or secular (*Threnody*), and by his turn (in the *St. Luke Passion*) towards a more direct manner of communication.

Career   Penderecki, who had studied violin by himself as a child, studied composition with Skolyszewski and then at the Krakow Conservatory with Arthur Malawski and Stanislaw Wiechowicz. His career began at a fortunate time, just as greater freedom was being granted to Polish artists and musicians. He became a teacher of counterpoint and later of composition. His compositions enabled him to travel to performances in West Germany and the United States, to attract significant commissions, to give lectures, and to live as he has wished. In 1972 he began to conduct his own works. The selection of Penderecki by the Lyric Opera of Chicago to compose an opera in honor of the American bicentennial indicates the size of his international reputation.

GLOSSARY

aleatory   refers to music in which the composer employs elements of chance, either in fashioning the composition itself or in prescribing conditions of performance, or both; also referred to as indeterminacy.

atonality   nontonal music and, in common usage, non–twelve-tone music. The term refers particularly to the pre–twelve-tone music of Schoenberg and his followers, which he preferred to describe as being "pantonal."

dodecaphonic   an ambiguous term referring to the use of the twelve chromatic pitches, but not making clear how they are being used. Nevertheless, it is commonly used synonymously with the word *serial.* (See **serial** below.)

electronic music   compositions produced exclusively by electronic means as well as some that include both electronic and natural sounds.

Expressionism   a word borrowed from art history to describe German and Austrian composers of the early twentieth century who shared a deeply subjective approach to their craft, most prominently Schoenberg and Berg.

glissando (It.)   a sliding movement through several notes of the scale.

Impressionism   a term borrowed from painting to refer to the supposedly objective tone-painting employed by Debussy. Impressionistic music is characterized by parallel chord movement, unresolved dissonance such as seventh and ninth chords, whole-tone scales, and subtle, unusual timbral effects.

indeterminacy   See **aleatory**.

musique concrète (Fr.)   music made on tape with sounds drawn from nature and man-made noises (including human voices) rather than musical instruments; often altered electronically.

Neo-classicism   a twentieth-century tendency to assume the attitude and employ the techniques and forms of pre-Romantic periods, principally Baroque and Classical.

pentatonic   refers to music which employs only (or primarily) the notes of a five-note scale.

polytonality   music in which more than one tonality is present at the same time; **bitonality** — when only two keys are employed simultaneously.

retrograde   the procedure by which a line or melody is read from the last note to the first; prominent in twelve-tone music and also found in the Renaissance.

serial   neither a system nor a style of composition, but simply music in which a fixed series of tones (usually twelve) generates the entire structure of a composition. No one set of twelve pitches is the model series, nor need the series be based on twelve. Total serialism finds the parameters of duration, timbre, dynamics, perhaps even articulation, placed in series as well. See also **twelve-tone method** and **dodecaphony**.

Sprechstimme (Ger.)   a vocal style halfway between singing and speaking, in which the voice touches the indicated pitches and then quickly moves away from them. Often found in expressionistic music.

sul ponticello (It.)   bowing a stringed instrument near the bridge.

tone cluster   the simultaneous sounding of a number of adjacent pitches.

twelve-tone method   a twentieth-century method of composition invented by Arnold Schoenberg in which one fixed form of the chromatic scale serves as the basis for a composition, subject to certain rules governing transposition of the row, among them being variation by **inversion**, **retrograde**, and retrograde inversion. See **serial**, **dodecaphonic**, and **atonal**.

whole-tone scale   a symmetrical scale made up of nothing but whole steps.

Unidentified Musical Examples

Study of both a Romantic and a Twentieth-Century anthology of music from those listed in the chapter bibliography is strongly recommended. In addition, the analytical notes for the compositions chosen to represent these periods should be read prior to studying the scores. Before attempting to identify the musical examples that follow, the Comparative Style Table for this chapter requires study. For those requiring still more assistance with a specific example, a list of hints is given below. Once again, the student should answer in writing the questions below for each mystery example:

1. What is the style period of the example, and what evidence supports your answer?
2. What kind of composition is it—Opera, symphonic piece, concerto, character piece or sonata for piano, song, chamber work, etc.?
3. Who among the major composers of the periods in question is the most likely composer?

Hints for Score Examples

Ex. 1. Note particularly the language (the original is the uppermost text), the size of the orchestra, and the ranges of the vocal parts.

Ex. 2 Find the tune (first violin part, m. 46) and sing it through. Note the nature of the accompanying keyboard part.

Ex. 3. Observe closely the orchestration; note the language of the performance indications.

Ex. 4. See particularly mm. 46 and 47, which are highly characteristic of the composer. Notice the dynamic markings and the octave passages.

Ex. 5. The title of this piece is its instrumentation. The changing and irregular meters are one of this composer's calling cards.

Ex. 6. Note the alternation of regular meters over a steady beat with much use of ostinati and a unique instrumentation. To whom do these point?

UNIDENTIFIED HISTORICAL SOURCES

After studying the opening essays and entries in Chapters 5 and 6, mark the clues in the following sources and answer the questions below. Hints are given after the sources.

1. What kind of source is it, and what is your evidence?
2. What is the style period (Early Romantic, Late Romantic, Early Twentieth Century, Middle Twentieth Century), and what is your supporting evidence?
3. Summarize the message of the source as briefly as you can.
4. What composers might be the authors of Nos. 1, 3, and 4? the subjects of Nos. 2 and 6?
5. How might you interpret or apply what you have learned from the historical source?

Consult the chapter glossaries for definitions of unfamiliar terms.

HISTORICAL SOURCE NO. 1

For me, as a creative musician, composition is a daily function that I am compelled to discharge. I compose because I am made for that and cannot do otherwise. Just as any organ atrophies unless kept in a state of constant activity, so

(continued on p. 206)

	TONE COLOR	TEXTURE	HARMONY
Early Romantic Period: 1800-60	Gradual expansion of string-dominated Classical orchestra (by adding some brasses such as trombones and making greater use of the brass timbre), partly to aid in depiction of extra-musical programs. Traditionalists (Brahms) build on Classical framework, while radicals (Berlioz) introduce special effects (mutes, col legno).	Variable, but essentially homophonic approach (largely melody with accompaniment) with richer, fuller chords and constantly changing textures, including counterpoint in development sections or for tone painting.	Harmonic color very significant, with vocabulary expanded through chromaticism, third relationships, new altered and borrowed chords (diminished sevenths and augmented sixths) — all with less resolution of dissonance and increasing instability of key.
High Romantic Period: 1860-1910	Greatly expanded orchestra in all families with love for dark colors (horn and cello) and completion of full range through contrabassoon, etc. Orchestral families used separately, intermixed, or blended with very large but also chamber effects and even soloistic use of strings. Wider range of dynamics and much concern for special effects and personal palettes (Wagner).	Greater degree of variability, perhaps linked with programmatic content; more richness through doubling, enhanced accompaniments, and revival of counterpoint (Mahler and Strauss). Parallelism and Impressionistic planing of chords (Debussy).	Proportion of dissonance growing, as composers write around dominant instead of tonic and use more 7th chords, 9ths, tritones, enharmonic relationships, and much-delayed suspensions. Obscuring of cadences, empirical harmonists (Mussorgsky), and non-functional use of chords (Debussy).
Early Twentieth-Century: 1900-50	Extremes and contrasts of color with less concern for euphony. Emancipation of percussion and use of instruments in unusual ranges with great virtuosity (Stravinsky), use of new sonorities (from folk (Copland) to "noise"), and ideal of *Klangfarbenmelodie* (Webern). Evolution of virtuoso orchestras & conductors.	Traditional textures available through Neo-classicism. Renewal of contrapuntal fabric in serialism (with new emphasis on retrograde and retrograde inversion), while Impressionistic textures remain viable.	Neo-classical music still achieves stability through consonance but within expanded contemporary vocabulary. Modal and pseudo-modal colors derive from nationalism, serialism negates tonal foundation of Western music, and eclectics draw from all sources.
Later Twentieth-Century: 1950-	Adventuring among new timbres, including electronic ones: serialized use of color and dynamics, non-pitched sounds, glissandi and special effects, pointillism, and new use of conventional instruments (as in tone clusters). Law of resonance explored and yet all the traditional possibilities remain. Timbres drawn from non-Western musics.	Extremes of density and transparency through the search for original textures produced by collage-like or over-dubbing techniques. Counterpoint remains strong as the heart of serialism. Aleatory approaches vary texture of piece with every hearing.	Co-existing remnants of traditional harmony with wide variety of new pitch-combinations, ranging from total serialism to aleatory freedom and from tone-clusters to electronically produced and mathematically determined pitch formations.

194

RHYTHM	MELODY	FORM
Wider range of pace and motion, with preference for extremes, or simply for a slower pace. Clear periodization likely in small pieces with symmetrical structures, but asymmetrical phrasing normal in larger works. Loosening of basic concept of regular pulse and firm tempo through use of rubato freedom.	Use of a wider range of pitches and moods, ranging from the intimate and the lyrical to the grand and the passionate. Phrase structure often asymmetrical and irregular. Voice dominant in vocal music, with accompaniment supportive rather than competitive.	Traditional, especially Classical, ways of organizing structure through tonal relationships and standard principles enhanced by an episodic approach to form and development of the cyclic principle and thematic transformation. Small works gathered in sets.
Greater freedom of pulse along with preference for extremes of pace and motion, for simultaneous rhythmic contrast at different levels, or simply for a slower pace. Reintroduction of cross-rhythms, hemiola, syncopation; much use of folk, march, and waltz rhythms. Adoption of poetic rhythms and rhythms drawn from East European or other folk musics.	Still larger melodic range and larger leaps, along with greater emphasis on chromaticism and thematic transformation (character variation), leading at one extreme to extraordinary lyricism. Use of folk-influenced modes and speech inflections as one aspect of irregular melos and phrasing.	Expanded time-scale reflected in innovative large-scale unity through freely-shaped dramatic intensity and graded dynamic climaxes, sometimes overlaid on greatly distended Classical formal principles. More frequent episodic quality and inception of so-called progressive tonality.
Contrasting approaches, ranging from post-Romantic character to a style based on irregular or additive meters (from nationalism) or simply emancipated from regular metric accent and periodic phrasing through polyrhythms, ostinati, and organic rhythmic cells (Stravinsky), to traditional Neo-classic use of spun-out or periodized motion.	Varied melodic styles according to orientation towards post-Romanticism, Nationalism (use of non-Western or folk-derived modes), individualistic use of fragmentation, rearrangement, and superimposition of motivic cells (Stravinsky), or Neo-classicism (with more dissonance).	Freely variational or episodic forms on a programmatic basis, architectural on symmetrical or asymmetrical basis (as in serialism or in Bartok's arch forms), organized around arbitrary pitch centers within a greatly expanded tonality. Traditional principles revive.
Retention of all traditional concepts (including ostinati, regular and irregular meters, continuous and discontinuous motion), but with renewed emphasis on the new: declamatory, serialized, and non-retrogradable rhythms, Eastern rhythmic complexity and Western polyrhythms, metric modulation, computer-dependent rhythms based upon elapsed time or fixed on tape.	All traditional scales and modes available (even together), enlargement of possibilities through Eastern influences (such as Indian ragas), synthetic modes, acoustically based new systems (Partch's 43-note octave). Highly influential mathematical approaches, including total serialization.	Renewed reliance upon traditional principles (perhaps in transformed manner), as well as use of highly intellectual (though not always inaudible) symmetrical, geometrical, and mathematical approaches. New frontiers lie in aleatory and improvisational concepts such as mobile form and procedurally controlled indeterminacy.

Ex. 1

Ex. 2

Ex. 3

Ex. 4

Ex. 5

Ex. 6

the faculty of composition becomes enfeebled and dulled unless kept up by practice
5   and effort. The uninitiated imagine that one must await inspiration in order to
create. That is a mistake; I am far from saying that there is no such thing as inspiration; quite the opposite. It is found as a driving force in every kind of human
activity, and is in no wise peculiar to artists. But that force is only brought into action by an effort, and that effort is work. Just as appetite comes by eating, so work
10   brings inspiration, if inspiration is not discernible at the beginning. But it is not simply
inspiration that counts. It is the result of inspiration — that is, the composition.
At the beginning of my career as a composer I was a good deal spoiled by the
public. Even such things as were at first received with hostility were soon afterward
acclaimed. But I have a very distinct feeling that in the course of the last fifteen
15   years my written work has estranged me from the great mass of my listeners. They
expected something different from me; . . . they are astonished to hear me speaking in another idiom. They cannot and will not follow me in the progress of my
musical thought. What moves and delights me leaves them indifferent, and what
still continues to interest them holds no further attraction for me. For that matter, I
20   believe that there was seldom any real communication of spirit between us. If it
happened — and it still happens — that we liked the same things, I very much doubt
whether it was for the same reasons. Yet art postulates communion, and the artist
has an imperative need to make others share the joy which he experiences himself.
But, in spite of that need, he prefers direct and frank opposition to apparent agree-
25   ment which is based on misunderstanding.
It is very doubtful whether Rimsky-Korsakov would have ever accepted
_____ or even _____. Is it any wonder, then, that the hypercritics of today should be dumbfounded by a language in which all the characteristics of their
aesthetics seem to be violated? What, however, is less justifiable is that they
30   nearly always blame the author for what is in fact due to their own lack of compre-
hension, a lack made all the more conspicuous because in their inability to state
their grievance clearly they cautiously try to conceal their incompetence in the
looseness and vagueness of their phraseology.
Their attitude certainly cannot make me deviate from my path. I shall as-
35   suredly not sacrifice my predilections and my aspirations to the demands of those
who, in their blindness, do not realize that they are simply asking me to go backwards. It should be obvious that what they wish for has become obsolete for me,
and that I could not follow them without doing violence to myself. But, on the
other hand, it would be a great mistake to regard me as an adherent of "Zukunfts-
40   musik" — the music of the future. Nothing could be more ridiculous. I live neither
in the past nor in the future. I am in the present. I cannot know what tomorrow will
bring forth. I can know only what the truth is for me today. That is what I am
called upon to serve, and I serve it in all lucidity.

HISTORICAL SOURCE NO. 2

The *signor Duca* Sforza-Cesarini, impresario of the aforementioned theater,
engages the *maestro* _____ for the forthcoming Carnival season of the year
1816; said _____ promises and binds himself to compose and stage the second opera (*buffa*) to be presented during the aforementioned season at the theater
5   indicated, and to whichever libretto, be it new or old, shall be given him by the
aforementioned *Duca*, impresario.
Maestro _____ binds himself to deliver the score by the middle of the
month of January and to adapt it to the voices of the singers; and further binds

himself to make all those changes which may be considered necessary both to the
10   good success of the music and to the advantage and demands of the singers.

      Maestro _____ also promises and binds himself to be present in Rome
to carry out the present contract not later than the end of the current December,
and to turn over to the copyist the first act of his opera, entirely completed, by
January 20, 1816. (January 20 is specified to the end of being able to carry out the
15   rehearsals perfectly and to be able to go on stage the day that shall please the impresario, the performance being fixed for about Feburary 5.) And also Maestro
_____ equally, must deliver his second act to the copyist at the desired time,
so that there may be time to prepare it and carry out the rehearsals early enough to
be able to go on stage on the evening indicated above; otherwise Maestro
20   _____ will expose himself to all damages, as it should be thus and not otherwise.

      Further, Maestro _____ will be obliged to conduct his opera as is cus-
tomary and to be present in person at all the vocal and orchestral rehearsals as
often as may be necessary, whether in the theater or elsewhere, at the demand of
25   the director, and also binds himself to attend the first performances to be given
consecutively and to conduct the performance at the *cembalo*, etc., because it should
be thus and not otherwise.

      In payment for his labors, the director binds himself to pay the total sum and
quantity for 400 Roman *scudi* once the first three performances that _____
30   should conduct at the *cembalo* have been concluded.

HISTORICAL SOURCE NO. 3

      I have already told you that I am at work on a great composition. Can't you
understand how that takes up all of a man? At such times I no longer belong to myself—the labor pains of the creator of such a work are terrible.

      My symphony is going to be something the like of which the world has not
5   yet heard. All nature is voiced therein, and tells of deeply mysterious matters. . . .

      I tell you, at certain passages I myself am sometimes overcome with an un-
canny feeling and can hardly believe that I could have written them. . . .

      You will see: I shall never live to see the victory of my cause. Everything I
write is too new, too strange, for the people; they find no bridge across to me,
10   because even the first that I have offered them is connected in no way with what
formerly was. My earliest works, from my study period, in which I still cling to the
past, and which were more or less of the past, have been lost, or have never been
produced. And what came later—beginning with _____—is already so
"_____-like," so sharply marked by my own style, and so different from any-
15   thing else, that there is no connection any longer. In addition to that: I have not
created much and—except for a few songs—no smaller works. Only at long intervals did I write a few—it is true—enormous works. Even Beethoven was "Mozart-
ish" at first, and Wagner leaned towards the Meyerbeer form of opera. But with me
there is nothing of the sort. All understanding between the composer and the lis-
20   tener is based on the convention that the latter approve of this or that motive or
symbol as the expression of this or that thought, or rather—in a few words—of the
spiritual content. That is particularly true of Wagner. But Beethoven also, and
more or less every other composer, has his especially accepted expression for everything he wishes to say. The people, however, have not yet accepted my language.
25   They have no idea of what I want to say, and what I feel, and it seems senseless to
them and incomprehensible. This also applies to the musicians who perform my

works; it takes them quite a time to understand me. Why must I suffer all this? Why take upon myself this fearful martyrdom? And not only for me, but for those who before me have been crucified because they wanted to give to the world their
30   best; and for all those coming after me, I feel immeasurable pain.

HISTORICAL SOURCE NO. 4

For us musicians, Beethoven's work is like the pillar of cloud and fire which guided the Israelites through the desert—a pillar of cloud to guide us by day, a pillar of fire to guide us by night, "so that we may progress both day and night." His obscurity and his light trace for us equally the path we have to follow; they are
5   each of them a perpetual commandment, an infallible revelation. Were it my place to categorize the different periods of the great master's thoughts, as manifested in his sonatas, symphonies, and quartets, I should certainly not fix the division into three styles, which is now pretty generally adopted and which you have followed; but, simply recording the questions which have been raised hitherto, I should
10   frankly weigh the great question which is the axis of criticism and of musical aestheticism at the point to which Beethoven has led us—namely, in how far is traditional or recognized form a necessary determinant for the organism of thought?
The solution of this question, evolved from the works of Beethoven himself, would lead me to divide this work, not into three styles or periods—the words *style*
15   and *period* being here only corollary subordinate terms, of a vague and equivocal meaning—but quite logically into two categories: the first, that in which traditional and recognized form contains and governs the thought of the master; and the second, that in which the thought stretches, breaks, recreates, and fashions the form and style according to its needs and inspirations. Doubtless in proceeding thus we
20   arrive in a direct line at those incessant problems of *authority* and *liberty*. But why should they alarm us? In the region of liberal arts they do not, happily, bring in any of the dangers and disasters which their oscillations occasion in the political and social world; for, in the domain of the beautiful, genius alone is the authority, and hence, dualism disappearing, the notions of authority and liberty are brought
25   back to their original identity. Manzoni, in defining genius as "a stronger imprint of Divinity," has eloquently expressed this very truth.
This is indeed a long letter, my dear Lenz, and as yet I am only at the preliminaries. Let us then pass on to the deluge—and come and see me at Weimar, where we can chat as long and fully as we like of these things in the shade of our fine
30   park. . . .

HISTORICAL SOURCE NO. 5

There seems to be something about stagnation of repertoire that breeds stagnation of performance. With constant repetition of the same works, certain approaches to their interpretation are found preferable to others and become more or less standard. Performers, thereafter, defy convention at their own risk. Most ob-
5   servers would agree, probably, that there has been the same inhibition of striking individuality among today's singers as has been noted in the work of orchestras, solo instrumentalists and conductors. The level of competence is high—possibly higher than ever—but its effectiveness is compromised by uniformity. . . .
Nor does today's singer have a viable contemporary music—as the popular
10   singer does—in which he could feel sufficiently at home stylistically to do as he pleases. . . .

And there are other restrictive factors. Not only is the repertoire of the opera house stagnant; the popularity of the song and *Lieder* recital is declining. . . . The recital, with the singer alone at the bend of the piano, solemnly progressing from
15 the seventeenth century to the twentieth through four or five groups, with only the piano as an accompanying instrument, is a trial both for the singer and for the public.

Today's singer is further handicapped by being virtually cut off from the main stream of popular music. In the eighteenth century, and well into the nine-
20 teenth, the arias from the operas of Rossini, Donizetti, Bellini and Meyerbeer were the popular music of the time. Singers offered them without shame as the principal items of their concert programs, and instrumentalists capitalized on their popularity by paraphrasing them in elaborate virtuoso potpourris. . . .

The singer of today could not be truly popular even if he had a choice; for
25 popular music is now idiomatically different from the music he has been taught to sing. . . .

Recording has created problems, too. With records being made from a selection of the best of several "takes," and with more or less splicing, the singer may find himself hard put to live up to his records in his public appearances. He is at a
30 disadvantage as his own competitor. . . .

But the basic problem is repertoire. And with the contemporary composer failing to provide a contemporary style congenial to the general operagoing public, the singer seeking an escape from the endless repetition of favorite operas of Mozart, Verdi, Strauss and Puccini has followed the example of many instrumen-
35 talists in retreating into the past.

HISTORICAL SOURCE NO. 6

The Philharmonia Orchestra devoted its entire concert to a new symphony by _____. It is the eighth in a series and similar to its predecessors in form and mood. I found this newest one, as I have found the other _____ symphonies, interesting in detail but strange as a whole and even repugnant. The
5 nature of the work consists — to put it briefly — in applying Wagner's dramatic style to the symphony.

Not only does _____ fall continually into Wagnerian devices, effects, and reminiscences; he seems even to have accepted certain Wagnerian pieces as models for symphonic construction, as, for example, the Prelude to *Tristan and*
10 *Isolde* . . . . Wagnerian orchestral effects are met on every hand, such as the tremolos of the violins *divisi* in the highest position, harp arpeggios over muffled chords in the trombones, and, added to all that, the newest achievements of the Siegfried tubas.

Also characteristic of _____'s newest symphony is the immediate juxta-
15 position of dry schoolroom counterpoint with unbounded exaltation. Thus, tossed about between intoxication and desolation, we arrive at no definite impression and enjoy no artistic pleasure. Everything flows, without clarity and without order, willy-nilly into dismal long-windedness. In each of the four movements, and most frequently in the first and third, there are interesting passages and flashes of
20 genius — if only all the rest were not there! It is not out of the question that the future belongs to this muddled hangover style — which is no reason to regard the future with envy. For the time being, however, one would prefer that symphonic and chamber music remain undefiled by a style only relatively justified as an illustrative device for certain dramatic situations.

25   Even before the performance we had heard such provocative reports of the
extraordinary profundity of the new symphony that I took care to prepare myself
through study of the score and attendance at the dress rehearsal. I must confess,
however, that the mysteries of this all-embracing composition were disclosed to me
only through the helpful offices of an explanatory programme handed to me prior
30   to the concert. The author of this dissertation is anonymous, but we easily dis-
cerned the fine hand of Schalk. From him we learned that the irksome humming
theme of the first movement represents the figure of the Aeschylean Prometheus.
An especially tiresome part of this movement is charmingly described as "most
awful loneliness and quiet."
35   What follows is even more exalted. In the Adagio we behold nothing less
than "the all-loving Father of Mankind in all His infinite mercy!" Since this Adagio
lasts exactly twenty-eight minutes or about as long as an entire Beethoven symphony, we cannot complain of being denied ample time for the contemplation of
the rare vision. At long last, the Finale — which, with its baroque themes, its con-
40   fused structure and inhuman din, strikes us only as a model of tastelessness. . . .
And the reception of the new symphony? A stormy ovation, waving of hand-
kerchiefs from the standees, innumerable recalls, laurel wreaths, etc.! For
_____ the concert was certainly a huge success. Whether Hans Richter performed a similar favor for his subscribers by devoting an entire concert to the
45   _____ symphony is doubtful. . . .

Hints for Historical Sources

1. How many famous composers achieve success early in their careers and then lose
   their audience by resolutely following their own pathways and changing their
   styles? In what ways do the attitudes of this composer represent a logical culmination of Romanticism, and in what ways do they break with it? Line 26 offers an important clue to the composer's identity: Why should he question whether Rimsky-
   Korsakov would have accepted two of his works?

2. This standard contract brought forth a very famous opera. Concentrate upon dis-
   covering and inferring from the source as much as you can about operatic life of the
   time.

3. Contrast this composer's attitude towards his creative work with that of such earlier
   musical craftsmen as Haydn and Brahms.

4. What does the author's view of Beethoven tell us about himself and about his era?
   Which features of Beethoven does he emphasize? Consider the evidence of his location (line 28), as well as his attitude towards authority and liberty in composition.

5. How valid does this statement of the case seem to you? (It is not necessary to identify the author.)

6. Solve two mysteries — the identities of composer and author. For the former, consult lines 2–13, 14–15, and 36–39; for the latter, consider his preparation for the
   concert (lines 25–27), his reasons for criticism (lines 20–24), and his fair-minded
   reporting (lines 41–45). Above all, consider him perhaps the foremost representative of his profession during his lifetime.

Chapter Seven

Writing about Music

ADVICE FOR WRITERS ON MUSIC

The key to writing lies in having something to express and in expressing it clearly. No one can learn to write well without exercising that skill. Fortunately, a steady and self-critical effort aimed at improvement will enable anyone to write adequately, and time spent with a knowledgeable teacher can work wonders. Whereas it is an arduous and sometimes fruitless task to learn how to think, it is relatively easy for someone who can think to learn how to write adequately.

Written language differs from spoken language. Spoken words are given emphasis, nuance, and rhythm, and they are accompanied by gestures. Repetition is expected in speech, and superfluous phrases are welcomed because they reduce the pace at which essential material passes. In writing, on the other hand, the choice of words, word order, and sentence and paragraph structure must communicate clearly without the aid of verbal nuances. A reader cannot be expected to divine the manner in which sentences would be spoken. Clarity of thought, logical flow from point to point, and economy of expression characterize good writing. In addition, the writer must not presume intimate acquaintance with the reader; the tone of his writing should be less familiar and somewhat more formal than his speaking.

Every writer requires a working collection of writing aids, beginning with a good dictionary and a thesaurus. Add to these a basic grammar,[1] a manual for writing research papers,[2] and — for the music student — a guide dealing with the special problems posed by writing about music.[3] Rather than an extension of this

---

[1]Highly recommended is William Strunk and E. B. White's *Elements of Style* (Macmillan).

[2]Perhaps Kate Turabian's *Manual for Writers of Term Papers, Theses, and Dissertations* (University of Chicago Press).

[3]Demar Irvine, *Writing about Music* (University of Washington Press).

list of basic books—the dedicated writer will want to investigate Wilson Follett's *Modern American Usage* (a Hill and Wang paperback), Theodore Bernstein's *The Careful Writer* (Atheneum), and others—a systematic outline summarizing the principal levels of writing may be helpful:

1. The Level of Argument and Organization
   a. Make an outline and follow it.
   b. Write a preface and a summary.
   c. Convey a message, if the project is a term paper or an essay.
2. The Level of Content and Explication
   a. Seek clarity of expression rather than eloquence, which comes unbidden if it comes at all, and use examples (including music examples) freely.
   b. Keep paragraphs to a reasonable length, and use topical and transitional phrases or sentences between one subject and the next.
   c. Footnote derivative material if it is not general knowledge.
3. The Level of Grammar and Good Sentence Structure
   a. Consult a good grammar book frequently and punctuate consistently.
   b. Strive for a balance between simple, compound, and complex sentences.
   c. Revise and rewrite sentences until they are as clear as possible.
4. The Level of Style and Manner
   a. Avoid intimidating or offending the reader by overestimating or underestimating his knowledge, or by using informal writing, colloquialisms, and such pointing phrases as "it is interesting to note that."
   b. Write with active verbs and nouns rather than with adjectives and adverbs, and do not rely too much upon the verbs *to be* and *to have*.
   c. Search for exactly the right word, consulting a dictionary or a thesaurus as needed.
5. The Level of Typing and Typography
   a. Follow the rules for writing a paper, as set forth in a source such as Turabian's *Manual for Writers of Term Papers, Theses, and Dissertations*.
   b. Spell words correctly, using a dictionary when necessary.
   c. Revise, rewrite, and proofread the paper several times with self-critical eyes.

Perhaps the major difficulty for a student is accounting for sources of information. No paper can be better than its sources. Not only must they be selected wisely, but what they say must be carefully separated from what the student says. Whereas general knowledge does not call for a footnote, a writer must not pass off another's ideas or points of view (and certainly not his words or phrases) as the writer's own. The ability to determine what constitutes general knowledge provides the best indication of a writer's mastery of a subject.

Learning by experience in writing is not the only way. Reading widely will expand the reader's vocabulary, offer common word-patterns and sentence constructions for his assimilation, and demonstrate the workings of prose logic. If his critical sense remains alert, the reader will also learn what to avoid in his own writing. The examples of writing that follow have the dual purpose of exemplifying the kinds of projects a music student might undertake and at the same time serving as objects for the student's own criticism; the author's critical comments appear in Appendix 1.

SMALL-SCALE WRITING PROJECTS

The historical research paper constitutes the traditional task for the music history student. For the advanced student, and even then only with close supervision and guidance, it remains valuable. Like the traditional textbook, however, it places the kinds of burdens upon an undergraduate that he is least able to bear. Instead of thinking about and assimilating new material, the student usually wastes his energies ploughing through endless sources and struggling with the demands of English composition. The dispassionate investigation and scholarly presentation of intellectually worthy research subjects is perhaps the most demanding form of writing about music. It is work for the scholar or the incipient scholar, not the average student of music. Rather than encouraging the student to form his own views on matters of some individual concern, the usual term paper demands application of historical perspective and synthesis far beyond his present powers. In addition, the term research paper represents a large-scale effort with at best only one opportunity for constructive criticism, and usually none at all for demonstrating subsequent improvement of skills. How much better to receive criticism for several small-scale projects calling for gradual development of his present capabilities.

What is required for most students of music history and literature are small-scale projects that remove the emphasis from scholarly judgment and place it upon listening or reading experience and competent expression of independent critical judgment. A student should first learn about the field—about music itself and about books on music—before being asked to don the mantle of omniscient scholarly objectivity. The first stage of the student's development might well be choosing a subject—say, a composer's music or a genre—and gathering information on it. Either an annotated bibliography or an annotated discography would serve this purpose well. For the second stage, a comparative study that deals with and, if possible, reconciles conflicting viewpoints is recommended; a suitable study would be either a comparative discography or a comparative bibliography. Finally, the student would take full responsibility for formulating and working out a thesis or subject of his own, perhaps in the form of an essay. If the student is principally a performer, a well-conceived concert program relevant to the thesis and accompanied by program notes would be an admirable project. Any of the types of projects discussed below can be adapted to suit most subjects and, with care, any of the stages of development explained above.

1) ANNOTATED BIBLIOGRAPHY

An annotated bibliography is a list of books and articles with commentary by the reader, including an explanatory preface and closing summary. Commentary normally includes criticism as well as a summary of the source's contents. Because it is oriented by subject and requires review of several or many books, it is a better learning tool than a book review. Like an annotated discography, it permits focus upon survey or comparison. For a student weak in music history, a very fruitful task is to compare the treatment of a specified period of music history in several standard books on the subject. Following the sample preface and entries for an annotated bibliography on *bel canto* given below, the reader is asked to consult the critical comments appended on page 222.

An Annotated Bibliography on the Subject of *Bel Canto*

Preface

While compiling this annotated bibliography, I became aware of the many divergent opinions held by singers, singing teachers, and musicologists concerning the term *bel canto* (beautiful singing). What was *bel canto* and when did it flourish? The term has been variously defined as a vocal method (referring to voice production), as a style (which was florid and embellished by ornaments), and as vocal concept (that is, round pear-shaped tone); on the other hand, it has been renounced as simply a myth. Conflicting opinions are also held concerning the period of music history in which *bel canto* actually existed, if it did indeed exist. To some writers, the only true *bel canto* period was during the Baroque and early Classical periods, when the celebrated *castrati* (male sopranos) dominated the operatic stage. Other writers feel that two periods can be distinguished, the aforementioned "early" *bel canto* period and the so-called "Golden Age" of Rossini, Bellini, and Donizetti. Still others contend that we are now in the midst of a *bel canto* revival, one marked by the artistry of such singers as Callas, Sutherland, Horne, Sills, and Caballé.

Because I feel that there is some validity in each of these viewpoints, and because many of the relevant books and articles present more than one concept of *bel canto* (for example, a book may be basically a *bel canto* method-book and yet may also stress appropriate style and the concept of beautiful tone), I have tried to select writings that represent each of these different approaches. The literature has been organized in four sections, the first being devoted to material that introduces the reader to the various definitions of *bel canto*. Sections II (Baroque–early Classical) and III (Romantic) are each subdivided into two groups: the first deals primarily with voice production, while the second deals with history, style, and performance practice. In each section, books are listed first, followed by periodicals, both materials in alphabetical order. Section IV deals with the twentieth-century renaissance of beautiful singing. It is hoped that the variety of views represented in the selected literature will enable the reader to draw his own conclusions about *bel canto*.

Sample Entries

Reid, Cornelius L. *Bel Canto Principles and Practices.* New York: The Joseph Patelson Music House, 1972 (reprinted from a 1950 edition). 202 pp.

A comprehensive treatment of *bel canto*. In the first five chapters, Reid discusses the history of *bel canto*, the *bel canto* ideal, and the basic principles of *bel canto*. Chapters six through nine deal with vocal training in a format based upon the teachings of Pietro Tosi and Giambattista Mancini. Vocal registers, scales and exercises, vibrato, and problems such as tremolo and wobble are discussed. "Decline of *Bel Canto*" and "Science vs. Early Tradition" are the titles of the last two chapters.

"What Cornelius Reid has to say about the principles on which the concept of *bel canto* rests is sound and valuable . . . . How successful the author has been in describing procedures designed to assist the student in learning how to sing beautifully is another matter." (Sergius Kagen in the February 24, 1951 *Saturday Review of Literature*.)

Donington, Robert. *The Interpretation of Early Music.* Second edition. London: Faber & Faber, 1965. 580 pp.

An exhaustive treatment of performance practices in early music. Similar in format to the same author's *Performer's Guide to Baroque Music,* this book is divided into sections covering "Style," "The Notes" (accidentals, embellishments, and accompaniment), "Expression," and "Instruments." It also contains an appendix with examples of ornamentation.

Of particular interest is Chapter LV (Book IV), "The Voice," which includes sections on "The Italian 'Bel Canto'," "Early Vocal Technique," and "The Castrato Voice." Part II, "Embellishment," contains the following noteworthy chapters: Chapter IX, which includes a section entitled "Vocal Ornamentation in Early Baroque Music," and Chapter XII, "The Cadenza."

Covering as it does 150 years of performance practices, this book is considered a standard on the subject. "Donington illustrates how performance can approach 'authenticity' by combining the results of exact research . . . with those of practical musicianship . . . . Although it is largely a work for scholars, it contains much of interest for performers and listeners." (*Economist,* September, 1974.)

Casselman, Eugene, "The Secret of Bel Canto," *Etude,* LXVIII, No. 9 (September, 1950), 20–22.

A summary of the basic principles and points of agreement of the so-called Old Italian Method of singing as indicated in the writings of Bovicelli, Caccini, Tosi, and Mancini. Casselman feels that a study of the old masters' writings is invaluable because "despite efforts to find a 'scientific' singing method," traditional rules of thumb remain the safest guide for teachers and students. "No one has explained how to teach singing any more clearly than the old masters, who hardly explained it at all."

2) ANNOTATED DISCOGRAPHY

An annotated discography is a list of phonograph recordings with critical commentary, again including an explanatory preface and closing summary. It may be a survey of a composer's works, or a performer's or conductor's career, or a genre (perhaps within one historical period), or a historical period. Or it may be of a comparative nature, comprising several different recordings of the same work or for the same medium (for example, violin). An annotated discography is a useful project for the inexperienced listener and writer. If it leads to research, as it should, it may require a bibliography and footnotes. There follows a portion of a comparative discography as an example for the reader to criticize and compare with the discussion and revision of the example in the Appendix (p. 222).

J. S. Bach's *Toccata and Fugue in D Minor* — A Comparative Discography

Preface

Coming from a small-town environment, my experience with music has been as a performer, not a listener. What I don't know about the subject would fill many volumes. In approaching the individual evaluations, I didn't try to compare every measure, but I tried to point out the things I didn't like, the really excellent passages, and the sections that differed most from version to version. I feel that although this piece is highly sectional, it is a musical whole and should be treated as

such. Changes in tempo should all be done in relation to what has come before. Ideally, it should be performed on a tracker organ, but I tried to remember that this is an ideal. I didn't comment too much on registration unless it was exceptional
10   (good or bad). I'm still not confident enough to say exactly what was being used. My main interest in this project was to see how other people played a work which I had studied and performed myself. This strongly implies a lot of subjectivity, but I tried to support my opinion with specific references and musical examples. I've tried in addition to take into account various ways of interpreting Bach. Whenever
15   I refer to the "traditional" method, it takes into account many years of learning how certain articulations are done and where they occur; why Bach isn't like Beethoven; what a tracker organ is and how it effects Baroque music; etc. All of this plus practical experience aided in my evaluations.

        This is a magnificent piece of music, and I tried to make a comparison of the
20   performance as a whole before dealing with specifics. There are no tables of tempo comparisons, because as a toccata and a fugue with a toccata-like ending, it is supposed to sound improvisatory. The tempo (and the dynamics, for that matter) vary not only between sections but within the sections themselves as well. Yet, as I mentioned before, in performance it's sections should create one musical whole.
25   Because of this undertaking, I feel that now, I could perform the work with more sensitivity and teach it with more understanding.

Sample Entry

"Bach Live in Los Angeles." Harvey Schmiffmeier, organist. Tape manufactured by Aztec LS-260. (c. 1973?)
        I must admit that before I heard this recording I was very biased against the performer, and this tape confirmed my prejudices. Besides some flaws in the tape itself, he does some perfectly awful things. This piece is preceded by a speech in which he says that purists (referring to interpreting Bach) are totally wrong be-
5   cause Bach was a living, feeling human being. Now, I am not a purist, but I do believe that Bach did not write like Chopin or Beethoven nor is he to be interpreted as if he had written that way. However, the performer proceeded to play a *very* romanticized and *very* dramatic *Toccata and Fugue in D Minor*. For example: he uses the swell pedal on the arpeggiated chords in measures 2 and 10 in the toccata. There is
10   a lot of accelerando and ritards to the point of where the piece loses its rhythmic playfulness. Also, there was much manual change; sometimes without any apparent reason.
        In the prestissimo, all concept of a beat was missing. It was a mass of fast-moving notes. The registration throughout the toccata was so loud and massive
15   that it overwhelmed you. He started the recitative and presto sections *very* slow and then accelerated into them. Before the subject is stated for the last time, there was a huge ritard and decrescendo. The vivace section was not vivace but very slow and deliberate. The thirty-second notes in the vivace section were sounded together instead of being clearly separated and were played on a softer manual. Instead of try-
20   ing to interpret Bach, the performer has set about to defy a composer and his style of writing. The former can be forgiven; the latter cannot.

3) CONCERT REVIEW

For stirring up controversy and student interest, nothing can compare with the concert review. Concerts by visiting performers are highly recommended as sources for review. There should also be an extensive training period—one spent partly in consulting published reviews. To be acquired are good taste in the expression of opinion, an understanding that evidence must support opinion, and a realization that a reviewer functions as an educator, a reporter, and perhaps even as a propagandist as well as a critic. Comments upon the following sample review may be found in the Appendix (p. 227).

A Review of a Percussion Recital

Despite the lack of stage help and the obvious lack of preparation on the part of the two accompanists, the recital given Tuesday evening, July —, by John Doe, percussionist, was quite an enjoyable experience. While it was merely unfortunate that Doe had to do all the stage work, it was totally inexcusable for the two accompanists to be so unprepared.

The concert began with John Bergamo's *Four Pieces for Timpani*. This is one of the few technically demanding yet musically interesting compositions that exist in the concert timpanist's repertory. Doe's performance of this piece would have proved to the world just how sensitive and meticulous a musician he is, had there been more than about forty people at his recital.

The second selection was Donald Erb's *Diversions for Two (other than sex)*. Doe performed this piece, written for multiple percussion and trumpet, with Wes Jones. This same duo had turned in a quality performance of *Diversions* last spring in a recital of contemporary music, however Jones had apparently not looked at the music since then.

The next piece on the program stole the show. *Liaisons* by Roman Haubenstock-Ramati is a no-nonsense, quasi-improvisational piece with many specified options open to the performer. In his interpretation Doe played the score backwards (counterclockwise) on vibraphone simultaneously with a prerecorded frontwards version realized on marimba. The effect was hypnotic, to say the least, the audience loved it, calling back Doe for two extra rounds of applause.

Doe and James Smith, alto saxophonist, opened the second half of the concert with George Heussenstamm's *Playphony, Opus 56,* a demanding, high-energy composition that these two players had premiered last spring in Kansas City. Last night it died. It died not from exhaustion but from Smith's obvious lack of interest and preparation. Throughout the performance Doe's exciting percussion lines were answered by Smith's dull and lackluster playing. Perhaps Smith just had an off night; this was the worst I have ever heard him play.

The concert ended with Doe's realization of *The King of Denmark* by Morton Feldman. This sensitive, ethereal bit of music explores the dynamic range from *p* to *pppp*. Here, Doe's playing (all done with the fingers) was definitely too loud, thereby mitigating the most important effect of the composition.

The highest praise goes to John Doe for his excellent selection of idiomatic music for percussion. I believe that this was the first percussion recital that I have heard without having to endure a transcription of "Greensleeves" or the like. Also of special note in this recital was Doe's effective staging. In addition to efficiently manipulating percussion instruments here and there, in itself quite a chore, Doe's use of lighting was very striking. Especially interesting was the use of two candles next to the vibraphone in *Liaisons*. The title of this piece took on an extra meaning when Doe extinguished the first candle after the taped part was finished and then blew out the remaining candle after his part was through. The effect on the audience was remarkable.

4) PROGRAM NOTES

Carefully researched and written program notes constitute a difficult assignment that encompasses the roles of music historian, music theorist, and music educator. At their highest level they are not merely informative but enlightening or at least thought-provoking, not merely descriptive of the music but analytical and penetrating. One of the greatest obstacles to writing good program notes is poorly conceived programs. Often the only cohesive point has to do with displaying a medium or an instrument through various historical periods. Almost as often the performers play or sing each work in precisely the same style. Nevertheless, a writer must seek a unifying thread or theme around which to focus his program notes. Whatever his difficulties, he must always remember to consider the level of his readers. After studying the program notes below, consult the Appendix (p. 227) for a critical commentary.

Sonata for Violin and Piano (Op. 47, the "Kreutzer") . . . .
. . . . Ludwig van Beethoven (1770–1827)
        Perhaps the greatest revolutionaries are those who transform their worlds from within, never ceasing to communicate with their contemporaries and yet bearing them, mostly unwilling, irresistibly along whatever paths genius dictates. So it was with Beethoven. His revolution lay in wedding his radically new seriousness of purpose to a self-conscious and truly Romantic view of music as a mode of self-expression. But his lines of communication with the listening public were firmly laid on the foundation of Classical tradition. The *Kreutzer Sonata* (1803) was written just before the composer's boldest work, the *Eroica Symphony*, and shares its indomitable vigor and its expansion (not explosion) of Classical concepts. Witness the juxtaposition of extreme dynamic levels, the sudden changes of tempo within movements, the sharp contrasts between principal themes, and the masterful manipulation of harmonic rhythm. Here is a brave new world of expression, and yet it is carved in the sturdy Classical molds of the sonata form (for the outer movements) and the theme with variations (for the middle movement). And witness the players exhibiting prowess hitherto reserved for the solo concerto. In fact, Beethoven's subtitle describes the composition as being "written in a very *concertante* style, like that of a concerto." Here is clearly discernible a factor of increasing technical proficiency that will eventually divide composers and performers into separate races of non-performing composers and non-composing performers. It seems ironic that a style aimed so successfully at captivating a larger audience should bring about the separation and, in the twentieth century, the alienation of the non-performing composer from that audience.

Sonata for Violin and Piano (Op. 13) . . . . Gabriel Fauré (1845–1924)
        Fauré was a traditionalist. How else explain a Romantic composer whose chamber works are comparable in number and scope to the chamber music of Schumann and Brahms? The extramusical appeal of program music had long since begun to throw chamber music into the shadows when, in 1876, Fauré composed his first violin sonata. In it he retains the structural principles of the Classical period but clothes them with a Romantic warmth and surging lyricism that speaks for itself to all kinds of listeners. The dreamers can float in the clouds of strangely beautiful modulations and subtle chromaticism, reflections of the composer's expanded harmonic vocabulary within bi-modal key centers. The co-creators can discern the underlying sonata principle in the first, second, and fourth movements, and the lively scherzo with trio in the third movement.

Sonata for Violin and Piano No. 2 . . . . Bela Bartok (1881–1945)

The great violinist Joseph Szigeti wrote in his autobiography that "Bartok and I made a point of playing this sonata, admittedly one of his most adventurous and problematic works, at all of the many concerts we gave together — in Budapest, London, Paris, Rome, and also in New York." Bartok certainly did not belong to the race of nonperforming twentieth-century composers. This sonata, however, just as certainly has never captivated large audiences. Perhaps, unlike Beethoven's revolutionary works, it lacks clear ties with tradition. Not only does it represent Bartok's greatest distance from tonality, but it also evinces a considerably greater emphasis upon rhythm and sonority than upon harmonic elements. Tone clusters, polychords, quartal chords, stress upon minor ninths and tritones — all bespeak harmonic austerity. The constantly changing meters and tempi, with much use of 5/8 and 7/8 and many cross-rhythms, lend the sonata an improvisatory air, while its rigorous avoidance of thematic relationship between the instruments extends no helping hand to the listener. Given the composer's reliance upon variation and transformation of a limited number of themes and their cyclic use throughout the entire sonata, the forms of the two movements (which run together without a break) bear only the loosest relationship to the rondo principle. Even the intermittent suggestions of Hungarian dances provide little relief from Bartok's highly concentrated expressionism. Perhaps hearing this sonata may help explain why — unlike Beethoven — Bartok was unable during his lifetime to impel his listeners along the path dictated by his genius.

5) ESSAY

An essay is usually an attempt to express a writer's own ideas or views on a subject rather than a vehicle for presenting research. It may be intended primarily to inform or to persuade, and therefore require considerable research; or it may be an essay in criticism; or it may be an essay answer to an examination question. If it takes up a well-known subject, the new ideas presented and the substance of the argument will be of more importance than the actual opinion expressed, whereas a fresh thesis may be of equal value with its presentation. The less original the thesis, the better the writing must be, considered on its own merits.

Just as verbal articulation is necessary for the cultivation of fluent critical thinking and convincing expression of opinion, so essay-writing is indispensable for the achievement of a prose style with discipline, logic, organization, and eloquence. Whether for an examination or simply to capture a point of view in writing, the essay on music will benefit if the writer observes the following steps:

1. Be sure either to formulate your hypothesis clearly or to understand fully the subject you are assigned (even defining it as you understand it, if necessary).
2. Organize your essay into a logical succession of points to be made or subjects covered *before* you begin to write, including only relevant material, connecting points that may not seem clearly related to the subject, and avoiding the danger of inserting information only because you happen to know it. Afterthoughts that occur during an examination should ordinarily be placed before the summary.
3. Exemplify points made with factual material, demonstrating thereby (but not for its own sake) your mastery of relevant historical and musical data. Appropriate exemplification is the key to good essay writing.

4. Summarize your argument firmly and cogently, a vital step that is best conceived during the time of organization and not left for the end.

Two sample essays follow. Both answer the same examination question:

Describe the major changes in the nature of music patronage in the Renaissance, and then discuss in meaningful detail the effects these changes had on the development of Renaissance styles and genres.

Essay A

The only important patron of music before the Renaissance was the Roman Catholic Church. It was also the only source of music education. Since control of music lay in its hands, the Church was able to limit the growth and development of music to appropriate sacred texts and styles. After the adoption of polyphony, Mass sections, other liturgical texts, and motets were set to music in great numbers. The style of this music rested upon the use of a cantus firmus drawn from Gregorian chant. Other parts were added one by one to make up a three or four-voice texture. This manner of composing has often been called additive. It seems closely related to the carefully structured chain of the Church hierarchy. Harmony was a secondary consideration for the Medieval composer, who built mainly upon the perfect consonances of the fourth, fifth, and octave. Rhythm was at first based on the rhythmic modes. Later, better music notation made possible both triple and duple meter and also the complexities of isorhythm.

During the Renaissance, the Church lost its hold on music and music education. Lacking such control, secular music flowered. Noble patrons wanted to hear secular music for their own entertainment. In response to this demand, secular vocal and instrumental music developed to replace the limited number of sacred genres. Musicians were hired to perform at court and to create new kinds of secular music. The invention of printing also aided the growth of secular music. With the increasing demand for secular music, composers turned to it more and more often. Each country, including France, Italy, and Germany, developed its own particular types of secular music.

New style features characterize the new Renaissance secular forms. A chordal or harmonic approach to sound, for example, replaces the linear approach of the earlier period. Tone-painting becomes important. Imitation begins to replace the cantus firmus in importance. Musical techniques like paraphrase and parody are used more often.

The patronage change was complete. The Church no longer controlled the style of music. What had been sacred became secular. Music was free to begin its progress from the Renaissance to the Baroque period and beyond.

Essay B

With the Renaissance came a major change in the nature of music patronage from the Church domination of Medieval music to the leadership of secular courts. It did not happen suddenly. Beset by schisms and political entanglements, the Church declined noticeably as a patron in the fourteenth century. The art of secular polyphony that took root then bloomed with the onset of Renaissance humanism. Among the human pleasures rediscovered by the humanists and welcomed by composers was that of vernacular poetry.

French chansons, Italian madrigals, German lieder—these were the secular fruits of courtly patronage. The fifteenth-century Burgundian dukes set an example followed widely by maintaining an elaborate musical establishment. At these enlightened courts, composers such as Dufay, Josquin, and Lassus wrote both sacred and secular music, and both flourished. Influenced by humanism, composers adopted new homophonic techniques that placed more emphasis on the text. As men assumed equality with those around them, so the voice-parts in their music found equality in imitative counterpoint. Cantus-firmus techniques, already transformed by the use of secular tunes, gave way before the new techniques of paraphrase and parody. In short, developments in musical style mirrored those in musical patronage.

Spurred by the general delight in secular music and by the new art of music printing, amateur music-making spread over Europe and reached the point of being a social necessity for well-bred gentlemen and gentlewomen. Perhaps the clearest indication of the change wrought by Renaissance patronage was the emergence of that most secular of musical arts—instrumental music. Canzoni, ricercari, toccate, fantasie, dance forms, and variations—all contribute to the late Renaissance and all lead towards further development in the future.

Before consulting the Appendix (p. 228), ask yourself the following questions:

Which essay makes more significant points in answer to the question? (Make a list of the main points raised in each essay.)

Which essay offers more explanatory data in support of its points?

Which essay is better organized? (Reconstruct the outlines from the essays and compare.)

Appendix One
Criticism
of Writing Samples

THE BIBLIOGRAPHY (page 214)

Without taking a stand, a permissible attitude in bibliographical writing, the author succinctly defines the term *bel canto* and then explains how he plans to organize the bibliographical entries that will constitute the body of his paper. The two paragraphs of the preface are both well written and well organized. The sample entries are evaluative as well as descriptive. Use of published reviews, as in the first entry, enable the writer to share the burden of evaluation with professional critics, and they help to retain the interest and the confidence of the reader. Use of just a portion of a large book is illustrated by the second entry, whose description degenerates, however, into a list. In addition, the reader might well prefer the quotation of a review from a musicological journal, particularly since the reviewer is not named, and would certainly welcome a more detailed periodical reference. The recommended form of a periodical entry is seen in the Casselman entry, in which the reader may also note once again that incomplete sentences are permissible in bibliographical annotations if the subject of a sentence is perfectly clear. Furthermore, selective quotation from a source is shown to be an excellent aid in description.

THE DISCOGRAPHY (page 215)

The author of the example commits errors at every level of writing. The preface is poorly organized. Various topics that require fuller discussion or explanation are scattered in fragments throughout the two principal paragraphs: the writer's limited background, his approach to evaluation of the performances, the nature of the piece to be evaluated, the nature of the instrument upon which the piece should be performed, the writer's reluctance to deal with organ registration, and, finally, styles of Bach-performance. By sorting this material into discrete subjects and presenting these subjects in logical succession, the writer could salvage most of his information. What is required is an outline, a plan of organization. Not only would an outline ensure order among the given materials, it would also reveal that two significant elements are missing — some historical, stylistic, and structural comments upon the composition under discussion and a statement indicating clearly the intended arrangement of the entries that will comprise the body of the paper. There follows a proposed outline for the entire annotated discography, including the preface.

Proposed Outline

  I. Preface
     A. Introduction of the subject and establishment of perspective
     B. Presentation of historical, stylistic, and structural material about the piece
     C. Explanation of the method and criteria for evaluation of each performance
     D. Discussion of the procedure and organization to be employed in the body of the paper
     E. Mention of the writer's limitations as a critic
  II. Discographical entries, each to be treated as follows:
     A. Information of a discographical nature, especially regarding the phonograph recording, its liner notes, and the performer
     B. Criticism of major performance elements in a systematic manner, including tempo, phrasing, articulation, and dynamics
     C. Criticism of secondary elements as appropriate (recording resonance and clarity, treatment of ornaments, choice of registration, etc.)
     D. Reference to published reviews of the selected performances
  III. Summary and conclusions, including a comparative table displaying clearly such elements as the performer's name, the date of recording, the label of each recorded performance, the exact tempo and the dynamic level at important points in the piece, the overall timing of the piece and of its main sections, the principal kinds of articulation employed, etc.

Errors of content or explication in the example's preface range from failure to indicate the published score consulted to enigmatic references to the so-called traditional manner of performing Bach and to an unnamed somebody's many years of learning about articulation. In addition, there is a lack of topic and transition sentences. Finally, the writer cannot possibly establish a link between the structure of the piece and such performance practices as articulation and phrasing without some analysis of the composition.

Whereas errors of style abound in the preface, grammatical and mechanical errors are relatively few. Sentence structure could be improved somewhat by ending sentences with important words. Both grammatical and stylistic errors are numbered and corrected in the revised preface that follows, with accompanying explanation where appropriate.

J. S. Bach's *Toccata and Fugue in D Minor, BWV 565*[1] — A Comparative Discography

Preface

My main purpose[2] in undertaking[3] this project was to hear[4] how other organists[5] play[6] a work that[7] I have[8] studied and performed myself. Naturally,[9] my comments are often highly subjective,[10] but I have[11] tried to support my opinions[12] by specific references to the music[13] and by the use of[14] music examples. In addition,[15] I have[16] tried to take into account the fact that[17] there are various ways of interpreting Bach's music.[18] Wherever[19] I refer to generally accepted performance practices, my primary point of reference is Hermann Keller's *Phrasing and Articulation* (London: Barrie and Rockliff, 1966).[20] When performance practice is influenced by the nature of the instrument itself, my own limited experience and my preference for a tracker mechanism — the only kind available to Bach — have governed my judgment.[21]

Bach's *Toccata and Fugue in D Minor*, S. 565, was apparently composed during the first decade of the eighteenth century. Its form and keyboard figuration clearly reveal its place in the North German tradition of organ toccatas . . . . [This paragraph represents an insertion of new material rather than revision of the original preface. Its completion would bring forth relevant historical, stylistic, and structural information about the composition and would also indicate which published edition of the score the writer used.]

In compiling the individual entries of the discography,[22] I have treated the composition as a whole before dealing with individual features.[23] Changes of tempo, for example, were considered in relationship to each other within an overall context.[24] Several important check points within the piece were established, and each performer's tempo at each point was noted. Also taken into account were phrasing, articulation, and dynamics.[25] For each performance I have indicated and given an explanation for the elements I judged to be excellent and then for those things I disliked. In particular, I tried to make note of the factors that varied most from performance to performance.

The entries in the body of the paper have been arranged according to my perception of each performance's quality, from the best to the least good.[26] Each entry follows the same basic format: discographical information, criticism, reference to published reviews if available. Never having criticized a performance in depth and in a systematic manner, I request the reader to consider my inexperience.[27] Owing to a lack of information and to my own ignorance, for example, I have been unable to do more than make isolated comments about organ registration in the various performances. In so far as possible, I have made use of published reviews of the performances to temper my judgments or simply to offer alternative viewpoints.[28] I do feel that what I have learned in writing this paper will enable me to perform the composition with more sensitivity and to teach it with more understanding.[29]

Revisions by Line

1 The *BWV* number, which indicates the location of the piece in the Schmieder thematic catalog of Bach's works, serves to identify this specific composition among all those with the same title.

2 The original opening sentence begins with a dangling participial phrase that does not refer to the grammatical subject of the sentence. In addition, apology for one's shortcomings should not begin a paper. The beginning proper is reached in line 11 of the original preface. The word *purpose* seems stronger and more accurate than *interest*.

3 Addition of the word *undertaking* makes the sentence read more smoothly.

4 *Hear* rightly replaces *see* in line 12 of the original.

5 The word *organists* is more specific than *people*.

6 A recorded performance can be replayed at any time, permitting the use of the present tense and helping to clarify the writer's difficulty with verb tenses.

7 *That* should be used as a defining or restrictive pronoun, and *which* as a nondefining or nonrestrictive one.

8 Using the present tense (number 6 above) permits the use of *have* here, a distinct improvement.

9 Use of the word *naturally* removes some of the emphasis upon the word *subjective*.

10 The change is made necessary by a *this* that does not refer back in a clear way to the preceding sentence.

11 The verb form is altered to agree with the previous sentence.

12 The plural form seems better.

13 *References* must be made *to* something.

14 The two phrases beginning with *by* now complement one another.

15 The words *in addition* should not be allowed to separate the subject of the sentence from its verb, particularly when they can be readily transferred to the beginning of the sentence.

16 Contractions should not be used in a formal paper.

17 The original statement places the emphasis on the ways of interpreting Bach, whereas the revision makes clear that the various ways themselves are of less importance than the fact of their existence.

18 The corrected statement does not leave the *music* of Bach to be assumed.

19 A paper unfolds in space (*wherever*) and not in time (*whenever*).

20 The original (line 15) employs the pronoun *it* in an unclear way, and it also leaves the point being made both unclear and unspecific.

21 The original is ungrammatical and unclear.

22 The use of the word *discography* is a way of maintaining perspective by reminding the reader of the nature of the paper.

23 The material of this third paragraph may be found in lines 3–8 and 19–24 of the original preface. However, unlike the original, tempo will be closely considered in the revised paper. *Specifics* (line 20) is an ugly and unnecessary noun.

24 This seems to express the sense of the original (lines 7–8), which is poorly worded.

25 Articulation and dynamics are mentioned separately in the original (lines 16 and 22), but phrasing not at all.

26 The arrangement and format of the entries is not indicated in the original preface.

27 All words of apology (lines 1–3 and 9–10 in the original) are best reserved for a place near the end of the preface, if they appear at all.

28 Published reviews were not mentioned in the original preface. Their mention here helps to counteract the effect of the preceding apology.

29 If it is true, such a statement does not seem out of place in a student paper. It brings us back full circle to the beginning of the revised preface.

Some errors in the original that are not corrected above are listed here:

9 The sentence should read "unless it was exceptionally good or exceptionally bad."

17 *Effects* is erroneously used in place of *affects*.

24 *Its* is a possessive pronoun, whereas *it's* is a contraction for *it is*.

25 The comma after *now* is misplaced, as is the word itself, which should follow *could*.

Discography Entry Revised

Schmiffmeier, Harvey. "Bach Live in Los Angeles." Aztec tape LS-260. (c. 1973?)[1]
     Highly romanticized and very melodramatic are the words that best describe this performance of Bach's *Toccata and Fugue in D Minor.*[2] Even before I heard this tape recording, I was already biased against the performer. Hearing the awful things he does to the piece only confirmed my opinion.[3] The performance is preceded by a speech in which the organist says that a purist approach to the performance of Bach's music is totally wrong, because Bach was a living, feeling human being.[4] Although I am not a purist, I do not believe that Bach's music must be interpreted in the style of Liszt or Franck in order to come alive and be expressive.[5]
     The performer destroys the rhythmic flow of the piece with his many gratuitous accelerandi and ritardandi.[6] Both the recitative and the *Presto* sections begin at a very slow tempo and then accelerate. In the *Prestissimo*, all concept of the beat simply disappears. Just as shocking, the last statement of the fugue subject is preceded by an enormous ritardando and accompanying decrescendo. Less offensive but more puzzling is the curiously slow and deliberate tempo of the *Vivace* section. Not unexpectedly, the thoroughly Baroque means of animating the rhythm by means of articulation and phrasing is almost entirely overlooked by the performer. Other elements of style reveal the same ignorance of Baroque performance practice. In measures 2 and 10, for example, as well as elsewhere in the piece, the swell pedal is used indiscriminately. In addition, the player changes manuals a great deal, sometimes with no apparent reason. Even worse, he changes registration in a manner impossible as well as tasteless for a Baroque organist. Throughout the performance the registration was overwhelmingly loud and massive. Rather than serving Bach, the performer clearly uses the composer's music as a means of indulgent self-expression.

Revisions by Line

1 Discographical form is not so clearly established as bibliographical form. Here, it makes sense to list the several performances of the same piece by performer. Comprehensiveness and consistency should be the watchwords.

2 This lively opening was found lurking in lines 7 and 8 of the original entry. Underlining adverbs or any parts of speech for emphasis is rarely appropriate in formal writing.

3 The two sentences are consolidated and their impact moderated. Nothing could be perfectly awful. A bias supported by fact does not remain a prejudice; since it is an aural fact, however, perhaps it should become an opinion.

4 Parenthetical insertions should not be used to stuff in essential explanatory information, and they should not be ungrammatical.

5 The word *nor* requires a preceding use of *neither*. The two composers mentioned are changed for greater impact.

6 The original review consists of two paragraphs, the second of which simply continues a rather desultory discussion of the performance. In the revision the second paragraph contains all of the specific performance criticism, rearranged so as to place similar points together. Note particularly how transitional phrases and sentences lead smoothly from one element of style to another.

Errors found in the remainder of the original entry are corrected below:

8 *For example* need not and should not be set off by a colon, especially where only one point follows it.

10 *Accelerando* is singular and Italian whereas *ritards* is plural and apparently English. "To the point of where" may possibly be colloquial, but in any case it is wrong.

11 Semicolons are not interchangeable with commas. There is only one sentence here. The noun-adjective *manual* is ugly and easily avoided.

15 There is no reason to bring the second person *you* into the account.

16–20 Sentence after unrelated sentence goes by with no attempt at a coherent account.

20–21 Being dead, Bach cannot be defied; being inanimate, neither can his style. Forgiveness of a performing sin lies as close at hand as the next performance.

THE REVIEW (page 216)

This sensitive and forthright student review of a student recital demonstrates the importance of preparation for a concert and how that foreknowledge and perspective can be effectively communicated. In the discussion of important points, the writer manages to convey several other facts in an incidental fashion, a useful writing technique. As for fulfilling his several functions, the writer does report, does educate, and does make a good argument for attending percussion recitals. He also criticizes and carefully supports his opinions. If the reviewer requires any advice, it would have to do with being discrete without failing to communicate his views. While undoubtedly deserved, the forceful derogation of the accompanists will cause many readers to take that as the writer's primary message.

One point of grammar needs to be made. The word *however* (at the end of the third paragraph) cannot be used as a conjunction. A semicolon or period is required before the word, and a comma afterwards. The reader should note especially that a somewhat freer, less formal, and more colorful style of writing is called for in a concert review than in a formal paper.

THE PROGRAM NOTES (page 218)

The sample program notes reveal several unifying threads, the most striking dealing with each of the three composers' relationships with tradition. A lesser but perhaps more provocative theme suggests that the wide gulf between composers and listening public in the twentieth century stems at least in part from the rise of the professional virtuoso and the demise of the performing composer. In the discussion of each composition, the presentation of essential data (such as date of composition, number of movements, and forms of the movements) is given incidentally in the course of an account focused on more significant matters. The nature of the notes and the level of the writing would seem to suit them for the intellectual environment of a university community. Those in the audience with technical knowledge of music would find in each brief account some information meant especially for them, but these technical matters do not prevent the basic message from reaching any interested music-lover. A large general audience would require quite a different set of program notes.

THE ESSAYS (pages 219-221)

Each of the questions given for consideration after the essay examples points to Essay B as the better essay. It is shorter because no space is wasted upon peripheral information. Essay A discusses Medieval music at length, perhaps because the writer happens to know a good deal about it, or at least about its style. On the other hand, perhaps because of this lengthy drift away from the thrust of the question, there is not nearly enough about the change in patronage, which should be the focus of the answer. In the simplified and overstated account of A, no reasons are offered for the decline of the Church's role and the rise of courtly patronage. Humanism goes unmentioned. Nowhere is there reference to such necessary supporting data as the types of secular genres composed or the leading composers. The amount of detail need not be large if it is well selected and accurate. In B, the reader encounters enough detail to grant the writer mastery of the subject. Incidental data for its own sake, or detail not closely linked to the major issues, does not help an essay. Even the best feature of A, its detailed discussions of style, are greatly weakened by the writer's failure to link style change with the changing nature of patronage. An outline would have given the writer of A a clearly organized structure within which to demonstrate his knowledge of the subject.

Appendix Two

Bibliographies

THE ANTHOLOGIES

BRANDT, WILLIAM and others, eds. *The Comprehensive Study of Music* **CSM** 4 vols. New York: Harper & Row, 1980.

DAVISON, ARCHIBALD T. and WILLI APEL, eds. *Historical Anthology of Music* **HAM** 2 vols. Cambridge: Harvard University Press, 1946.

GREENBERG, NOAH and PAUL MAYNARD, eds. *An Anthology of Early Renaissance Music* **AERM** New York: W. W. Norton, 1975.

HOPPIN, RICHARD H., ed. *Anthology of Medieval Music* **AMM** New York: W. W. Norton, 1978.

JANDER, OWEN, ed. *Music of the Classical Era* **MCE** New York: Thomas Y. Crowell, 1967.

KIRBY, F. E., ed. *Music in the Classic Period* **MCP** New York: Schirmer Books, 1979.

LANG, PAUL HENRY, ed. *The Concerto 1800–1900* **LC** New York: W. W. Norton, 1969.

LANG, PAUL HENRY, ed. *The Symphony 1800–1900* **LS** New York: W. W. Norton, 1969.

MARROCCO, THOMAS and NICHOLAS SANDON, eds. **OAM** *Oxford Anthology of Medieval Music*. London: Oxford University Press, 1977.

PALISCA, CLAUDE V., ed. *Norton Anthology of Western Music* **NAWM** 2 vols. New York: W. W. Norton, 1980.

PARRISH, CARL, ed. *A Treasury of Early Music* **TEM** New York: W. W. Norton, 1958.

ROBINSON, RAY, ed. *Choral Music* **CM** New York: W. W. Norton, 1978.

STARR, WILLIAM and GEORGE DEVINE, eds. *Music Scores Omnibus* **MSO** 2 vols. Englewood Cliffs, N.J.: Prentice-Hall, 1974.

WENNERSTROM, MARY H., ed. *Anthology of Twentieth-Century Music* **ATM** New York: Appleton-Century-Crofts, 1969.

CHAPTER 1: MEDIEVAL MUSIC

Chant

APEL, WILLI. *Gregorian Chant*. Bloomington: Indiana University Press, 1958.
Anthology Examples: CSM I; HAM I; AMM; OAM; NAWM I; TEM; CM; MSO I.

Mass

LOCKWOOD, LEWIS. "Mass," *New Grove Dictionary* XI, 783–790.
Anthology Examples: CSM I, 1; HAM I, 55; AMM 5–22; OAM 10, 11, 61–66; NAWM I, 21; TEM 13–14; CM 4; MSO I, 1, 22.

Motet

SANDERS, ERNEST. "Motet," *New Grove Dictionary* XII, 617–28.
Anthology Examples: CSM I, 48, 51, 55, 59, 62; HAM I, 28, 32–35, 43–44; AMM 38, 53–56, 59, 61; OAM 43–50; NAWM I, 13, 16–17; TEM 10, 12, 18; CM 10; MSO I, 16–21.

Chanson

BROWN, HOWARD MAYER. "Chanson," *New Grove Dictionary* IV, 135–45.
Anthology Examples: CSM I, 26, 28, 33, 67, 70, 71; HAM I, 36, 46–8; AMM 41–7, 69; OAM 18–26, 56–60, 68–73, 98; NAWM I, 5–7, 20, 22; TEM 13–14; MSO I, 12, 23.

Madrigal

ROCHE, JEROME. *The Madrigal*. New York: Charles Scribner's Sons, 1972.
Anthology Examples: CSM I, 74, 81; HAM I, 49–54; AMM 65–67, 70; OAM 74–81; NAWM I, 18–19; TEM 17; MSO I, 27.

Léonin

BENT, IAN D. "Léonin," *New Grove Dictionary* X, 676–77.
HUSMANN, HEINRICH. "The Origin and Destination of the Magnus Liber organi," *The Musical Quarterly* XLIX, 3 (July, 1963), 311–30.
Anthology Examples: CSM I, 37; HAM I, 29; AMM 33; NAWM I, 13; TEM 9.

Pérotin

BENT, IAN D. "Pérotin," *New Grove Dictionary* XIV, 540–43.
Anthology Examples: CSM I, 39; HAM I, 31; AMM 35; NAWM I, 14.

Machaut

REANEY, GILBERT. *Guillaume de Machaut*. London: Oxford University Press, 1971.
Anthology Examples: CSM I, 67, 70, 71; HAM I, 44–46; AMM 61–4; OAM 68–71; NAWM I, 20–1; CM 7; MSO I, 22, 25, 26.

Landino

FISCHER, KURT VON. "Landini," *New Grove Dictionary* X, 428–34.

Anthology Examples: CSM I, 81; HAM I, 53–4; AMM 67; OAM 77–8; NAWM I, 19; MSO I, 27.

General

HOPPIN, RICHARD H. *Medieval Music*. New York: W. W. Norton, 1978.

SEAY, ALBERT. *Music in the Medieval World*. Englewood Cliffs, N.J.: Prentice-Hall, 1965.

Recommended

MUNROW, DAVID. *The Art of Courtly Love*. 3-vol. set of recordings with accompanying booklet. Seraphim SIC-6092.

MUNROW, DAVID. *Instruments of the Middle Ages and Renaissance*. Recordings with accompanying booklet. Angel SBZ-3810.

Anthologies

CSM I; HAM I; AMM; OAM; NAWM I; TEM; MSO I.

CHAPTER 2: RENAISSANCE MUSIC

Mass

LOCKWOOD, LEWIS. "Mass," *New Grove Dictionary* XI, 783–90. Although the table is based upon this article, the number of Masses and techniques employed are generally drawn from the various composer entries in the same encyclopedia.

Anthology Examples: CSM I, 4 exs.; HAM I, 8 exs.; AERM 5 exs.; NAWM I, 6 exs.; CM 5 exs.; MSO I, 6 exs.

Motet

PERKINS, LEEMAN L. "Motet," *New Grove Dictionary* XII, 628–37. The estimated number of motets for composers are drawn from composer entries in the *New Grove Dictionary*.

Anthology Examples: CSM I, 16 exs.; HAM I, 23 exs.; AERM 14 exs.; NAWM I, 10 exs.; TEM 6 exs.; CM 8 exs.; MSO I, 6 exs.

Chanson

BROWN, HOWARD MAYER. "Chanson," *New Grove Dictionary* IV, 135–45.

REESE, GUSTAVE. *Music in the Renaissance*. 2nd ed., revised. New York: W. W. Norton, 1959.

Anthology Examples: CSM I, 8 exs.; HAM I, 13 exs.; AERM 7 exs.; NAWM I, 6 exs.; CM 27–9; MSO I, 5 exs.

Madrigal

KERMAN, JOSEPH. *The Elizabethan Madrigal*. American Musicological Society, 1962.

ROCHE, JEROME. *The Madrigal*. New York: Charles Scribner's Sons, 1972.

Anthology Examples: CSM I, 157, 266, 284; HAM I, 7 exs.; NAWM I, 7 exs.; TEM 33; CM 8 exs.; MSO I, 43.

Dunstable

BENT, MARGARET. "Dunstable," *New Grove Dictionary* V, 720–25.

BROWN, HOWARD M. *Music in the Renaissance.* Englewood Cliffs, N.J.: Prentice-Hall, 1976.

Anthology Examples: CSM I, 89; HAM I, 61–2; OAM 97; NAWM I, 25; TEM 18; CM 75; MSO I, 32.

Dufay

BROWN, HOWARD M. *Music in the Renaissance.*

HAMM, CHARLES. "Dufay," *New Grove Dictionary* V, 674–87.

Anthology Examples: CSM I, 4 exs.; HAM I, 65–8; AERM 1, 6, 19, 35; NAWM I, 26–7, 35, 41–2; CM 11; MSO I, 30, 31.

Ockeghem

BROWN, HOWARD M. *Music in the Renaissance.*

BUKOFZER, MANFRED. "Caput: A Liturgico-Musical Study," in *Studies in Medieval and Renaissance Music* (New York: W. W. Norton, 1950), pp. 217–310.

PERKINS, LEEMAN L. "Ockeghem," *New Grove Dictionary* XIII, 489–96.

Anthology Examples: CSM I, 102, 109; HAM I, 73–5; AERM 2, 9; NAWM I, 36, 44; CM 6; MSO I, 32.

Josquin

REESE, GUSTAVE. *Music in the Renaissance.*

REESE, GUSTAVE and JEREMY NOBLE. "Josquin Desprez," *New Grove Dictionary* IX, 713–39.

Anthology Examples: CSM I, 4 exx.; HAM I, 89–91; AERM 5 exs.; NAWM I, 29–30, 45; CM 7, 12; MSO I, 34, 37.

Willaert

BROWN, HOWARD M. *Music in the Renaissance.*

Anthology Examples: CSM I, 178; HAM I, 113, 115; NAWM I, 32, 52.

Palestrina

LOCKWOOD, LEWIS. "Palestrina," *New Grove Dictionary* XIV, 118–37.

REESE, GUSTAVE. *Music in the Renaissance.*

Anthology Examples: CSM I, 185, 195; HAM I, 140–2; NAWM I, 40; CM 8, 14; MSO I, 61.

Lassus

HAAR, JAMES. "Orlande de Lassus," *New Grove Dictionary* X, 480–502.

REESE, GUSTAVE. *Music in the Renaissance.*

Anthology Examples: CSM I, 231; HAM I, 143–5; NAWM I, 33; CM 13; MSO I, 56.

Byrd

HOLST, IMOGEN. *Byrd.* New York: Praeger Publishers, 1972.

KERMAN, JOSEPH. "Byrd," *New Grove Dictionary* III, 537–52.

Anthology Examples: CSM I, 225; HAM I, 150-1; NAWM I, 34; CM 9, 18, 25; MSO I, 50.

Marenzio

ARNOLD, DENIS. *Marenzio*. London: Oxford University Press, 1965.

LEDBETTER, STEVEN and ROLAND JACKSON. "Marenzio," *New Grove Dictionary* XI, 667–74.

Anthology Examples: CSM I, 266; HAM I, 155; CM 33.

Gabrieli

ARNOLD, DENIS. "Giovanni Gabrieli," *New Grove Dictionary* VII, 60–5.

ARNOLD, DENIS. *Giovanni Gabrieli and the Music of the Venetian High Renaissance*. London: Oxford University Press, 1979.

Anthology Examples: CSM I, 236, 301; HAM I, 157; CM 16; MSO I, 80.

General

BLUME, FRIEDRICH. *Renaissance and Baroque Music*. Trans. M. D. Herter Norton. New York: W. W. Norton, 1967.

BROWN, HOWARD M. *Music in the Renaissance*. Englewood Cliffs, N.J.: Prentice-Hall, 1976.

REESE, GUSTAVE. *Music in the Renaissance*. 2nd ed., revised. New York: W. W. Norton, 1959.

TROWELL, BRIAN, ANTHONY MILNER, and others. *Renaissance and Baroque*, Vol. II of *The Pelican History of Music*. New York: Penguin Books, 1963.

Recommended

MUNROW, DAVID. *The Art of the Netherlanders*. 3-vol. set of recordings with accompanying booklet. EMI SLS-5049.

WANGERMÉE, ROBERT. *Flemish Music*. Trans. Robert Erich Wolf. New York: Frederick A. Praeger, 1968. (Ch. 4 is suggested.)

Anthologies

CSM I; HAM I; AERM; NAWM I; TEM; CM; MSO I.

CHAPTER 3: BAROQUE MUSIC

Opera

GROUT, DONALD J. *A Short History of Opera*. 2nd ed., revised. New York: Columbia University Press, 1965. The estimated number of operas by each composer is drawn from the composer entries in *The New Grove Dictionary*.

BRODY, ELAINE. *Music in Opera: A Historical Anthology*. Englewood Cliffs, N.J.: Prentice-Hall, 1970.

Anthology Examples: CSM II, 6 exs.; NAWM I, 68–79; TEM 44-6, 50; MSO I, 91, 116, 119, 220.

Oratorio

SMITHER, HOWARD E. "Oratorio," *New Grove Dictionary* XIII, 656–78. Estimated oratorio totals are drawn from the composer entries elsewhere in the same encyclopedia.

Anthology Examples: CSM II, 34, 308; NAWM I, 83, 87; TEM 37, 42; CM 39, 44; MSO I, 100, 217.

Cantata

FORTUNE, NIGEL and others. "Cantata," *New Grove Dictionary* III, 694–718. Cantata totals are drawn from the composer entries elsewhere in the same encyclopedia.

Anthology Examples: CSM II, 85, 229; NAWM I, 88; TEM 304; CM 48, 49; MSO I, 121, 171.

Organ Music

KIRBY, F. E. *A Short History of Keyboard Music.* New York: The Free Press, 1966.

Anthology Examples: CSM II, 15, 54, 158; NAWM I, 94-7; TEM 41; MSO I, 7 exs.

Suite

FULLER, DAVID. "Suite," *New Grove Dictionary* XVIII, 333–50.

Anthology Examples: CSM II, 46, 108; NAWM I, 615, 617; TEM 39; MSO I, 112, 134, 157.

Sonata

NEWMAN, WILLIAM S. "Sonata," *New Grove Dictionary* XVII, 479–96.

Anthology Examples: CSM II, 62; NAWM I, 525, 530; MSO I, 131.

Concerto

HUTCHINGS, ARTHUR. *The Baroque Concerto.* New York: W. W. Norton, 1965.

Anthology Examples: CSM II, 114, 171; NAWM I, 536, 569; TEM 47; MSO I, 144.

Monteverdi

ARNOLD, DENIS. *Monteverdi.* London: J. M. Dent, 1963.

Anthology Examples: CSM II, 1, 2; NAWM I, 4 exs.; CM 38; MSO I, 91.

Frescobaldi

NEWCOMB, ANTHONY. "Frescobaldi," *New Grove Dictionary* VI, 824–35.

Anthology Examples: CSM II, 15, 21; NAWM I, 100; MSO I, 111.

Schütz

MOSER, HANS JOACHIM. *Heinrich Schütz.* Trans. Derek McCulloch. New York: St. Martin's Press, 1967.

Anthology Examples: CSM II, 25; NAWM I, 84; CM 46; MSO I, 105.

Corelli

> TALBOT, MICHAEL. "Arcangelo Corelli," *New Grove Dictionary* IV, 768–74.
> Anthology Examples: CSM II, 62; NAWM I, 91; MSO I, 131.

Purcell

> ZIMMERMAN, FRANKLIN. *Henry Purcell.* New York: St. Martin's Press, 1967.
> Anthology Examples: CSM II, 70, 77; NAWM I, 74; CM 43; MSO I, 116.

A. Scarlatti

> DENT, EDWARD. *Alessandro Scarlatti.* New impression of 1905 ed., with additional
> notes by Frank Walker. London: Edward Arnold, 1960.
> Anthology Examples: CSM II, 85; NAWM I, 76; TEM 261; MSO, 121.

Couperin

> MELLERS, WILFRID. *François Couperin and the French Classical Tradition.* New York:
> Dover Publications, 1968 (reprint of the 1950 edition).
> Anthology Examples: CSM II, 108; NAWM I, 102; MSO I, 134.

Vivaldi

> KOLNEDER, WALTER. *Antonio Vivaldi: His Life and Work.* Trans. Bill Hopkins.
> Berkeley: University of California Press, 1970.
> TALBOT, MICHAEL. "Vivaldi," *New Grove Dictionary* XX, 31–46.
> Anthology Examples: CSM II, 114; NAWM I, 92–3; TEM 47; CM 40; MSO I,
> 144.

Rameau

> GIRDLESTONE, CUTHBERT. *Jean-Philippe Rameau.* New York: Dover Publications,
> 1969.
> Anthology Examples: CM 42.

J. S. Bach

> GEIRINGER, KARL. *Johann Sebastian Bach.* London: Oxford University Press, 1966.
> Anthology Examples: CSM II, 10 exs.; NAWM I, 88–9, 95–7; CM 48–50; MSO
> I, 10 exs.

Handel

> DEAN, WINTON. "George Frideric Handel," *New Grove Dictionary* VIII, 83–140.
> LARSEN, JENS PETER. *Handel's Messiah.* 2nd ed. New York: W. W. Norton, 1972.
> Anthology Examples: CSM II, 298, 302, 308; NAWM I, 77, 79, 87; CM 44;
> MSO I, 119, 217, 220.

D. Scarlatti

> KIRKPATRICK, RALPH. *Domenico Scarlatti.* Princeton: Princeton University Press,
> 1953.
> Anthology Examples: CSM II, 335; CSM III, 32; MCE 5 exs.; MCP 7 exs.; LS 3;
> NAWM II, 6 exs.; MSO I, 6 exs.

General

BLUME, FRIEDRICH. *Renaissance and Baroque Music.*

BORROFF, EDITH. *The Music of the Baroque.* Dubuque: Wm. C. Brown Co., 1970.

BUKOFZER, MANFRED. *Music in the Baroque Era.* New York: W. W. Norton, 1947.

GROUT, DONALD JAY. *A Short History of Opera.* 2nd ed.

PALISCA, CLAUDE V. *Baroque Music.* 2nd ed. Englewood Cliffs, N.J.: Prentice-Hall, 1981.

RAYNOR, HENRY, ALEC HARMON, and DENIS STEVENS et al. *Renaissance and Baroque*, Vol. II of *The Pelican History of Music.*

Recommended

ABRAHAM, GERALD. *The Tradition of Western Music.* Berkeley: University of California Press, 1974.

STEVENS, DENIS (ed.). *The Art of Ornamentation in the Renaissance and Baroque.* Recordings. The Bach Guild BGS-7069718.

Anthologies

CSM II; NAWM I; TEM; CM; MSO I.

CHAPTER 4: CLASSICAL MUSIC

Opera

GROUT, DONALD J. *A Short History of Opera.* 2nd ed. Estimated opera totals are drawn from composer entries in *The New Grove Dictionary.*

BRODY, ELAINE. *Music in Opera: A Historical Anthology.*

Anthology Examples: CSM II, 429; MCE 235, 249; MCP 6 exs.; NAWM II, 118–20; MSO I, 236, 306.

Sonata

NEWMAN, WILLIAM and MICHAEL TILMOUTH, "Sonata," *New Grove Dictionary* XVII, 479–96.

Anthology Examples: CSM II, 291, 294; CSM III, 1; MCE 5 exs.; MCP 6 exs.; NAWM II, 4 exs.; MSO I, 222, 328.

Concerto

VEINUS, ABRAHAM. *The Concerto.*

Anthology Examples: CSM II, 375; MCE 4 exs.; MCP 16; LS 3, 68; NAWM II, 115–16; MSO I, 294.

String Quartet

TILMOUTH, MICHAEL. "String Quartet." *New Grove Dictionary* XVIII, 276–87.

Anthology Examples: CSM II, 326; CSM III, 8; MCE 3, 9; MCP 7 exs.; NAWM II, 107–08; MSO I, 4 exs.

Symphony

LaRue, Jan. "Symphony," *New Grove Dictionary* XVIII, 438-53. Symphony totals are drawn from composer entries in *The New Grove Dictionary*.
Anthology Examples: CSM II, 335; CSM III, 32; MCE 5 exs.; MCP 7 exs.; LS 3; NAWM II, 6 exs.; MSO I, 6 exs.

Gluck

Einstein, Alfred. *Gluck*. Trans. Eric Blom. New York: McGraw-Hill, 1972.
Anthology Examples: MCP 6; NAWM II, 119; MSO I, 236.

Mozart

King, Alexander Hyatt. *Mozart*. London: Anchor Books, 1970.
Anthology Examples: CSM II, 4 exs.; MCE 7 exs.; MCP 9 exs.; NAWM II, 116, 120; CM 56-8; MSO I, 288, 294, 306.

Haydn

Geiringer, Karl. *Haydn: A Creative Life in Music*. 3rd ed. Berkeley: University of California Press, 1982.
Anthology Examples: CSM II, 321, 326, 335; MCE 6 exs.; MCP 8 exs.; NAWM II, 111-12; CM 59-61; MSO I, 4 exs.

Beethoven

Tovey, Donald Francis. *Beethoven*. London: Oxford University Press, 1965.
Lang, Paul Henry. *The Symphony 1800-1900*.
Anthology Examples: CSM III, 1, 8, 32; MCE 7 exs.; MCP 7 exs.; LC 3; LS 3, 68; NAWM II, 108, 114; CM 62; MSO I, 4 exs.

General

Blume, Friedrich. *Classic and Romantic Music*. Trans. M. D. Herter Norton. New York: W. W. Norton, 1970.
Heger, Theodore E. *Music of the Classic Period*. Dubuque: Wm. C. Brown Co., 1969.
Ottaway, Hugh. "The Enlightenment and the Revolution," *Classical and Romantic*, vol. III of *The Pelican History of Music*. New York: Viking/Penguin, 1968.
Pauly, Reinhard G. *Music in the Classic Period*. Englewood Cliffs, N.J.: Prentice-Hall, 1965.
Wellesz, Egon and Frederick Sternfeld (eds.). *The Age of Enlightenment: 1745-1790*. vol. VII of *The New Oxford History of Music*. London: Oxford University Press, 1973.

Recommended

Rosen, Charles. *The Classical Style*. New York: W. W. Norton, 1971.
Rosen, Charles. *Sonata Forms*. W. W. Norton, 1980.

Anthologies

CSM II; MCE; MCP; NAWM II; CM; MSO I.

CHAPTER 5: ROMANTIC MUSIC

Symphonic Poem

> MACDONALD, HUGH. "Symphonic poem," *New Grove Dictionary* XVIII, 428–33.
> Anthology Examples: CSM IV, 6; NAWM II, 3 exs.; MSO II, 3 exs.

Symphony

> TEMPERLEY, NICHOLAS. "Symphony," *New Grove Dictionary* XVIII, 453–62.
> Anthology Examples: CSM III, 180; LS 7 exs.; MSO II, 74, 116.

Concerto

> NELSON, WENDELL. *The Concerto*. Dubuque: W. C. Brown Co., 1969.
> Anthology Examples: LC 9 exs.; MSO II, 9, 41.

Piano Music

> KIRBY, F. E. *A Short History of Keyboard Music*. New York: The Free Press, 1966.
> Anthology Examples: CSM III, 7 exs.; CSM IV, 1, 3; NAWM II, 4 exs.; MSO II, 6 exs.

Art Song

> STEVENS, DENIS (ed.). *A History of Song*. New York: W. W. Norton, 1961.
> Anthology Examples: CSM III, 12 exs.; NAWM II, 4 exs.; MSO II, 7 exs.

Opera

> GROUT, DONALD J. *A Short History of Opera*. 2nd ed. Opera totals are drawn from composer entries in *New Grove Dictionary*.
> BRODY, ELAINE. *Music in Opera: A Historical Anthology*.
> Anthology Examples: CSM III, 6 exs.; NAWM, 6 exs.; MSO II, 205, 253.

Schubert

> HUTCHINGS, ARTHUR. *Schubert*. Revised edition. London: Octagon Books, 1973.
> Anthology Examples: CSM III, 4 exs.; LS 98; CM 63–4; NAWM II, 129; MSO II, 4 exs.

Rossini

> TOYE, FRANCIS. *Rossini: A Study in Tragi-Comedy*. New York: W. W. Norton, 1963.
> Anthology Examples: CSM III, 77; CM 75; NAWM II, 133.

Berlioz

> BARZUN, JACQUES. *Berlioz and the Romantic Century*. 3rd ed. New York: Columbia University Press, 1969.
> Anthology Examples: CSM III, 120, 126; LS 130; CM 66; NAWM II, 125; MSO II, 74.

Chopin

ABRAHAM, GERALD. *Chopin's Musical Style*. London: Oxford University Press, 1968.
Anthology Examples: CSM III, 3 exs.; LC 194; NAWM II, 122; MSO II, 3 exs.

Schumann

WALKER, ALAN (ed.). *Robert Schumann*. London: Barrie and Jenkins, 1972.
Anthology Examples: CSM III, 155, 168; LC 319; LS 348; CM 72; NAWM II, 130; MSO II, 3 exs.

Liszt

SEARLE, HUMPHREY. *The Music of Liszt*. 2nd ed., revised. New York: Dover Publications, 1966.
Anthology Examples: CSM III, 175, 180; LC 413; NAWM II, 123-4; MSO II, 110.

Wagner

NEWMAN, ERNEST. *Wagner As Man and Artist*. 2nd ed. London: Peter Smith, 1974 (originally published in 1924).
Anthology Examples: CSM III, 187, 192; NAWM II, 137; MSO II, 205.

Verdi

MARTIN, GEORGE WHITNEY. *Verdi: His Music, Life and Times*. New York: Dodd and Mead, 1963.
Anthology Examples: CSM III, 219; CM 76; NAWM II, 138; MSO II, 253.

Brahms

DALE, KATHLEEN. *Brahms*. London: Archon Books, 1970.
Anthology Examples: CSM III, 6 exs.; LC 589, 656; LS 587; CM 70-1; NAWM II, 128; MSO II, 5 exs.

Mahler

RAYNOR, HENRY. *Mahler*. New York: Macmillan and Co., 1975.
Anthology Examples: NAWM II, 132.

Debussy

LOCKSPEISER, EDWARD. *Debussy*. 4th ed. New York: McGraw-Hill, 1972.
Anthology Examples: CSM IV, 4 exs.; NAWM II, 140; MSO II, 304.

R. Strauss

DEL MAR, NORMAN. *Richard Strauss*. London: Free Press of Glencoe, 1973.
Anthology Examples: NAWM II, 142; MSO II, 276.

General

ABRAHAM, GERALD. *A Hundred Years of Music*. 3rd ed. Chicago: Aldine Publishing Co., 1964.
BLUME, FRIEDRICH. *Classic and Romantic Music*.

EINSTEIN, ALFRED. *Music in the Romantic Era*. New York: W. W. Norton, 1947.

LONGYEAR, REY M. *Nineteenth-Century Romanticism in Music*. 2nd ed. Englewood Cliffs, N.J.: Prentice-Hall, 1973.

RIEDEL, JOHANNES. *Music of the Romantic Period*. Dubuque: Wm. C. Brown Co., 1969.

Recommended

LOESSER, ARTHUR. *Men, Women, and Pianos*. New York: Simon & Schuster, 1954.

MORGENSTERN, SAM (ed.). *Composers on Music*. New York: Pantheon Books, 1956.

Anthologies

CSM III; LC; LS; NAWM II; CM; MSO II.

CHAPTER 6: TWENTIETH-CENTURY MUSIC

Debussy

LOCKSPEISER, EDWARD. *Debussy*. 4th ed. New York: McGraw-Hill, 1972.
Anthology Examples: CSM IV, 4 exs.; NAWM II, 140; MSO II, 304.

Bartók

STEVENS, HALSEY. *The Life and Music of Béla Bartók*. London: Oxford University Press, 1964.
Anthology Examples: CSM IV, 5 exs.; NAWM II, 150; CM 94; ATM, 2, 11, 13.

Ravel

ARBIE ORENSTEIN. *Ravel, Man and Musician*. New York: Columbia University Press, 1975.
Anthology Examples: CSM IV, 44, 46; NAWM, 141; MSO II, 324.

Schoenberg

REICH, WILLI. *Schoenberg: A Critical Biography*. New York: Praeger, 1971.
Anthology Examples: CSM IV, 28, 33; NAWM II, 149; CM 81; ATM, 3 exs.

Stravinsky

WHITE, ERIC WALTER. *Stravinsky: The Composer and His Works*. Rev. edition. Berkeley: University of California Press, 1966.
Anthology Examples: CSM IV, 3 exs.; NAWM II, 143-44; CM 95-6; MSO II, 347; ATM, 4 exs.

Berg

REICH, WILLI. *The Life and Works of Alban Berg*. Trans. Cornelius Cardew. New York: Harcourt, Brace and World, 1965.
Anthology Examples: NAWM II, 156; ATM 30, 35.

Varèse

OUELETTE, FERNAND. *Edgard Varèse*. Trans. Derek Coltman. New York: Orion Press, 1968.

Carter

NORTHCOTT, BAYAN. "Carter," *New Grove Dictionary* III, 831–36.

ROSEN, CHARLES. "Elliott Carter," Vinton, John (ed.). *Dictionary of Contemporary Music*. New York: E. P. Dutton, 1971.

Anthology Examples: CSM IV, 195; CM 106; ATM 45, 47.

Penderecki

POCIEJ, BOHDAN. "Penderecki," *New Grove Dictionary* XIV, 349–50.

ZIELINSKI, TADEUSZ. "Krzysztof Penderecki," Vinton, John (ed.). *Dictionary of Contemporary Music*.

Anthology Examples: CSM IV, 258; CM 97.

General

AUSTIN, WILLIAM. *Music in the Twentieth Century*. New York: W. W. Norton, 1966.

GRIFFITHS, PAUL. *A Concise History of Avant-Garde Music*. New York: Oxford University Press, 1978.

GRIFFITHS, PAUL. *Modern Music: The Avant-Garde since 1945*. New York: George Braziller, 1981.

PEYSER, JOAN. *The New Music: The Sense behind the Sound*. New York: Dell Publishing Co., 1971.

SALZMAN, ERIC. *Twentieth-Century Music: An Introduction*. 2nd edition. Englewood Cliffs, N.J.: Prentice-Hall, 1974.

Recommended

HODEIR, ANDRÉ. *Since Debussy; a View of Contemporary Music*. Trans. by Noel Burch. New York: Da Capo Press, 1975.

MEYER, LEONARD B. *Music, the Arts, and Ideas*. Chicago: University of Chicago Press, 1967.

Anthologies

CSM IV; NAWM II; CM; MSO II; ATM.

SELECTED GENERAL HISTORIES

ABRAHAM, GERALD. *The Concise Oxford History of Music*. New York: Oxford University Press, 1979.

CROCKER, RICHARD L. *A History of Musical Style*. New York: McGraw-Hill, 1966.

GROUT, DONALD J. *A History of Western Music*. 3rd edition. New York: W. W. Norton, 1980.

LANG, PAUL HENRY. *Music in Western Civilization*. New York: W. W. Norton, 1941.

RAYNOR, HENRY. *Music & Society since 1815*. New York: Schocken Books, 1976.

RAYNOR, HENRY. *A Social History of Music from the Middle Ages to Beethoven*. London: Barrie and Jenkins, 1972.

ROSENSTIEL, LÉONIE (ed.). *Schirmer History of Music*. Riverside, N.J.: Schirmer Books, 1982.

REFERENCE TOOLS

DUCKLES, VINCENT (ed.) *Music Reference and Research Materials*. Third ed. New York: The Free Press, 1972.

MARCO, GUY A. *Information in Music: A Handbook of Reference Sources in European Languages*. Vol. 1: *Basic and Universal Sources*. Littleton, Colo.: *Libraries Unlimited*, 1975.

APEL WILLI. *Harvard Dictionary of Music*. Second ed. Cambridge, Mass.: Belknap Press, 1969.

BOHLE, BRUCE (ed.) *The International Cyclopedia of Music Musicians*. Tenth ed. New York: Dodd and Mead, 1972.

The Music Index: the Key to Current Music Periodical Literature. Detroit: Information Service, 1949-

Répertoire international de littérature musicale (International Inventory of Musical Literature). **RILM** Abstracts of Music Literature. New York: International RILM Center, 1967-

SADIE, STANLEY (ed.)*The New Grove Dictionary of Music and Musicians*. Sixth ed. New York: Schirmer Books, 1978.

Appendix Three
For Further Study

The list that follows contains suggestions that — with some thought — can be employed with regard to the music of any of the historical periods.

1. Listen to each composition analyzed with score in hand, being sure to understand every point made.
2. Study thoroughly each of the Comparative Style Tables.
3. Use the various Overview Tables and prepare more detailed ones for each period.
4. Make a tape with carefully chosen recorded examples from each historical period and swap it with a friend, keeping the identification sheet yourself.
5. Photocopy carefully chosen score pages from each historical period and swap them with a friend.
6. Make a comparative study (possibly in a table) of the treatment of each historical period in the selected general histories of music.
7. Write entries for additional composers: Vitry, Ciconia, Cordier; Victoria, Gesualdo; Lully, Carissimi; C. P. E. Bach, Clementi; Mendelssohn, Bruckner; Shostakovich, Britten, Boulez, Ginastera, Lutoslawski, Cordero, Stockhausen.
8. Copy in your own hand representative masterpieces from each historical period.
9. Read appropriate selections in Carl MacClintock, *Readings in the History of Music in Performance* (Bloomington: Indiana University Press, 1979); Ruth Halle Rowen, *Music through Sources and Documents* (Englewood Cliffs, N.J.: Prentice-Hall, 1979); Oliver Strunk, *Source Readings in Music History* (New York: W. W. Norton, 1950).
10. See representative art and read representative poetry from each of the historical periods.

SUGGESTED RESEARCH PAPERS

Medieval

Isorhythm — The Quintessential Musical Manifestation of the Medieval Mind
The Cantus Firmus as Musical *Auctoritas*
The Evolution of the Cadence from Chant to Landino
The Ars Nova: New Art But the End of an Era?
Music Education during the Medieval Period

Renaissance

Implications of the Decline of Cantus-Firmus Technique and the Rise of Systematic Imitation as the Major Principle of Form in the High Renaissance
The Lute in the Cultural Life of the Late Renaissance
The Role of Music in the Plays of Shakespeare
Parody Technique as a Revelation of the Mind of the Renaissance Composer
Competition in Renaissance Music: A Study of Various *L'homme armé* Masses

Baroque

The Problem of the Repeats in Baroque Music
One Concerto 400 Times? Vivaldi Reconsidered
Handel's Oratorios — Operas in Disguise?
The Triumph of the Concerto over the Trio Sonata — Its Significance for Music History
The Problem of Reviving Baroque Opera

Classical

Music Patronage in the Careers of Haydn, Mozart, and Beethoven
Orchestral Facts and Modern Performance Practice — The Actual Makeup of Orchestras in the Classical Period
The Impact of *Opera Buffa* on the History of Music
Gluck: Important Reformer or Timely Opportunist?
Baroque versus Classical Elements in the Style of C. P. E. Bach

Romantic

The Nature of Programs and Concert Life in the Romantic Period
The Curious Career of the Opera *Carmen*
Three Coins in the Fountain: Noble Patronage in the Nineteenth Century
The Birth of Musical "Genius"
Tracing the Career of Mahler on the Musical Stock Exchange of Popularity

Twentieth-Century

Expressionism — A Manifestation of the Twentieth-Century Mind
The Problem of the Cadence in Twentieth-Century Music
Neoclassicism — A Fruitful Avenue Or a Blind Alley?
Art Music and Jazz: A Fruitful Cross-fertilization?
Shostakovich — His Stature and Significance As a Composer and Soviet Citizen

Appendix Four

Scores and
Historical Sources Identified

UNIDENTIFIED MUSICAL EXAMPLES: CHAPTER 2

1a. Early Renaissance because of its simple, flowing triple meter and conjunct melody, and especially by its careful regulation of a small amount of typical dissonance, the disguised **V-I** Burgundian-type cadence, and the still popular Landino cadence.
  b. Chanson by texture (ballade style), French text, and rondeau form.
  c. Dufay, "Adieu ces bon vins de Lannoys" (ed. Heinrich Besseler), *Opera omnia*, vol. VI, in *Corpus Mensurabiliis Musicae* (Rome: American Institute of Musicology, 1964), p. 50.

2a. High Renaissance because it is an idiomatic keyboard piece with a variable number of voices and many scale passages, because of its major tonality and simple tonal chord patterns, and because of its regular subdivision of the beat and closing 4-3 suspension.
  b. Suite (actually a dance-pair), with balancing four-measure phrases and firmly metrical instrumental setting, tonal unity, as well as contrast in rhythm (slow duple/fast triple) and variation of theme.
  c. The dances are a pavan and a galliarde by an unknown composer (printed in 1530 by Pierre Attaingnant), ed. Arnold Schering, *Die Geschichte Musik in Beispielen* (Leipzig: Breitkopf & Haertel, 1931), p. 86.

3. Mid-Medieval by its monophonic texture and free rhythm, which—along with its Latin text ("Viderunt omnes")—points to Gregorian chant (composer unknown), as edited in William Brandt et al, *The Comprehensive Study of Music: Anthology of Music from Plainchant through Gabrieli*, vol. I (N.Y.: Harper and Row, 1980), p. 7.

4a. Late Medieval from the incidental treatment of dissonance, the rhythmic independence and irregular motion of the voices, and the double leading-tone cadence in mm. 23–4.
  b. A chanson is indicated by the ballade-style texture and French text.
  c. Machaut, "Honte, paour, doubtance," (CSM I, p. 69).

5a. High Renaissance by its evident chordal conception in four voices with syncopation and a 4-3 suspension in the cadence.
   b. Chanson in its lively homophonic Parisian variety.
   c. Sermisy, "Pourtant si je suis brunette", eds. Gaston Allaire and Isabelle Cazeaux, *Opera Omnia*, vol. iv (Rome: American Institute of Musicology, 1974), p. 62.

6a. High Renaissance because of its six-voice imitative polyphony with fully regulated dissonance treatment and smoothly flowing quarter-notes.
   b. Mass, by the text "Agnus Dei."
   c. Palestrina by the smooth flow, the conservative harmonic idiom, and the lack of tone-painting; *Missa Papae Marcelli* as edited by Arnold Schering (N.Y.: Eulenburg, 1923), pp. 44–5. Used by permission of European American Music Distributors Corporation, sole U.S. agent for Eulenburg Miniature Scores.

7a. Late Medieval by its four voices in the rhythmic modes with a measured and then unmeasured tenor voice, and by its perfect consonances and incidental dissonances.
   b. Organum in discant-style, then sustained-note organum on the word "omnes," but a textual trope in the contratenor makes it motet-like.
   c. Pérotin, "Viderunt omnes," CSM I, p. 43.

8a. High Renaissance, featuring much expressive chromaticism in five voices with a basically chordal texture and a chain of 7-6 suspensions.
   b. Madrigal, by an Italian text and unusual, even bizarre, tone-painting.
   c. Gesualdo, "Itene, o miei sospiri," (ed. Erwin Leuchter) *Florilegium Musicum* (Buenos Aires: Ricordi Americana, 1964), p. 153.

9a. Early Renaissance, in fact precisely in the non-imitative, four-voice style of Ockeghem, with its continuous but irregular rhythmic flow, its characteristic dissonances (anticipations and escape-tones), and its avoidance of internal cadences.
   b. Mass, from the text "Kyrie eleison."
   c. Ockeghem, *Missa Caput*, ed. Gabor Darvas (Edition Eulenburg, 1972), pp. 2-3.

10a. Late Medieval on the basis of its perfect consonances on strong beats and incidental dissonance on weak ones, its irregular rhythmic flow and narrow range of voices with some part-crossing, and its cadence.
   b. Mass, from the text "Benedictus" (part of the Sanctus).
   c. Machaut, *Notre Dame Mass*, ed. Leo Schrade, *Polyphonic Music of the Fourteenth Century* (Monaco: Éditions de L'Oiseau-Lyre, n.d.), vol. III, p. 58.

11a. Mid- or Late Medieval, with two-voice polyphony in the first rhythmic mode and perfect consonances favored.
   b. An instrumental dance movement (a *nota*) by its lack of text, strong rhythmic flow in balanced phrases, and sectional structure.
   c. Anonymous, "Nota." Reprinted from *Music in Medieval and Renaissance Life* edited by Andrew Minor, (p. 9) by permission of the University of Missouri Press. Copyright 1964 by the Curators of the University of Missouri Press.

12a. Mid-Medieval, with narrow vocal range and in the dorian mode.
   b. Minnelied by its German language, the form AAB (as in the German bar-form), and the stress on the third (a secular trait).
   c. Walther von der Vogelweide, "Allererst leb' ich mir werde." The rhythm, unclear but not unmeasured, is transcribed here in a definite meter by Barbara and W. Thomas Seagrave in *The Songs of the Minnesingers* ©1966 The Board of Trustees of the University of Illinois. Reprinted by permission of the University of Illinois Press, pp. 95–6.

13a. High Renaissance, featuring use of inversion and tonal answer in a five-voice imitative texture with an apparent cantus firmus (note the long rests), which is commented upon phrase by phrase in the other voices.

   b. A motet (its Latin text is not part of the Mass Ordinary).

   c. Lassus, "Da pacem Domine," as edited by Wolfgang Boetticher in *Vier Motetten*, 3rd ed. (Kassel: Barenreiter, 1963), p. 12.

14a. Mid-Medieval by its monophony of narrow vocal range in the dorian mode with apparent difficulties in the rhythmic notation.

   b. Either a troubadour or trouvère chanson by its use of Medieval French.

   c. Guiraut de Bornelh, a noted troubadour listed in the Medieval Overview table, "Reis gloria," as edited by Pierre Aubry in *Trouvères and Troubadours* (N.Y.: Cooper Square Publishers, 1969), p. 71.

15a. Mid-Medieval because the two-voice polyphony emphasizes perfect consonances, including the fourth, and apparently uses the rhythmic modes.

   b. Organum by its sustained-note, or melismatic style (with a contrasting passage in discant style), and Latin text.

   c. Léonin, the master of discant style, "Viderunt omnes," CSM I, p. 38.

16a. High Renaissance through its regularly flowing four-voice imitative polyphony in which the themes are freely varied by changing note-values (diminution), inversion, and alteration of metrical position.

   b. Instrumental, probably for keyboard, but lacking the metrical accent and balanced phrasing of dance music; in fact, the one principal theme suggests its genre, ricercare.

   c. Cabezon, "Fuga al contrario" (ed. Arnold Schering), GMB, p. 112.

UNIDENTIFIED HISTORICAL SOURCES: CHAPTER 2

1a. Primary (practical theory treatise).

   b. High Renaissance because the art of composition is described as simultaneous conception of four voices, and 3rds and 6ths (but *not* the 4th) are called consonances.

   c. Definitions of counterpoint and consonance, as well as description of simultaneous process of composing.

   d. Renaissance homogeneous approach offers striking contrast to the linear freedom, authoritative cantus firmus, and heterogeneity of Medieval music.

   e. Pietro Aaron, *Toscanello in musica* (1523), Book II, Chs. 13 and 16, as translated by Peter Bergquist (Colorado Springs: Music Press, 1970), pp. 21–2 and 27–8. In *The New Grove Dictionary* ("Aron"), Bergquist writes that it is "probably the best general treatise of its generation."

2a. Primary, a command (with penalty specified) from a powerful churchman.

   b. Late Medieval, since it mentions hockets, prolations, secular cantus firmi, and preference for the perfect consonances (including the 4th).

   c. Innovations corrupt church music.

   d. A stand was made against new music; although it failed, it may help explain the increasing emphasis on secular music, especially in Italy, thereafter.

   e. A papal bull issued by Pope John XXII in 1324 or 1325 at Avignon (trans. H. E. Woolridge), *The Oxford History of Music* (2nd ed.), vol. I (London: Oxford University Press, 1929), pp. 294–6.

3a. Primary, from a practical theory treatise.

   b. Late Renaissance: the author treats his subject (musical theme) in imitation with obvious concern for expressing the meaning of the text.

   c. The practical problems of composition are foremost, these centering upon working out one theme in all voice-parts.

   d. Mastery in composition rests on craft (not originality, a later view).

e. Gioseffo Zarlino, *Istituzioni armoniche* (1558), Book III (trans. Oliver Strunk, *Source Readings in Music History* (N.Y.: W. W. Norton and Co., Inc., 1950, 1965), pp. 229–31 — one of the great monuments of music theory.

4a. Primary, a theory treatise that also describes performance practice.

  b. High Renaissance by its reference to more than four-voice polyphony and concern for tempo and dynamic changes in secular music to express the passions of the words.

  c. Singers often failed to suit their performance to the piece; secular music required embellishment, but the harmony had to be kept clear.

  d. The author states that madrigals were customarily performed by an ensemble of soloists (versus choral sacred polyphony) with tempo and dynamic changes (which some found strange and in error).

  e. Nicola Vincentino, *L'antica musica ridotta alla moderna prattica* (Rome, 1555), Book IV, Ch. 42, as translated in Carol MacClintock (ed.) *Readings in the History of Music in Performance* (Bloomington: University of Indiana Press, 1979), pp. 76–8. Although in advance of his contemporaries in his chromatic and enharmonic theories, the author appeals to the ear rather than the mind and his views on performance may have been widely shared.

5a. Secondary, being a summary of a primary source (a theory treatise) with quotations included.

  b. Early Renaissance, with an apparent concern for vertical texture (3rds, 6ths, and 4ths as consonances, the last with care, and parallel perfect consonances basically prohibited) and emphasis on need for improvisation.

  c. Practical guidance for composers.

  d. Proper recognition of contemporaneous emphasis on improvisation would cast different light on early music.

  e. Johannes Tinctoris, *Liber de arte contrapuncti* (1477), as summarized in Gustave Reese, *Music in the Renaissance*, rev. ed. (N.Y.: W. W. Norton and Co., Inc., 1954, 1959), pp. 141–4.

UNIDENTIFIED MUSICAL EXAMPLES: CHAPTER 4

1a. High Classical by the progressive subdivision of the beat, subtle phrasing, chord vocabulary (including the diminished-seventh), and the genre itself.

  b. Piano concerto (by the instrumentation).

  c. Mozart, *Piano Concerto in B-flat*, K. 595 (N.Y.: Eulenburg, n.d.), pp. 16–7. Note the typically Mozartean lightly-textured piano figuration, thin scoring, and the dramatic modal change to the parallel minor.

2a. High Baroque because of the long-breathed phrases, figured bass, and instrumentation (3 trumpets).

  b. Church cantata with chorus and orchestra (note the familiar chorale tune in the tenor voice, second system).

  c. J. S. Bach, *Ein' feste Burg* (eds. William Starr and George Devine), *Music Scores Omnibus, Part 1,* 2nd ed. (Englewood Cliffs, N.J.: Prentice-Hall, Inc., 1974), pp. 174–5. This is Bachian imitative counterpoint.

3a. High Classical, featuring clearly articulated phrasing and melody-with-accompaniment texture as well as grace-notes and the augmented-sixth chord.

  b. String quartet (Why must they be stringed instruments?)

  c. Haydn, *String Quartet* Op. 71, #3, I, *83 string quartets*, vol. 3 (Eulenburg, N.D.), pp. 4–5.

4a. High Baroque from the genre, the regular rhythmic flow, the chain of suspensions over a figured bass, and functional harmony with secondary dominants.
 b. Concerto grosso, with trio sonata-like concertino and four-part ripieno.
 c. Corelli, *Concerto Grosso* Op. 6, #3, IV, ed. by Hans Engle, *The Concerto Grosso,* (*The Anthology of Music,* vol. 23), p. 64 (Cologne: A. Volk Verlag, 1958). The composer helped consolidate functional harmony as well as the genre of concerto grosso.

5a. Early Baroque on account of the irregular rhythmic motion, expressive dissonance, and unpredictable harmonic progressions.
 b. Toccata (or fantasia, a good guess); for organ, because of the large note-values and the nature of the dissonance.
 c. Frescobaldi, "Toccata ottava," ed. by Erich Valentin, *The Toccata* (*The Anthology of Music,* vol. 17), p. 26 (Cologne: A. Volk Verlag, 1958). The composer was noted for his slow, expressive toccatas.

6a. High Classical because of its wide tonal and dynamic ranges, weak beat sforzandi, abrupt tempo changes, and expressive recitative-like passages.
 b. Piano sonata (by the keyboard score).
 c. Beethoven, *Piano Sonata in D Minor,* Op. 31, #2 (ed. by F. E. Kirby), *Music in the Classic Period* (N.Y.: Schirmer Books, 1979), pp. 636–37.

7a. Early Classical by reason of the light scoring (which was standard), the repetition of short phrases and simple diatonic motives, and the Mannheim crescendo.
 b. Symphony (by the instrumentation).
 c. Johann Stamitz, *Symphony in E-flat,* I (ed. Lothar Hoffmann-Erbrecht), *The Symphony,* vol. 29 in *The Anthology of Music* (Cologne: Arno Volk Verlag, 1967).

UNIDENTIFIED HISTORICAL SOURCES: CHAPTER 4

1a. A secondary source (a music history book), since it embodies a Twentieth-Century perspective and reflects access to archival information.
 b. High Baroque/Early Classical, a transitional time.
 c. It is made clear how a noble's musical interests affected his realm.
 d. Can one depict the history of music as an orderly sequence in which composers created for the common man? Note how the nature of opera reflects societal factors.
 e. This excerpt is drawn from Henry Raynor, *A Social History of Music* (London: Barrie and Jenkins, 1972), pp. 96–8.

2a. A primary source, being a preface to an edition of toccatas.
 b. Early Baroque from the reference to the "newer madrigals" and especially to changing tempi in the performance of toccatas.
 c. Tempi change in the newer madrigals and in toccatas as well, according to the expressive nature of a passage.
 d. Here is justification for freedom of tempo on the part of a performer of toccatas and by a madrigal ensemble in the performance of "newer madrigals."
 e. Frescobaldi, preface to a collection of toccatas, as translated in Paul Nettl, *The Book of Musical Documents* (N.Y.: Philosophical Library, 1948), pp. 52–3.

3a. Primary, for it is music criticism (in the form of a letter).
 b. High Classical (long and noisy symphonies).
 c. Criticism of the latest symphonies of a highly influential composer with the conclusion that he has been injurious to the art of music.
 d. Another traditionalist affronted by the new in music objects to the taste of a master.

e. An anonymous letter to the editor of the *Quarterly Musical Magazine and Review* (1827), as quoted by Nicolas Slonimsky in his *Lexicon of Musical Invective*, 2nd ed. (Seattle: Washington State Press, 1965) pp. 45–6.

4a. Primary, being a travel journal or diary (actually written in English).

b. High Baroque—a time when conservatories of music for boys flourished, as did castrati and clarino trumpet-playing.

c. A first-hand account of life in an eighteenth-century music conservatory.

d. Training in music was available for those talented and strong-willed enough to endure it, but they had to acquire taste and expression elsewhere.

e. Charles Burney, *An Eighteenth-Century Musical Tour in France and Italy*, as edited by Percy Scholes (London: Oxford University Press, 1959), pp. 269–70.

5a. Primary, since it is taken from a travel journal or diary; many clues are given as to the identity of the mystery composer.

b. High Classical, with the early limit being fixed by the performance of piano concertos and symphonies and the late one by the presence of a castrato.

c. An eye-witness account of a public concert features a virtuoso pianist-composer assisted by some singers and a very small orchestra.

d. The nature of the concert (which reveals the omnipresence of opera in the period by being in two acts!) deserves discussion, as does the comparison of castrati with female singers. The concert documents the sad decline in popularity of a great Classical composer.

e. Count Ludwig Von Bentheim-Steinfurt kept a travel diary and thus left this account of a Mozart concert of October 15, 1790, in Frankfurt. Otto Erich Deutsch (ed.), *Mozart: A Documentary Biography* (Stanford University Press, 1965), pp. 375–76.

6a. Primary, being a letter of music criticism dealing with a great keyboard virtuoso who demonstrates an excess of compositional art.

b. High Baroque, a fact confirmed by the presence of great virtuosity and masterful use of counterpoint while taste has turned to lighter things.

c. Unfortunately, says the writer, the most eminent keyboard player of the time cultivates an unnatural and difficult contrapuntal style.

d. However good this composer may be, musical style and taste seem to have changed around him, the chief complaints being his addiction to counterpoint, his practice of covering the melody with written-out ornaments, and his use of an instrumental style in vocal parts.

e. J. A. Scheibe, an anonymous letter of May 14, 1737, criticizing J. S. Bach, in *The Bach Reader*, Hans T. David and Arthur Mendel, eds. W. W. Norton & Company, Inc., 1944, 1966, p. 238.

UNIDENTIFIED MUSICAL EXAMPLES: CHAPTER 6

1a. High Romantic from the complex texture, extravagant vocal lines, and the large orchestra.

b. Opera (actually symphonic drama).

c. Wagner, *Tristan und Isolde*, Act II duet (Leipzig: Breitkopf and Hartel, 1905), pp. 420–21.

2a. Early Twentieth-Century because it is dodecaphonic (principal and subordinate themes are indicated by symbols), yet scored in a traditional manner.

b. Piano concerto (note the layout of the score).

c. Schoenberg, *Piano Concerto*, Op. 42, I (ed. Tadeusz Okuljar), *Samtliche Werke*, vol. XV (Vienna: Universal Edition, 1975), p. 165.

3a. High Romantic from its variable tempo and subtle rhythms, enharmonicism, and unique tone colors.

b. A symphonic piece whose instrumentation seems to indicate a tone poem.

c. Debussy, *Prelude to "The Afternoon of a Faun."* Reproduced from the Norton Critical Score, Claude Debussy, Prelude to "The Afternoon of a Faun" edited by William Austin by permission of W.W. Norton & Company, Inc. Copyright© 1970 by W.W. Norton & Company, Inc., pp. 52-3.

4a. Early Romantic by its limited harmonic vocabulary with occasional chromaticisms and its wide-ranging lyrical melody (not expressive marking) over an idiomatic chordal accompaniment with many octaves.

b. Character piece for piano somewhat more likely than a piano sonata.

c. Chopin, Ballade in F Minor, Op. 52. Ed. Ewald Zimmerman. (Munich: G. Henle: 1976), p. 45.

5a. Early Twentieth-Century by its irregular and changing meters, dissonant but tonal idiom, and unique instrumentation.

b. A symphonic piece with characteristics of both tone poem and symphony.

c. Bartok, *Music for Strings, Percussion and Celesta*, IV. Copyright 1937 by Universal Editions. Renewed 1964. Copyright and renewal assigned to Boosey & Hawkes, Inc. for the U.S.A. Reprinted by permission. pp. 132-33.

6a. Early Twentieth-Century because of its changing meters, dissonant harmonies, and unique chamber scoring, yet tonal and reliant on ostinati.

b. A Neo-Classical chamber piece with mixed winds and strings.

c. Stravinsky, *L'histoire du soldat* (London: J. and W. Chester, 1924), pp. 22-3.

KEY TO UNIDENTIFIED HISTORICAL SOURCES: CHAPTER 6

1a. Primary source, in the form of an autobiography.

b. Early Twentieth-Century, since there is only gradual estrangement between composer and audience and the writer mentions Rimsky-Korsakov.

c. The composer feels a calling for his profession and a need to search for artistic truth, wherever that leads.

d. Although he pursues art for art's sake, the composer assumes a craftsmanlike approach to his calling.

e. Stravinsky, *Autobiography* (1935), as quoted by Paul Nettl, *The Book of Musical Documents*, pp. 324-26. The titles left out in lines 27-28 are *Le Sacre* and *Petroushka*. Reprinted by permission of Philosophical Library.

2a. Primary, a contract to compose and produce an opera buffa.

b. Early Romantic.

c. The terms of the contract are specified, revealing a great deal about operatic life in Italy.

d. Note the stringent deadlines and restrictions, which together produced eminently facile men of the theater (not just composers) with little incentive and less likelihood of producing enduring masterpieces.

e. Rossini: *The Barber of Seville* resulted from this contract, which is quoted in *Rossini: A Biography* by Herbert Weinstock. Copyright © 1968 by Herbert Weinstock. Reprinted by permission of Alfred A. Knopf, Inc. pp. 377-78.

3a. Primary, being excerpts from two letters (each containing intimate material).

　b. High Romantic from the composer's self-consciousness, originality and attitude towards his art.

　c. Someone is told to leave this genius alone and that he feels his day in the sun will come.

　d. This composer regards himself as a special being, who is doomed to misunderstanding in his lifetime.

　e. Mahler, whose goal was to voice all nature and whose time did come. The first part is from a letter of August 18, 1896, concerning *Symphony No. 3* and the second is undated; both are quoted by Paul Nettl, *Book of Musical Documents,* pp. 335-36. Reprinted by permission of Philosophical Library.

4a. Primary, a letter.

　b. Early (actually Middle) Romantic, since it is clearly post-Beethoven by only one or two generations.

　c. Reverence for Beethoven as a progressive (liberty is to be welcomed in the liberal arts), the criticism for the division of his career into three style periods.

　d. The author goes straight to the heart of the Romantic dilemma — liberty versus authority (tradition) in composition. How does he resolve the duality, and what does his removal of social responsibility from the sphere of the artist portend?

　e. Franz Liszt, quoted from a letter of December 2, 1852, to Wilhelm Lenz, who had just published *Beethoven and His Three Styles.* The excerpt is drawn from Irving Kolodin (ed.), *The Composer As Listener* (N.Y.: Horizon Press, 1958), pp. 27-8.

5a. Primary, a critical essay.

　b. Later Twentieth-Century because of the references to phonograph recordings and to mid-century concert practices.

　c. The failure of contemporary composers causes stagnation of repertory and binds performers to an acceptable, but not very creative, conventionality. The author is critical of the institution of the song recital, the separation of art music from popular, and the art of recording.

　d. Is the contemporary composer, abetted by the art of recording music, responsible for the decline of singing and of later Twentieth-Century music, especially of singing and of opera?

　e. Henry Pleasants, *The Great Singers* Copyright© 1966 by Henry Pleasants. Reprinted by permission of Simon & Schuster, a Division of Gulf & Western Corporation, pp. 348-49. The same author wrote a book entitled *The Agony of Modern Music* (N.Y.: Simon and Schuster, 1955.)

6a. Primary, being an article by a famous music critic attacking a composer whose identity should not be difficult to guess.

　b. High Romantic, since the influence of Wagner seems overwhelming.

　c. A new symphony is said to apply to Wagner's dramatic style to that genre.

　d. The writer reports, saying honestly that the concert was a success. He also educates, duly explaining that the composer's symphonic style is not inherently musical but tied to programmatic meaning. Finally, he foretells the decline of the symphony and of chamber music owing to the departure from traditional principles. Consider the frequently unhappy role of the music critic and the fact that only the reviews — not the performances — remain.

　e. The composer is Bruckner. The author, clearly well-prepared for his task, is Eduard Hanslick, as quoted (in a somewhat condensed version) by Henry Pleasants (ed.), in *Music Criticisms 1846-99* (N.Y.: Penguin Books, 1963), pp. 288-90.